D1480419

In no country save our own could such a
career as that of Roger A. Pryor be possible.
—from an editorial in
The New York *Herald*, March 16, 1919

General Roger A. Pryor
Courtesy Eggleston Library, Hampden-Sydney College in Virginia

Adapt
or
Perish

THE LIFE OF GENERAL ROGER A. PRYOR, C.S.A.

by Robert S. Holzman

Archon Books   1976

Library of Congress Cataloging in Publication Data

Holzman, Robert S
   Adapt or perish.

   Bibliography: p.
   Includes index.
   1. Pryor Roger Atkinson, 1828-1919. I. Title.
KF368.P78H64   347'.73'3634 [B]   76-6988
ISBN 0-208-01585-X

© Robert S. Holzman 1976
First published 1976 as an Archon Book,
an imprint of The Shoe String Press Inc.,
Hamden, Connecticut 06514

Printed in the United States of America

Contents

Illustrations

Acknowledgements. The frontispiece is reproduced by permission of the Eggleston Library, Hampden-Sydney College in Virginia. The other three illustrations have been made available through the courtesy of General Pryor's granddaughter, Mrs. Sara Dodge Kimbrough.

Preface

Adapt or perish. During Roger A. Pryor's formative years, Charles Darwin was developing his principles of evolution. What cannot adapt to changing circumstances does not survive.

The adaptation of a general officer of a defeated power to civilian life is not easy. The problem is compounded when this defeated general is forced by economic necessity to earn his bread in the realm of the conqueror. Adaptation to a new profession and way of life is all the more difficult when one is regarded as an enemy in his new home and a traitor in his old. But because he *could* adapt, Pryor survived—with distinction and honor.

Roger A. Pryor was of an old-line, blue-blooded Virginia family, but his acquaintances were not confined to the local aristocracy. His friends included political and artistic figures of the day. He was one of the outstanding prewar Southern journalists, whose thoughtful editorials (admitted Lincoln) were the origin of the phrases "Irrepressible conflict" and "a house divided." He was one of the principal Southern hotheads, and was widely famed as a duellist. It was he who made the irreversible ultimate decision to fire on Fort Sumter, thus triggering the Civil War; and in recognition of his ardor, he was offered the "opportunity" of firing the first Confederate shot of the war upon that occasion.

His fire-brand speeches had helped Southerners decide to secede, and he was quickly made a Confederate congressman and colonel (later, brigadier-general). He saw considerable action early in the war, bloodstaining a bayonet himself when necessary; but when he received no higher promotion, he resigned his general's stars, to enlist immediately as a private in the cavalry. He served the remainder of the war as a confidential scout for Lee, until captured in November, 1864. He was released from a New York prison by Lincoln's personal intervention, over the vehement protests of the Secretary of War (who wanted Pryor to be hanged) and of General Grant (who wanted to hold him as a prisoner).

When the war ended, Pryor was one of the first of the prominent Confederates to realize that continued opposition to the North was pointless. He moved to New York and, under conditions of absolute poverty, studied law while he worked (incognito) as a journalist. He lacked the means to bring along his wife and children. His fight was against frightful odds, for most Northerners wanted nothing to do with this notorious Secessionist hothead. By dint of superhuman efforts, he developed into one of New York's greatest and most respected lawyers. In a day of legal giants in that city, he held his own with the best of them, participating in some of the most famed cases of his time. Representing the people of the State of New York, he won the first of the great antitrust suits. He became a criminal court judge and, later, a justice of the New York State Supreme Court. The terrible fight to shift from fire-breathing Secessionist to distinguished New York jurist was successful.

This Virginian spoke powerfully in favor of the South's accepting the North's victory and the resultant postwar legislation. His speeches and acts did much to bring North and South together again. Here was a professional Rebel who successfully undertook integration after the war, winning at the same time the respect and confidence of both North and South.

R.S.H.

I

In the Beginning

Roger Atkinson Pryor was born on July 19, 1828. His roots in Virginia were deep; many of his ancestors were colorful personages in that colony.

In 1654, Theodorick Bland, the first of the line in America, purchased the Westover estate in Virginia. Here he built a church and gave the county ten acres of land, a court house, a prison. He was one of the King's Council for the colony and "was both in fortune and understanding inferior to no person of his time in the country."[1] His father-in-law, Richard Bennett, was governor of Virginia. Bland had three sons: Theodorick, Richard, and John. Richard married Elizabeth, the daughter of Colonel William Randolph of Turkey Island (which, in 1814, was to become by purchase the ancestral home of the Pickett family, including the future General George E. Pickett).[2] The children of this marriage were Mary, Elizabeth, Anna, Theodorick, and Richard. Mary married Henry Lee and thus was an ancestress of the future General Robert E. Lee.[3] Her brother, Richard, was named by Thomas Jefferson as "the wisest man south of the James River." Another brother, Theodorick, was sent to England for his education and returned to Virginia at age ninety-three, a physician, who served with distinction in the American Revolution. A friend and counselor of Washington, Jefferson, and Lafayette, he was a member of Congress and of the convention that framed the constitution.[4] His son, the Reverend William Bland (an Episcopalian) married Elizabeth Yates, daughter of the president of William and Mary College. Their daughter, Nancy, married Richard Pryor, a descendant of John Pryor, who had come to Hanover County, Virginia, from England in the early seventeenth century. (John, a successful farmer, gave his name to a celebrated Virginia tobacco, "blue and medley Pryor," as well as to a fine apple.)[5] Their oldest son, Theodorick Pryor, married Lucy Atkinson of Dinwiddie, whose first boy, Roger, was born near Petersburg, in Dinwiddie County. Through blood and marriage, the lad was decended from the greatest families in colonial Virginia: Bland, Poythress, Cary, Randolph, Isham, Gates, Atkinson, and Pleasant. Through them, his lineage extended to noble families in England and France.[6]

Young Roger's father, Theodorick Pryor, had been a lawyer. When Roger was two years old, his mother died, and the grief-stricken widower entered Union Theological Seminary at Hampden-Sydney, Virginia, on January 9, 1831, as a student of theology under Dr. John Holt Rice. Theodorick was licensed by the East Hanover Presbytery in April, 1832, at Portsmouth. He came to Nottoway as a licentiate until fall; and in September, he was installed by the presbytery at East Shiloh Church in Nottoway. On December 2 of that year, he took a second wife, Frances Epes.[7]

Dr. Theodorick Pryor, as a pastor, was "eminent for piety, eloquence, and usefulness."[8] An observer remembered him as "a man cast in the mould of which martyrs were made in the olden time, and whether roasted, broiled, or boiled, he would never have yielded one iota in the confession of that faith which he so long held and so strongly defended."[9] In 1853 he was to go to the Third Presbyterian Church in Baltimore, but the following year he returned to the Second Presbyterian Church in Petersburg, in that area where he was to devote most of his life.[10]

Young Roger spent much of his youth at the Old Place in Nottoway County, Virginia. This was situated on the road from the Poor House by Frank's Shop to Nottoway Court House. The original house had been built in about 1760 upon 400 acres of land.[11] Nottoway Court House thus was described in Martin's *Gazeteer of Virginia* in about 1835: a post-village 67 miles west of Richmond and 189 miles from Washington. It was on the Nottoway River, one mile east of Hendersonville. The community contained the court house, clerk's office, and criminal and debtors' prison, as well as fifteen dwellings, one mercantile house, one hotel, one saddler, one tailor, and one blacksmith shop. The population was seventy persons, including one physician and one attorney.[12]

Roger attended the Classical Academy of Ephraim Dodd Saunders in Petersburg.[13] At the age of twelve, he was recorded as saying what could have been the blueprint of his life: "I am going to make my mark at whatever I do; if it is blacksmithing, I will be a good blacksmith."[14]

In 1843, he entered Hampden-Sydney College, where he was noted for his love of general reading.[15] He joined the Union Hall, a literary society, [16] and, more importantly, he met Sara Rice.

The Rices could trace their Virginia ancestors almost as far back as could the Pryors; Thomas Rice had come from England in about 1680.[17] Sara was born in Halifax County, Virginia, on February 19, 1830, the daughter of the Reverend Samuel Blair and Lucinda Walton (Leftwich) Rice. She was educated privately.[18] In view of the many Rice children and the frail state of her mother's health, she made her home in Charlottesville, where she was "practically adopted as the only child of my aunt and uncle, Dr. and Mrs. Samuel Pleasants Hargrave."[19] "The general impression I retain of the world of my childhood," she was to recall, "is of gardens—gardens everywhere; abloom with roses, lilies, violets, jonquils, flowering almond-trees which never fruited, double-flowering peach trees which also bore no fruit, but were, with the almond trees, cherished for their blossoms."[20]

It was an isolated, self-sufficient existence. "Everything the family and the plantation needed was manufactured at home, except the fine fabrics, the perfumes, wines, etc., which were brought from Richmond, Baltimore, or Philadelphia."[21] Nothing was very close. "There was no railroad to bring us luxuries from the nearest town—Richard—twenty-five miles distant. . . ."[22]

The meeting of Roger Pryor and Sara Rice took place in 1844, when he was sixteen years of age and she was fourteen. It was the isolation of her town that was responsible: A large convention of Presbyterian clergymen was held in Charlottesville, where there was no hotel. "The landlord was ruined by the hospitality of the citizens. As soon as a pleasant stranger 'put up' at a private house, he was claimed as a guest by the first man who could reach him.

"When large religious or political or literary meetings convened in our town, my uncle would send to the chairman asking for the number of guests we could entertain. Until they arrived, we were as much on the *qui vive* as if we had bought numbers in a lottery. . . ."[23]

Sara was frankly disturbed to learn that a visiting clergyman and his son were to be quartered at her uncle's home. "Mercy! Worse and worse! There's no hope for us! A strange man is to be entertained in our little parlor!"

But it was not to be so bad after all. "The name of this unwelcome intruder was Roger A. Pryor. He made himself charming. I had not yet tucked up my long braids, but he treated me beautifully. He was so alert, so witty, so amiable, that he was unanimously voted the freedom of our sanctum."[24] He had made a lasting impression. When the visit was over and the Pryors took their departure, she listened to the winding horn of the stage until it could be heard no more. Then she prayed for Roger's care. "According to my Presbyterian training, I was taught that every prayer must be followed by efforts for its fulfillment. It was clearly my duty 'to take care of him.' He needed it."[25]

The following year, young Pryor was graduated from Hampden-Sydney College at the head of his class[26] as the valedictorian.[27] Then he returned to Charlottesville for the 1846-1847 session. The University of Virginia student records for that year showed that he studied Modern Language under Professor M. Schele de Vere, Moral Philosophy under Professor William H. McGuffey, and Mathematics under Professor Edward H. Courtenay. In Professor Schele de Vere's classes, stated the bulletin for that year, "The method of instruction is by lectures, examinations, written exercises, and comments on the text-books as read in the lecture-room, the principal classic authors in each language being used for this purpose." In Moral Philosophy, a number of texts was listed in the bulletin. "The examinations will be on the Professor's Lectures and the text-books, that is, those books enumerated above, names of which are not included in parentheses. Those so included are to be consulted, but are not required to be studied as text-books." In Mathematics, "The instruction in each class is conveyed partly by lectures, and partly by the systematic study of approved text-books, the student being assisted by full and frequent explanations from the Professor, and being constantly subjected to rigid examinations. The progress of the student in every class is also tested by his being required to perform written exercises, in which the principles acquired are applied to the solution of particular problems."

During the session 1847-1848, Pryor studied law under the tutelage

Sara Rice
Courtesy Sara Dodge Kimbrough

of Professor John B. Minor.[28] Minor had become professor of law
that very year and had entire charge of the law school. He disliked
being called "professor," saying that this title was "the property of the
bootblacks, tonsorial artists, patent medicine quacks, and dancing
masters, to the exclusion of its true proprietors."[29] Each student's
opinion, according to the bulletin of that year, "is required on supposed
cases; he is called upon to devise and to institute remedies, by suit or
otherwise, to conduct suits at law, to draw wills, conveyances, and
assurances; and, in short, to discharge most of the functions devolving
upon a practitioner of the law." Logically (but unfortunately for
Pryor's later career), the emphasis was upon "the Statute Law of
Virginia. . . ."

The young law student found plenty of time to be concerned with
Sara's education. He gave her a gorgeous edition of Shakespeare,
Macaulay's *Essays*, Hazlitt's *Age of Elizabeth*, Leigh Hunt's *Fancy And
Imagination*. He read his gifts to her, along with Shelley, Keats, Byron,
and Coleridge.[30] But she was doing right well with her own literary
endeavors. When she was sixteen, she sold a story, "The Birthnight
Ball," to *The Saturday Evening Post*, although the editor tried to get her
to waive a fee when he learned of her tender age.[31]

Pryor received his law degree from the University of Virginia in
1847 and was admitted to the Virginia bar before he was twenty-
one.[32] But the event that he always regarded as the most important
of his life took place the following year. He was twenty and she was
eighteen when Roger and Sara were married at Charlottesville on
November 8, 1848. They were married at the home of her father, the
Reverend Samuel Blair Rice in a ceremony performed by the Reverend
Dr. Frederick Pryor. Only a small wedding was held, as Sara's mother
was ill. The bride wore a wedding dress of India muslin, with flounces
of handsome thread lace. She wore a silver Tiffany comb, and a
wreath of white roses held in place a long white veil.[33] George Loyal
Gordon served as the best man.[34] (The Pryors' first child, who was
born a year and a half later, was named M. Gordon, presumably in
honor of the best man.)

On his wedding day, Pryor also took time to cast his first vote, which,
he said, was *against* Zachary Taylor,[35] the Whig candidate for president, which meant that the vote was fruitlessly cast for the Democratic candidate, Lewis Cass.

Pryor set up a tiny law office at a corner of the court green in Charlottesville. But within two years, he sustained a serious throat affliction; and Dr. Green, an eminent Philadelphia specialist, ordered him to a warmer climate, with strict instructions not to speak in or out of court until the disability was cured.[36] This apparently meant the end of the young man's brief career as an attorney, for "In those days a Virginia lawyer without speaking was no lawyer at all."[37] Pryor could not exist without an occupation and so, in 1850, he moved to Petersburg, near his birthplace, to become a journalist. Petersburg in that year had a population of 14,603, of whom about 6,000 were white. "A more hospitable and warm-hearted people did not live," noted a contemporary townsman, "but a stranger was required to bring character and cultivation as his credentials. Money, with its meretricious adornments and its vulgar display, was not the sesame to open any gentleman's door."[38] But Roger A. Pryor had the proper credentials.

II

The Journalist

Pryor established the *Southside Democrat* and served as its editor for three years.[1] He purchased the equipment of a defunct newspaper, Drinkard's *Republican*, paying $1,200 for all the fixtures, types, forms, presses, printing material, and good will on October 3, 1850.[2] The editor handled virtually every phase of the undertaking himself, even soliciting subscribers.[3] His editorials "were a revelation of strength and purity in classic English," according to one reader of the newspaper.[4]

Journalism was to have a lasting appeal to Pryor. Late in life, he declared: "That was fascinating work. Do you know that I'd be in it to this day if it hadn't been for an accident?"[5] The accident was the Civil War.

A considerable charm of journalism to Pryor was the opportunity of meeting the important men of the day. One visitor to the offices of the *Southside Democrat* was Stephen A. Douglas, the "Little Giant." He was below average height, yes. "But the word *insignificant* could never have been applied to him," noted the editor's highly literary wife. "There was something in his air, his carriage, that forbade it. His massive head, his resolute face, more than compensated for his short stature."[6] Another prominent visitor who came to the editor's office was Louis Kossuth, the distinguished Hungarian patriot, who was actively soliciting the support of the United States newspapers. He gave Pryor a cigar. But the *Southside Democrat* came out for nonintervention in Austria-Hungary's affairs.[7]

In 1853, Pryor was called to a more formidable journalistic post. He

[15]

was by now regarded as "talented, studious, ambitious, bold to contempt of consequences, and a fitting leader of the young Democracy which was springing up in the decadence of the Whig party, tainted at that time with free-soilism and abolition at the North, and ready on that account for dissolution at the South."[8] He sold the *Southside Democrat* to A. D. Banks and J. R. Lewellen[9] and moved to Washington.

Pryor had been a Virginia delegate to the Democratic Party convention that had nominated Franklin Pierce for President of the United States in Baltimore in 1852;[10] and when the new Pierce administration sponsored the Washington *Union* as the party organ, two editors were desired, one to represent the North and the other the South. Charles Eames of Massachusetts and Roger A. Pryor of Virginia obtained these assignments.[11]

The Pryors lived in a large boarding house maintained by Mrs. Tully Wise, a Virginian.[12] "I remember Washington only as a garden of delights," recalled Sara Pryor, "over which the spring trailed an early robe of green, thickly embroidered with gems of amethyst and ruby, pearl and sapphire. The crocuses, hyacinths, tulips, and snowdrops made haste to bloom before the snows had fairly melted."[13] But her pleasures were not limited to the bucolic, and the Pryors' widening circle of acquaintances included such diverse personalities as General Winfield Scott, Sam Houston, and Washington Irving.[14]

Roger Pryor soon became embroiled in an international issue of extreme delicacy. In the spring of 1853, he wrote a scathing review of *The War of Ormuzd and Ahriman* by Henry Winter Davis, a politician and a leader in the Whig and Know-Nothing Parties. Davis had set forth the United States and Russia as the respective champions of the principles of liberty and of despotism, foreseeing a mighty and persistent conflict. Pryor, in his review, declared that this was impossible, as "in every element of national strength and happiness Russia is great and prosperous beyond any other country in Europe." Instead of becoming enemies, these nations "will consolidate and perpetuate their friendly relations by the same just and pacific policy which has regulated their intercourse in times past." This review was distasteful to many readers of the *Union*, who already were taking sides with England in the threatening dispute with Russia in the Crimea, and the owner of the newspaper, General Robert Armstrong of Tennessee, denounced the critique. Pryor defended himself in the columns of a rival newspaper, the *National Intelligencer*, stating that while he was not the eulogist of the Russian Empire, he did see Russian good will towards the United States. He pointed out that "in Russia the maudlin, mock philanthropy of Uncle Tom's Cabin is an unknown disease." Noted the clerk of the Senate Printing Records: "It was the general belief at Washington that Mr. Pryor had been inspired by some one connected with the Russian Legation."[15] But Congressman Caleb Cushing thought that Pryor's Crimean article was "unanswered and unanswerable."[16]

At about the same time, Pryor wrote an article in the Washington *Union* on the relations among the United States, Great Britain, and Russia, as affected by the pending Crimean War. The tone of his article was decidedly anti-English. Appearing in the journal supposed to be the organ of the ruling Democratic party, the article suggested that President Pierce was sympathetic to Russia.[17] The owner of the newspaper suggested that Pryor disavow his article "upon further consideration"; but the fiery young editor replied that he must write according to his convictions or not at all. The matter might have been settled amicably, but General Armstrong advised Pryor to "think twice before giving up a large salary." The editor resigned at once. When his wife asked him what he actually had declared, he replied, "Well, if you *will* have it—I said, '*damn* the money!' "[18] Another version of the dispute had it that Armstrong discharged Pryor because of the disagreement.[19]

On August 23, 1853, Pryor accepted an editorial position with the Richmond *Enquirer*, which was edited by Thomas Ritchie and his two sons, William and Thomas, Jr.[20] But he took a leave of absence to handle a delicate matter for Franklin Pierce. The president of the United States had been attracted to Pryor by his articles in the Washington *Union* and had consulted him on some of his own speeches.[21] In 1855, he sent the editor to Greece as special commissioner for the adjustment of a long-standing dispute with that country.[22] The Reverend Jonas King had gone to Greece as a relief worker during the Greek War of Independence. He bought land while Athens was in a virtual state of ruin; but this land was involved in rehabilitation plans, and for sixteen years it remained under a government injunction against sale or use for building purposes. The United States minister at

Constantinople was detached from his post in 1852 in order to try to settle the dispute. But the matter was not settled; in July, 1855, Pryor was sent to Athens to see that the assurances of Paicos, the Greek foreign minister, were carried into effect.[23]

Sara could not accompany her husband to Europe as her mother was seriously ill.[24] And there were her two infant children: Gordon and the first son, Theodorick, who had been born on July 8, 1851.

The amateur diplomat apparently was not awed by the majesty of his status; and when he called upon the United States minister to France, John Y. Mason, en route to Athens, it was recorded that Pryor "created great amusement with a toy mouse."[25]

Pryor was able to get the Kingdom of Greece to release the Reverend Jonas King and to pay him $36,000 for the disputed land.[26] This was regarded as a "satisfactory" settlement, amounting to about one-fourth of the original claim. But Pryor did not leave the country upon the completion of this assignment, for he had been instructed by Secretary of State William L. Marcy on July 18 to gather all the data on Greece that could be obtained.[27] The travelling editor was asked by King Otho at a state banquet what problem most interested the United States at the time. "The problem, may it please your majesty, of how we shall govern our superfluous territory and invest our superfluous treasure." He charmed Queen Mathilde with discussions about night-blooming cereus.[28]

His mission accomplished, Pryor used his generous expense allowance and visited Venice, Rome, Constantinople, and Egypt.[29]

Pryor booked passage back to the United States on the *Pacific* and had so advised his wife. Somewhere in the Atlantic, the vessel sank and he was believed to have perished. But he was to return to a startled wife, for he had left the ship at Marseilles when he discovered that his baggage had been opened. This ministerial discourtesy, in his judgment, required redress; and he took a later vessel home in safety.[30]

After the Greek success, he was offered a mission to Persia, which was declined.[31] He returned to the Richmond *Enquirer*. Here he received $5,000 annual compensation, the largest salary in the country for a staff editor.[32]

Pryor, the journalist, "was a slight figure, with a set of features remarkable for their intellectual cast; a profusion of dark hair falling from his brow in long, straight masses over the collar of his coat gave a student-like air to his whole appearance. . . . [H]e might pass for a student of divinity or a young professor of moral philosophy. . . ."[33] But this description was misleading, for his "aggressiveness and passionate oratory" brought him many duels along with national prominence.[34]

The Reverend Dr. Theodorick Pryor became greatly disturbed by the number of duels in which his son Roger was becoming embroiled,[35] and there was good reason for his disturbance. A Virginian of that era noted that "Whilst filling the office of editor, Pryor was principal in several affairs of honor, as the duel was then called, but he came out of all unhurt. The duello was the fashionable mode of settling differences between gentlemen at that day; and although indefensible from some points of view, was less reprehensible and less barbarous than the present system [1904] which places a revolver in the hip pocket of the aggrieved citizen and bids him open battle upon the street or elsewhere, as much to the danger of the innocent bystander as to his opponent."[36] The church, of course, vehemently disapproved of duels, and one clergyman declared in a sermon delivered in St. Peter's Church in Charleston in 1844: "Let the patriot resolutely determine never to countenance, in any way, the man, who by his practice, sanctions duelling. Let the sober man turn with silent censure from the man of blood."[37] But to other men, the *code duello* was the quintessence of justice. Noted an attorney: "When gentlemen go to the field they are on terms of absolute equality, and nothing can be devised by man fairer and more equitable."[38]

In his later life, Pryor acknowledged two duels as youthful indiscretions.[39] But he overlooked a few. His first duel was with Charles Irving; no shots actually were exchanged on the field of honor. His second match was with Robert Ridgway, a student of the classics. Five years older than Pryor, he also was a lawyer and journalist; he edited the Richmond *Whig*. The encounter took place at Blair's Mill, near Washington, and Pryor intentionally fired his pistol into the ground. Next he met a son of John Minor Botts, a congressman from Virginia, whom he also declined to shoot at because of his opponent's infirmity. Pryor challenged Colonel Thomas F. Goode at Boydton, but no match took place.[40] Pryor almost fought a duel with Robert W. Hughes of the Richmond *Examiner* about the former's secretly working for the nomination of Franklin Pierce for President of the United States, but friends successfully intervened.[41]

In 1815, while editor of the Richmond *Enquirer*, Pryor got into a rabid controversy with Dr. Oswald R. Finney after a caustic editorial. Finney, a Whig member of the Virginia Senate,[42] was a wealthy bachelor who resided at Onancock, Accomac County. The only possible solution, according to the Virginia code of honor, was a duel, and Finney sent the editor a challenge. They met one morning in Manchester, near the Free Bridge. At the first shot, Finney fell, badly wounded; a bullet had struck a rib and was deflected towards his spine.[43] He was expected to die of the wound, but he lived with his disability for more than forty years. Of these two men who faced each other's fire, the winner lived to the age of 90 and the vanquished, to 91.[44]

The great historian of Southern fighting men, Douglas Southall Freeman, wrote of Pryor that "he was perhaps the most notorious duellist of his day."[45] But his most notorious duel, with Representative John Fox Potter of Wisconsin, never took place. This will be considered in its proper context when the career of Congressman Pryor is examined.

Pryor was willing to see a compromise of an affair of honor, so long as it was not his. Senator Stephen A. Douglas of Illinois, a friend of the fiery editor, was greatly disturbed when the president of the United States sent to the Senate for approval various nominations of Illinois men, without first obtaining the customary courtesy approval of the senators of that state. In high dudgeon, Douglas declared that many of these nominees were dishonest and corrupt. Senator Graham N. Fitch of Indiana announced in the strongest language that this was a slur upon his own son, who had been nominated for United States Attorney in Chicago. Fitch *père* was a well-known marksman, but Pryor and Major Hawkins demanded that he withdraw his offensive language.[46] Then Pryor persuaded Douglas to substitute a more conciliatory letter for the challenge he had written when no retraction was forthcoming. In time a mutually satisfactory explanation was worked out.[47] The Illinois senator should have been grateful to Pryor for having negotiated the settlement, for Douglas's friend, David C. Broderick, recently had been killed in a duel with David S. Terry.

But the less martial side of the Virginia editor generally attracted such attention as he drew. Noted a senator who had seen and heard him frequently: "Roger A. Pryor was a man of striking and graceful presence, of most fascinating manner and irresistibly charming. He was orator, editor, politician, leader of popular assemblages, tribune of the people."[48] Another prominent Washingtonian recalled that "Virginia always had a supply of good speakers . . . [such as] Roger A. Pryor, with his impetuous and dazzling temperament . . ."[49] Yet it was primarily as a journalist that he was noted in the 1850s.

One perspicacious individual who carefully read Pryor's editorials was a rising Illinois politician, Abraham Lincoln. Several of Lincoln's most important speeches used phrases which Honest Abe freely attributed to the editor. During one of his peripatetic debates with Douglas (at Cincinnati in September, 1858) Lincoln referred to the famous phrase about the gathering storm, "the irrepressible conflict," which even today most historians attribute to William H. Seward.[50] Explained Lincoln: "But neither I, nor Seward . . . is entitled to the enviable or unenviable distinction of having first expressed that idea. That same idea was expressed by the Richmond *Enquirer* in Virginia, in 1856—quite two years before it was expressed by the first of us. And while Douglas was pluming himself that in his conflict with my humble self, last year, he had 'squelched out' that fatal heresy, as he delighted to call it, and had suggested that if he only had the chance to be in New York and meet Seward he would have 'squelched' it there also, it never occurred to him to breathe a word against Pryor. . . . That same Roger A. Pryor was brought to Washington City and made the editor of the *par excellence* Douglas paper, after making use of that expression, which, in us, is so unpatriotic and heretical."[51] Lincoln gave Pryor substantially the same credit in a speech delivered at the Palladium in New Haven on March 6, 1860.[52] Curiously enough, Pryor overlooked his own authorship and later gave the credit to Seward in a Congressional speech.[53]

At the Republican State Convention in Springfield, Illinois, on June 17, 1858, Lincoln declared: " 'A house divided against itself cannot stand.' I believe this government cannot endure permanently half slave and half free. I do not expect the Union to be dissolved; I do expect it will cease to be divided. It will become all one thing, or all the other."[54] Lincoln informed Henry C. Whitney that an editorial in the May 6, 1856, issue of the Richmond *Enquirer* was largely responsible for the keynote of this speech. "In this issue the editor, Roger A. Pryor, drew a vivid picture of the war between the two systems."[55]

During the great financial panic of 1857, Pryor stated in the Rich-

·mond *South:* "As Southern men, we look with great equanimity upon this financial revulsion. It will tend to elucidate the great problems, whether the North or the South is the most dependent upon each other. . . . We can now ask, where are the boasted resources of the North?

"The present crisis will show that the *slave labor staples of the South* will furnish the means of extrication from commercial indebtedness. It will show the South—comparatively free from distress or embarrassment—able to ride out the storm which the speculation of the North has caused."[56]

Pryor was a leader in the fight against the Know-Nothings or American Party. This nativist, anti-foreigner, anti-Catholic party nominated ex-president Millard Fillmore and A. J. Donnelson as its national slate in the 1856 elections. Although there were few foreigners and Catholics in Virginia, Pryor opposed the party as a matter of principle,[57] and his editorials in the Richmond *Enquirer* were the "argument and text" of the Democratic Party.[58] He was one of a group of eminent speakers that defended the cause of the Democrats throughout Virginia; the anti-nativist campaign was preached by Pryor, Stephen A. Douglas, Robert M. T. Hunter, John B. Floyd, James Y. Mason, and John Letcher.[59] (Pryor was moving in distinguished company now: Senator Douglas was regarded as presidential timber, Senator Hunter was one of the South's best-regarded spokesmen, Floyd was Buchanan's Secretary of War, Mason had been Minister to France, and Letcher was soon to be Governor of Virginia.) The Know-Nothings seemed irresistible until they reached Virginia, where Pryor's candidate, Henry A. Wise, won election by 10,000 votes.[60] The grateful Governor Wise wrote that he owed more to Pryor than to any other man in Virginia, and state Democrats gave the editor a silver service,[61] which subsequently was to be the only asset between him and starvation. The magnitude of the accomplishment of the Virginia Democrats was indicated by the fact that the Know-Nothings captured more than one-fifth of the total national vote.[62] After the election, there were five members of the party in the United States Senate and fourteen in the House of Representatives.[63]

After the Know-Nothing campaign, Pryor became the editor of a new paper, *The South.*[64] Volume 1, Number 1 was issued on March 28, 1857, as a daily.[65] A weekly periodical thus greeted its compatriot:

"That the paper will be ably conducted there cannot be a doubt, but how far its purposes will be sustained by the people whose interests it especially advocates remains to be seen. Mr. Pryor is a bold writer, and unfolds his designs without fear and asks for no favors. His paper will undoubtedly be the acknowledged organ of the extremists of the South, and if they allow it to fail for want of support, the moral effect will be destruction to the political strength supposed to be possessed by the friends of the measures advocated by Mr. Pryor."[66] Sara Pryor selected the paper's motto: *"Unum et commune periclum una salus"*[67]— "the one safety in the one and common peril."

The new editor thus described the purpose of his paper: "To that institution which distinguishes the slaveholding States in the confederacy,[68] divides them into a separate community, makes them an object of fanatical hatred and the victim of Federal injustice; to that institution which exposes them to the same danger and unites them in the same destiny, and to the vital interests of public policy, education, agriculture, commerce, and industrial development which engage the thought and energies of their people, and constitute them a distinct and peculiar commonwealth: in short, to those institutions and interests, to those political principles, social characteristics and intellectual tendencies; to those common necessities and aspirations which are embraced and suggested in the word South, the paper acknowledges a primary and paramount allegiance, and pledges inflexible fidelity and a zealous service."[69]

The South was regarded on both sides of the Mason and Dixon line as being a distinct and separate section long before Pryor,[70] although it was during the period of his bitter pen that sectionalism became most rampant. "A mild anti-slavery sentiment, born of the philanthropic spirit, had existed in all parts of the country from the first."[71] It is the thesis of one book that the South first was arrayed against the North in the years 1775-1789, rather than in the generally accepted period of "about 1820." The peculiar problems of the South were not only those related to slavery, according to this author, but also concerned climate, specialized farming, and the "Southern way of life."[72] But as it was intended to do, *The South* was a unifying newspaper of the Southern point of view. According to one observer, Pryor "was among the most brilliant of the young editors of the Southern press. His newspaper, the Richmond *South*, had a large and growing circulation in the cotton states. . . ."[73] He was one of the Southern editors who preached economic and political preparedness.[74] His paper backed the position of Robert M. T. Hunter that the loss of Kansas would end all hopes of extending slavery and of achieving equality in the nation.[75]

But *The South* did not flourish as it should have. On September 8, 1857, the daily slipped to a semi-weekly edition. On November 19 of the following year, publication was discontinued.[76] After the newspaper failed, Pryor joined the staff of the Washington *States*.[77]

III

The Politician

Roger A. Pryor abandoned his incipient law career before it could get fairly started by reason of an apparently serious throat ailment, and journalism became his career of necessity. On numerous occasions, however, he was called upon to explain or to defend a positive position which he had taken. He did so with fluency and fire. His fame as an orator soon matched his renown as an editor, and Pryor became a familiar figure on the hustings. A man with a decided point of view, the courage of his convictions, and the ability to communicate with large groups of persons naturally gravitated, or was catapulted, into politics. The South then was a geographic term, rather than a political entity, but Pryor (perhaps without conscious intendment) set about establishing *his* views as the South's point of view.

Pryor was "one of the most eloquent speakers upon the hustings. . . ."[1] A classmate at Hampden-Sydney College was later to write of him: "With long hair, classic face, dressed in the finest style; with gestures which he practiced as a boy before a glass; with a fire of genius in his eye and his clear, well-tuned and penetrating voice; and with a speech carefully prepared and, it is said, committed to memory and the same nearly all over the district, he came from the editorial chair in Washington, entered the lists, and beat all the old political leaders. He certainly produced the greatest effect before the people ever produced here by any man except Randolph."[2]

In 1856, Pryor wrote that "It is evident that the North will give us no guaranties. . . . The Black Republicans are beginning to be embold-

[25]

ened by the evidence of submission in certain Southern States."[3] To combat that tendency, it was necessary to teach the North that the South would resist any hostile actions.

The most important of the educational influences devised by the more advanced leaders of the slave states was the Southern Commercial Convention, held annually.[4] At the 1856 convention in Savannah, many Southerners favored a resolution objecting to Federal subsidies for mail steamers, as they operated exclusively from Northern ports. Pryor moved to amend this vague protest by adding the words, "but this convention does not approve the policy of Federal bounties to steamship lines."[5]

At the 1857 convention in Knoxville, Pryor was named to be a member of a three-man committee to report on the reopening of the African slave trade.[6] Article I, Section 9 of the Constitution of the United States prohibited Congress from interfering with the importation of slaves before 1808; but both Northern and Southern congressmen had voted in 1807 to end the importation of slaves in the following year. For several decades after this, there was no serious proposal to reopen the foreign slave trade.[7] At the 1858 convention in Montgomery, William Lowndes Yancey of Alabama demanded that the foreign slave trade be reopened. The delegates from the Gulf states backed the proposal.[8] Pryor led the border and conservative states in opposition. At first he had been in favor of reopening the foreign slave trade, but he concluded that such a policy was repugnant to grave and sensible men. The material interests of the South would not be benefitted, he decided, by the importation of nonvoting Negroes; for if the South needed a larger voting population to defeat the political schemes of the North, white people would have to be imported. Mere numbers were not a real source of political and social strength.[9]

The greatest curse of the South's domestic economy, Pryor explained to the convention, was excessive household labor, and Negroes then were not skilled workmen. Training of the Negroes would present opportunities to breed discontent, and white mechanics would resent the effort to retrain house workers to master trades—workers who would compete with existing skilled workers. Furthermore, world opinion would be outraged by the revival of international slave trade, "and those who profess to be Christians should not throw the gauntlet in the face of the Christian world."

[26]

Yancey's proposal to reopen the slave trade, continued Pryor, was actually a move to dissolve the Union. "If you intend dissolution, declare it boldly and manfully. Present your proposition with your preamble and resolutions, and we will meet you upon it, and either acquiesce and go with you heartily and zealously, or give you our reason for not doing so."[10]

John A. Jones of Georgia called to Pryor: "Will the gentleman go now, today, for a dissolution of the Union?" The audience applauded the question. Pryor replied that he would not take a position outside of the Union until the South was united. "Give me a cause of oppression and tyranny," he demanded, "sufficient to justify a dissolution of the Union, and give me a united South, and then I am willing to go out of the Union." The crowd applauded again.

Jones insisted that if Pryor had to wait for a united South, he never would secede. The Virginian retorted: "I will not so stigmatize any style, or any class of my fellow citizens, by believing that when a case arises sufficient to justify a dissolution of the Union, any state of the South will stand back. In no case has the Old Dominion ever been recreant to her duty."[11]

Later, Yancey asked, "Will the gentleman from Virginia say what is the issue upon which the South should contest their rights?"

"Should a Black Republican president be installed in the executive chair in Washington," Pryor answered, "and the power of the government be palpably in his hands," and if the South were satisfied to justify the movement, he was willing to secede and would pledge Virginia to do so.[12]

"The scene was a brilliant on," reported a delegate; "a very large building had been prepared for the accommodation of the convention. The great body of delegates represented the whole South; there were visitors from distant points, and the seats were crowded with ladies who felt as deep an interest in political affairs as the friends of contending statemen in England did when those of the highest rank thronged the hustings. . . . Roger A. Pryor, of Virginia, then in the full ardor of his course, in vindication of the Southern policy as defined by its great exponent, the late John C. Calhoun,[13] was present, and made a speech of great interest."[14] Pryor was given the credit for defeating Yancey's efforts to reopen the foreign slave trade.[15]

Pryor was thoroughly known in the South by now, and when Congressman William O. Goode of the Fourth District of Virginia died before he could take his seat, the editor resolved to return to Washington as a legislator. He was opposed for the Democratic nomination by Colonel Thomas F. Goode. Pryor's campaigning was vigorous, and he was "unsurpassed for fiery invective, for thrilling eloquence, for immoveable logic," in the judgment of an earwitness.[16] Elderly men (even Whigs) rode as far as forty miles to hear him.[17] On September 21, 1859, he was nominated by acclamation by the convention of the Democratic Party, which met at Farmville.[18]

Pryor's admirers staged a great celebration for him. A Petersburg tobacco manufacturer named a new brand of his product in the congressman's honor,[19] the second Pryor to be identified with a tobacco.

Early in December, 1859, Pryor reported for service in the House of Representatives of the United States Congress. Rather in awe, one of the congressmen reported: "But what a company of conspicuous men answered to the roll-call on the 6th of December . . . in the Thirty-sixth Congress. . . . Considered by results, it was, perhaps, the most important congregation of men that ever assembled upon our continent. It held the destinies of our institutions and races in the hollow of its hand."[20] This congress embraced the temporal span March 4, 1859 to March 3, 1861, although actually the legislators were not in service for much of that time. The first session was from December 5, 1859, to June 25, 1860; the second, from December 3, 1860, to March 3, 1861.[21]

This House of Representatives contained many distinguished figures. Among the more important were Robert Toombs (Georgia); Schuyler Colfax (Indiana); William Barksdale and Lucius Q. C. Lamar (Mississippi); Owen Lovejoy, Elihu B. Washburn, John A. McClernand, and John A. Logan (Illinois); Francis P. Blair, Jr. (Missouri); Daniel P. Sickles and Roscoe Conkling (New York); Clement L. Vallandigham, Samuel S. Cox, and John Sherman (Ohio); Thaddeus Stevens (Pennsylvania); H. Winter Davis (Maryland); Charles F. Adams (Massachusetts); John H. Reagan (Texas); Justin S. Morrill (Vermont); W. Porcher Miles (South Carolina); and Zebulon B. Vance (North Carolina). On the first day of the term, the House of Representatives was composed of 109 Republicans, 101 Democrats, and 27 Know-Nothings.[22] There was a great feeling of strain and tension; John Brown had been hanged three days before.

The setting was precisely the same as the one described by a member at the opening of Congress two years earlier. "The scene is intense in a rare dramatic quality. Above shine in vari-colored light, the escutcheons of thirty states; around sit the members upon richly-carved oaken chairs. Already arrayed upon either side are the reactions in mutual animosity. . . . The times were then sadly out of joint."[23]

Pryor took his seat on December 7. He at once made his presence felt with a long, impassioned speech, in which humility was not a characteristic, nor, he said, a necessity. Representative Nelson of Tennessee, a member of the Know-Nothing Party, declared that "we want no abolition, no secession, no disunion, no nullification, no civil wars, no reeking carnage, no blazing fields, no burning cities, no military despots. . . ."Pryor could not see it that way. His opening words in Congress were:

> I believe, Mr. Clerk, it was a saying of Edmund Burke's, a consummate master in the science of political philosophy, that "public calamity is a mighty leveler." But even under the impression of that maxim, I do not think I would have ventured to thrust myself into the presence of this august body, conscious as I am of the critical exigencies of the Republic, if I were not impelled, indiscreetly perhaps, by a feeling of surprise and indignation at the position assumed in the speech of the gentleman who preceded me. . . . Mr. Clerk, some gentlemen of the other side have endeavored to make light of this controversy. Nero fiddled while Rome was burning. . . . These men are essaying to force the South to disunion. . . . The Representative from Tennessee to-day catches up and reechoes the assertion, that it is southern agitators who are clamorous for disunion. But he modified his statement subsequently and said that the people of the North, in that respect, were quite as bad as the people of the South. I thank him for that poor compliment. I thank him for certifying that the secessionists of the South are no worse than the Abolitionists of the North.[24]

The new congressman's words were not addresses in the customary manner to "Mr. Speaker," for there was none. So great was the animosity between the evenly matched Republicans and Democrats that a speaker could not be elected for two months, and it was not even possible to agree upon a speaker *pro tempore* to preside over meetings until the House could get organized. Thus, of necessity, the Clerk of the House sat in the speaker's chair.[25]

The first order of business was organization: selection of the speaker. The Republicans put forth John Sherman of Ohio, while the Democrats fought to elect Thomas S. Bocock of Virginia. Although the House had been using the plurality rule up to that time, this procedure was now not satisfactory to the majority. As far as the South was concerned, Sherman was unacceptable for many reasons. In general, he was a Northerner and a Republican; specifically, he had joined others of his party in endorsing an 1857 book by a Southerner, Hinton Helper, *The Impending Crisis*, which took the view that slavery was uneconomical and doomed.[26] This book, said Pryor, was "riotous in rebellion, treason, and insurrection, precisely in the spirit of the act which startled us a few weeks since at Harper's Ferry."[27]

"The nomination of Sherman for the Speakership," declared Pryor, "was, in itself, a proclamation of war, and gave the signal of hostilities. . . . If you do not desire the agitation of the slavery question, why did you nominate a man whose mere candidacy is an affront to southern feeling and a challenge to southern resistance?"[28]

Week after angry week, the House devoted its attention to the election of a Speaker and to nothing else. Tempers rose to the boiling point. When members of the House exchanged notes about floor strategy, spectators hopefully thought that challenges to duels were being passed.[29]

On January 30, 1860, just before the thirty-ninth ballot for Speaker, Sherman withdrew his name.[30] Two days later, on the forty-fourth ballot, William Pennington, a New Jersey Republican, received 117 of the 233 votes cast. This was one vote more than half of the total number cast and he was consequently elected. Meanwhile, at this crucial session, with war or peace hovering on the brink, the House of Representatives had to that date performed no function except to vote for Speaker and to discuss the political implications of election of a particular candidate.[31] As to the new Speaker himself, "He was a man of splendid presence," recorded a fellow congressman, "with a great talent for humor, a capital stump-speaker, and perhaps the most thoroughly unaccomplished man in parliamentary law who ever wielded the gavel."[32]

Congressman Pryor rented a large house on New York Avenue in Washington, which he staffed with servants from Virginia.[33] Sara served as her husband's private secretary.[34] She sensed fully the passions of the day. "Nor can I pause to do more than hint at the spirit of the Thirty-sixth Congress, the struggles, vituperation, intemperate speech, honest efforts of the wise members."[35] On the second day of the session, she saw that "Members from their seats crowded down the aisles, and the clerk was powerless to preserve order. 'A few more such scenes,' said one, 'and we shall hear the crack of the revolver and see the gleam of the brandished blade.'"[36] She was not the only Southern woman who faithfully attended the bitter sessions. "The wives, daughters, and other female connections of Southern members were in the galleries constantly," a congressman recollected. "They cheered, by their presence and smiles, the fervid efforts of the secession orators. For impetuous debate, there was Lamar, of Mississippi, scholarly and defiant; . . . for vituperative philippic, there was Roger A. Pryor. . . ."[37] "The clever women of the South met . . . to urge on their slow-moving husbands in what they considered the path of duty."[38]

"The entire South seems to have been very rich then in buds of beauty and women of distinction. . . . Mrs. Roger A. Pryor is Virginia's own."[39] She did not play a conspirator's role in these trying days. "Mrs. Pryor," observed a contemporary, "adorned Washington society at a time when our national history was drifting into its most tragically dramatic stage, but not yet released from the primitive era which regarded the White House as a structure of classic magnificence. . . . It was an era of political and social brilliance, when eloquent men still thundered forth heroic sentiments in classic periods, and lovely women had the sloping shoulders and oval faces which have since given place to the square build and commerical profile of a business age."[40] The conversational scope of these social functions was not restricted. "We talked," Mrs. Pryor noted, "of art and artists, galleries in Europe, shops in Paris—anything except what we were all thinking about."[41]

In the House, Pryor "had only time to work up his reputation as an impassioned speaker and as a fearless defender of the rights of the States."[42] "My husband was probably the first congressman to wear 'the gray,' a suit of domestic cloth having been presented to him by his constituents. Immediately a Northern member said, in an address on the state of the country, 'Virginia, instead of clothing herself in sheep's wool, had better don her appropriate garb of sackcloth and ashes.' In pathetic contrast to these scenes were the rosy, cherubic little pages, in white blouses and cambric collars, who flitted to and from bearing, with smiling faces, dynamic notes and messages from one representative to another."[43]

The secessionist threat was never far from any congressman's lips. Representative Nelson of Tennessee declared in debate that he loved the whole country, its mountains and hills and valleys, but that his country was being corrupted by separationist sentiments. Pryor sprang to his feet. "Allow me to protest most emphatically that I am no disunionist. Allow me to protest that I am as warm an admirer of the Union, in the spirit of the Constitution, as the gentleman from Tennessee. I do not yield even to him in the ardor of my attachment to the Confederacy; but I do say that my patriotism is of a different character and different policy. Sir, by a sort of perverse idolatry, he worships our mountains and hills, our valleys, our rivers, and lakes; he worships, in other words, the visible senseless symbol. I worship the spirit of the Constitution; but when that spirit has departed, when the divinity has been dethroned from the altar, I no longer pay my homage there."

The debate became more personal, and Nelson cried that he was able to protect himself. "I will not violate parliamentary procedure," replied Pryor. "I say to the gentleman that he may dismiss his apprehensions; I am not going to assault him." There was laughter and applause at this reassurance,[44] for the Virginia congressman's reputation as a duellist had preceded him.

Pryor was no less emphatic in explaining to the House that the South as a whole was no more an aggressor than was he personally. "In fact, the entire history of this sectional struggle exhibits the South in a uniform attitude of defense; and exhibits the North pursuing an invariable policy of insult and encroachment. No man will dare deny this statement. The most adventurous and unscrupulous Representative on the other side, will not undertake to advance a single instance wherein the South has impaired the interests, or trampled on the rights of the non-slaveholding states."[45]

In this aggressive atmosphere, Pryor was anything but conciliatory himself. When he asked another congressman when he would complete his remarks and was told that the speaker had not really begun as yet, the Virginian declared: "I do not know that I have greater powers of endurance than the other gentlemen. At any rate, I prefer that when a gentleman obtains the floor, his speech should not be like the campaigns of the old Austrian generals—beginning one year, and concluding several years afterwards. I think a speech should be, as the classical dramatists said, all of a unity—of time, place, and action." On one occasion, Representative Bingham objected during debate that Pryor was interrupting him too frequently. "I claim my rights here," proclaimed Bingham, "and I intend to enforce them."

"Very well," agreed Pryor, "the right of silence is one."[47]

Pryor had gone to Congress to fill the vacancy caused by the death of William O. Goode. When the new congressman offered a resolution expressing the House's regrets at Goode's demise, acceptance was prompt,[48] for by this time most Northerners had learned to regret that Goode had died. If he had not perished, Pryor would not have been present.

Representative Pryor wished to concentrate on the states' rights issue. Thus, he asked unanimous consent of the House to be excused from serving on the Committee for the District of Columbia.[49] But he did participate in debates on any issues that interested him; for example, he opposed the privilege of unlimited franking of mail.[50]

A fellow congressman noted that "Pryor was at first with, and at last against, the Union. He was not as eager as he seemed for a separate Confederacy. His career is known, with its vicissitudes. The extremes he once advocated seemed now to be as alien to his cautious and heroic nature, as moderation would have been in his earlier ardent years, when he sought no exemption from any attack."[51]

In his earlier speeches, Congressman Pryor took the position that the nation needed both North and South. "In fact," he declared, "the resources of one section are exactly responsive to the deficiencies of the other. Our economy of labor, disciplined and steady and unfailing, is an indispensable auxiliary to the adventurous and educated industry of the North. We plant and produce; they fetch and fabricate. We supply the solid basis; they the decoration of the Corinthian capital. The ever active and turbulent spirit of free labor in the North would precipitate the social system into anarchy, if it were not counteracted and controlled by the conservative interests of slave labor in the South."[52]

But it did not take long for the Virginian to conclude that sectional differences could not be settled with speech. "We have threatened and resolved," he announced, "and resolved and threatened, and backed out from our threats, until, so help me God! I will never utter another threat or another resolution; but as the stroke follows the lightning's flash, so, with me, acts shall be coincident and commensurate with words."[53]

Pryor explained what had changed his attitude. "Sir, it is idle and unmeaning mockery to talk of *preserving* the Union; and they who indulge in this strain of declamation betray little of the candor demanded by the urgency of the occasion. . . . The issue before the country, I repeat, sir, is the simple question of peace or war. . . . The party into whose hands the control of the Administration is passing, so far from a recourse to conciliatory measures and a recognition of the right of secession, obdurately reject all overtures of compromise, and avow a purpose to employ all of the resources of Government for the subjugation of the retiring States. And so it is that the calamities of civil war are about to be precipitated upon the country."[54]

But he insisted almost until the last that he was a unionist. "For answer, I have only to give the gentleman assurance that the southern States do not now intend to abandon the Union, whatever ultimate recourse events may impose upon them. . . . They are resolved, in the first instance, to vindicate their rights in the *Union*, peaceably if possible, by force if necessary."[55]

It took Pryor a full year to conclude that force was not the solution. "I offer the following resolution: *Resolved*, That any attempt to preserve the Union between the States of this Confederacy by force would be impracticable, and destructive of republican liberty."[56] His motion failed.

Of what war could do to the United States, Pryor had no doubts. "What, then, I would entreat of gentlemen on the other side, do they propose by kindling the flame of civil war? No matter what may be the issue, liberty cannot survive the conflict. The frail fabric of a system constructed for the abode of peace, would perish under the shocks and concussions of intestine strife."[57]

It was the doings of the North, Pryor believed, that brought the nation to the brink of war. "As a body, the people of the South are in no way concerned in the violation of the law against the slave trade.

[34]

They are not more guilty of the crime than the people of the North. In fact, and notoriously, it is in northern ships, by northern men, and for the aggrandizement of northern capital, that the slave trade is prosecuted in defiance of legal prohibition."[58]

The North, he persisted, was the aggressor. "It is an express, solemn stipulation of the constitutional compact, that fugitive slaves should be returned to their masters. How does the North redeem this obligation? . . . Above all, as avowed in the preamble to the Constitution, the Constitution was formed to 'establish justice and insure domestic tranquillity'; and yet we of the South are pillaged by compatriots, while fellow-citizens incite our slaves to insurrection!"[59]

A bill was introduced in the Thirty-sixth Congress "to protect and support the Republic of Liberia," specifically, to regulate that republic's slave trade. Pryor opposed the measure on the ground that what was going on in Africa was not for the United States to legislate. He used this opportunity to restate his acceptance of the Constitution's prohibition against importation of additional slaves.

> I am not of those who deny altogether the authority of the Federal Government to suppress the slave trade. I admit the power; nay, I affirm it. . . . But, sir, the bill before us . . . makes provision for the suppression of the slave trade between the Island of Cuba and the dominions of Dahomey—an extension of power for which no man can adduce constitutional authority. . . . The point that I made was this—and perhaps my colleague's misapprehension was the effect of my own ambiguous language: that this Government has the authority to prohibit the slave trade, and punish those engaged in it, as between this country and Africa; but that the bill before us provides resources to prohibit the trade between Africa and foreign countries. My second point was, that while it was perfectly constitutional to prohibit the slave trade, it is unconstitutional to establish colonies and employ missionaries in the interior of Africa.[60]

When a cargo of illegally imported Africans was seized and taken to Key West, a bill was introduced in the House of Representatives to return the Negroes to Africa. Pryor opposed it.[61] He had a different solution to offer. "Last year I suggested, without much thought, the idea of adopting the policy already practiced by the Government of Great Britain, and that is the policy of reducing captured Africans to a quasi-slavery—a species of apprenticeship. I have thought much upon the question since; I have read somewhat upon it, and I am only confirmed in the idea I then advanced."[62]

Congressman Pryor was the epicenter of the mounting North-South fury in the House of Representatives. "While in Congress his aggressiveness and passionate oratory led to several duels," noted one of his contemporaries,[63] but actually the only "duel" resulted in a near miss. A member of that legislature recalled that "The summer of 1860 was ominous of domestic discord and civil war. . . . [T]he violent scenes in the House, notably those between Potter, Pryor, Barksdale, and Lovejoy, were indicative that the south was aggressive, and that the north would fight."[64] Early in April, Congressman Owen Lovejoy, chairman of the Public Lands Committee, angered the Southerners with a characterization of slavery. "It has the violence of robbery," he exclaimed, "the blood and cruelty of piracy, it has the offensive and brutal lusts of polygamy, all combined and concentrated in itself." Pryor left his seat and moved quickly towards Lovejoy, "with a gesture full of menace," according to the official reporter. "The gentleman from Illinois," cried the Virginian, "shall not approach this side of the House, shaking his fists and talking in the way he has talked. It is bad enough to be compelled to sit here and hear him utter his treasonable and insulting language; but he *shall not*, sir, come upon this side of the House shaking his fist in our faces."[65]

John Fox Potter, a Wisconsin Republican, chimed in: "We listened to the gentlemen on the other side for eight weeks, when they denounced the members upon this side with violent and abusive language. We listened to them quietly and heard them through. And now, sir, this side *shall* be heard, let the consequences be what they may."

Pryor rose to a point of order: these Republicans must speak from their seats. Thirty or forty congressmen gathered around Lovejoy and Pryor, gesticulating and shouting. At length, Lovejoy was permitted to continue his oration, while Barksdale of Mississippi shouted, "The meanest slave in the South is your superior."[66] Martin J. Crawford of Georgia cocked his revolver.[67]

The matter did not end there. A few days later, Pryor rose to a question of privilege in the House. He charged that at the office of the *Con-*

gressional Globe, Potter had added to his own speech the brave words about being heard, "let the consequences be what they may." Actually those words had not been uttered on the floor, claimed Pryor. Potter replied that he would stand by his language. "I will put what construction I please upon it," announced Pryor, "and whether or not he stands by it the sequel will demonstrate." The Republicans jeered derisively.[68] But Pryor was in deadly earnest. He named A. R. Chisholm of Kentucky to be his best man, to deliver a challenge to a duel. Potter selected as his second a transcontinental explorer, soldier, and poet, Frederick West Lander, who transmitted the Wisconsin congressman's terms; as the challenged party, he had the choice of weapons. Under Potter's stipulations, the duel would be fought with Bowie knives in a closed room in the District of Columbia, in the presence of an armed friend of each contestant.[69] "But Pryor was not fool enough to accept any such tom-cat terms," a Confederate veteran later observed.[70] In actual fact, it was Chisholm who refused the terms in the name of his principal. Pryor was disappointed and wrote Potter that he disapproved of Chisholm's action and would accept these terms. But Potter declined to reopen the matter.[71]

Potter's friends did not question his courage. Noted one: "He was not very tall, but remarkably square-shouldered and broad-chested, and the movements of his limbs betokened that elastic, muscular poise which usually denotes not only power, but also quick readiness of action. He might have been called a fine-looking man, of the virile style of beauty, with his strong, regular features framed in blond hair and beard, his aquiline nose, and a pair of blue eyes which in repose would charm with their honest and kindly gaze, but could shoot forth flashes of lightning when in excitement—the whole man the very picture of strength and courage."[72]

At a Congressional roll call, when Potter's name was reached, some one shouted, "He is keeping a Pryor engagement." When Pryor's name was called, a voice replied, "He has gone to be made into Potter's clay."[73]

The altercation was widely noted and discussed. According to a newspaper in the North, its people had "long been deluded with the notion that every Southerner was a walking, pent-up volcano, ready to belch forth fire and death at a touch; that he was the embodiment of courage and high-strung fortitude; and to cross his path was as good as death." But now "the chivalric, ferocious ogres" were shown to be "a very harmless set of blusterers who are brave only when they have a very decided advantage." But on the other hand, a Southern newspaper declared: "That man gains a great deal of credit who eludes a bargain, a pledge, or gets out of any sort of scrape by a quibble . . . such as men in the North wink their eyes at and say, 'devilish clever, isn't it?' and such as men in the South blush at, and are tabooed by all honorable men."[74] Potter was regarded as a hero in the North and as a coward in the South. W. A. Graham, a senior at Princeton College at the time, thought he could see the meaning of the altercation: the North was willing to argue with the South but not to fight.[75]

Representative Thad Stevens of Pennsylvania suggested that the Potter-Pryor duel should have been fought, with dung-forks.[76]

IV

Secession

Because of its dynamic personalities and issues, the Thirty-sixth Congress trod slowly through history. The days were not long enough for all the exhortation, invective, and sarcasm that was to be vented. With increasing frequency, the illuminating gas in the House of Representatives had to be turned on for night sessions. There came a time when many exhausted members no longer could drag themselves to the chamber. Then a rule was adopted which ordered the sergeants-at-arms to bring recalcitrant representatives to Congress, by force if necessary. Ever alert to the violation of personal rights, Roger A. Pryor objected. "[A] handful, a miserable minority, sustained by extraordinary powers of endurance, or by artificial stimulants, have, in the majesty of their power, issued a peremptory summons to other gentlemen, who have, as became good and prosperous persons, retired to bed at a proper hour. What has been done in the interest of the country? Has business been forwarded? You have effected an expensive consumption of gas. You have put an intolerable burden upon those unfortunate gentlemen who are noting and transmitting to a disgusted posterity the drivel of this night's proceedings."

Representative Lovejoy interrupted to object to those words "miserable" and "drivel" as being disrespectful to the House. "Then," Pryor replied, "I will say, what is obvious to everybody, that I intended no offense to the House. By a 'miserable minority,' I mean that you are paltry in numbers. When I said 'drivel,' I meant the nonsensical utterances of jaded and befuddled members."[1] This substitution for his word "drivel" apparently was inoffensive. Or perhaps the members were just too tired to care.

In the spring of 1860, the national political conventions began. Curiously enough, Pryor's name was prominently mentioned at the National Republican Convention, which opened at The Wigwam in Chicago on May 15. Noted an observer: "The curiosity of the town—next to the 'wigwam'— is a bowie-knife seven feet long, weighing over forty pounds. It bears on one side the inscription, '*Presented to John F. Potter by the Republicans of Missouri.*' On the other side is this motto, 'Will always keep a "Pryor" engagement.' This curiosity is gaped at almost as much as Greeley, and it is a strange and dreadful looking concern. It will be formally presented to Potter at Washington, by a committee from Missouri."[2] Also at this convention, a curtain was dropped, adorned with a full-length picture of Potter and the words, "He always meets a Pryor engagement."[3]

The National Democratic Convention met in Charleston on April 23. The convention broke up heatedly when delegates from seven Southern states refused to accept a popular sovereignty plank in the party platform. Stephen A. Douglas was nominated for President of the United States, with Benjamin Fitzpatrick of Alabama in the second slot. The dissident delegates went to Baltimore, where they reconvened on June 18. The Southern wing of the Democratic Party here nominated John C. Breckenridge of Kentucky for President of the United States, with Joseph Lane of Oregon as his running mate.[4] The Douglas Democrats in Virginia held a convention of their own in Staunton, while the Breckenridge Democrats held a convention in Charlottesville, where the principal speakers were Hunter, Mason, and Pryor. This convention met for the last time on August 18, and Pryor was named to a five-man committee that was to prepare an address to the people of Virginia.[5]

Pryor was very active in this campaign and his oratory reached a high level. At Nottoway Court House, said a reporter, "Never man spake like this man."[6] "Here in 1860, Roger Pryor made the finest speech of his career for Breckenridge."[7] On Election Day, November 6, Virginia's vote was:

Bell (Constitutional Union Party)	74,681
Breckenridge	74,323
Douglas	16,290
Lincoln	1,929[8]

Pryor was elected to the Thirty-Seventh Congress.[9]

Lincoln was elected President of the United States, a signal to the ardent secessionists that the parting of the ways had come. The day after Election Day, a young Southern girl was making a journey from Charleston to Florida. "On the train, just before we reached Fernandina, a woman called out: 'That settles the hash!' Tanny touched me on the shoulder and said: 'Lincoln's elected.' 'How do you know?' 'The man over there has a telegram.' Someone cried: 'Now that the black radical Republicans have the power I suppose they will [John] Brown us all.' "[10] When she reached Florida, "I saw a few men running up a wan Palmetto flag, and shouting, though prematurely: 'South Carolina has seceded!' "[11]

The reaction *was* premature, but not by many days. One week after Election Day, on November 13, South Carolina passed a law calling for a convention to consider "the dangers incident to the position of the State in the Federal Union."[12] On December 20, by unanimous vote, the convention adopted an ordinance stating that "the union now subsisting between South Carolina and the other States, under the name of the 'United States of America' is hereby dissolved."[13]

News of South Carolina's secession reached Washington that same day. President Buchanan, attending the wedding of Miss Parker and Mr. Bouligny, was disturbed by a commotion outside; and Sara Pryor went to investigate. She reported back to him: "It appears, Mr. President, that South Carolina has seceded from the Union." He collapsed into a chair, then asked her to call his carriage. No one thought more of the bride or the wedding cake.[14]

Outside, an excited woman called to a naval officer, "South Carolina has seceded, and, O captain, we will have a glorious monarchy, and you must join it!" "Yes," he replied, "and be made Duke of Benedict Arnold."[15]

Certainly it was not a day for rejoicing. Later Sara Pryor was to note: "This was the tremendous event which was to change all our lives,—to give us poverty for riches, mutilation and wounds for strength and health, obscurity and degradation for honor and distinction, exile and loneliness for inherited homes and friends, pain and death for happiness and life."[16]

Should Lincoln's election have been taken by South Carolina as the signal for secession? "Any attempt to answer the question, 'Was there a reasonable probability that the election of Lincoln meant an attack

upon the institution of Slavery within the States?' must be made with
a clear realization that probabilities are after all mere conjectures."[17]
"[I]n view of the increasingly unsound economics of slave labor, the
doom of slavery in the Southern states was sealed more by the social
and economic forces that had gained headway in nineteenth-century
America than by the immediate implications of the political resolution of 1860."[18] "The South," wrote an eminent Southern historian,
"had avowedly staked everything, even her allegiance to the Union,
upon this election. The triumph of Mr. Lincoln was, in her eyes, nothing less than the establishment in power of a party bent upon the
destruction of the southern system and the defeat of southern interests,
even to the point of counternancing and assisting servile insurrection."[19] In the opinion of a Richmond editor who lived through that
day, "The election of Abraham Lincoln to the Presidency of the United
States might have precipitated the Secessionist movement of the
Southern States; but it certainly did not produce it. . . . The mind
of the South . . . suffered from a general apprehension rather than
a specific alarm; and the election of Abraham Lincoln was a vague
addition to this uneasiness rather than a particular cause of complaint."[20]

South Carolina's secession was followed by that of six other states:
Mississippi (January 9, 1861), Florida (January 10), Alabama (January 11), George (January 19), Louisiana (January 26), and Texas (February 1).[21] Pryor was tremendously disturbed by these developments,
and his words were the most intemperate of his career. He referred to a
"a hireling soldiery . . . concentrated [in Washington] to impose an
obnoxious ruler on an unwilling people."[22] He promised that if a
coercion policy were imposed by the Federal government, without any
apparent effort on the part of the South to resist, he alone and single-
handed would plunge a dagger in Lincoln's heart.[23] Pryor's vehemence
and outspokenness were noted by a hostile Northern press. Said the
New York *Herald*: "Time was, until PRYOR, when 'Virginian' was
synonymous with 'gentleman.' "[24] In Congress the next day, Pryor
rose to a point of personal privilege. "No gentleman," he declared, "can
desire a more significant and satisfactory compliment than the abuse of
James Gordon Bennett. His applause is an argument of suspicion; his
invective is a title of honor."[25]

To consider the parlous state of the Union, the Committee of Thirty-three was formed in the House of Representatives, comprised of sixteen Republicans, fifteen Southern Democrats, and two Northern Democrats. A similar Committee of Thirteen was formed in the Senate.[26] The Committee of Thirty-three carefully studied a compromise proposal offered by John J. Crittenden of Kentucky: slavery would be prohibited in national territory north of the line 36° 30′; south of the line, slavery would be Federally protected. Any states to be admitted in the future would make their own choice as to the status of slavery within their borders. Existing fugitive slave laws would be enforced, but the Congress of the United States would endeavor to have the states abrogate their personal liberty laws. When all this was accomplished, Congress would agree that the slavery issue henceforth must be outside the jurisdiction of the Federal legislature.[27]

Etheridge introduced a watered down version of Crittenden's proposal when it appeared that the original compromise offer could not be passed. On January 7, 1861, Pryor wrote to Lewis E. Harvie, the president of the Richmond & Danville Railroad in Richmond: "The last hope extinguished to-day. Even Etheridge's compromise voted down by Black Republicans nearly unanimously. . . ."[28] The following day he wrote to J. Wilcox Brown in New York: "No chance of compromise. Republicans will not yield."[29]

The stern Republican Representative Thad Stevens shared Pryor's view. "I regret, Sir, that I am compelled to concur in the belief stated yesterday by the gentleman from Virginia, that no compromise which can be made will have any effect in averting the present difficulty. When I see these states in open and declared rebellion against the Union, . . . when I see our flag insulted, and that insult submitted to, I have no hope that concession, humiliation, and compromise can have any effect whatsoever."[30]

Pryor vigorously opposed all pending legislation that seemed to be discriminatory towards the South. He voiced his objections to the Naval Appropriation Bill. "Mr. Chairman, so long as the American Navy was engaged in the lawful and beneficent enterprise of protecting the interests of commerce, enlarging the boundaries of discovery, and maintaining the honor of our flag against foreign attack, I voted to accord it a generous support. But now, sir, when it is to be employed for the inhuman purpose of subjugating sovereign States, and imposing the yoke of military despotism upon a people who are guilty of no other

[43]

crime than a gallant resistance to wrong and oppression, I would sink
it in the abyss of ocean before I would grant it a farthing. A bulwark
of national defense, it invokes the nation's gratitude; the dread instru-
ment of death and desolation in fratricidal strife, it deserves the nation's execration."[31]

When the Committee on Military Affairs wanted to give the incoming President greater powers, Pryor objected. The measure proposed

> submits to the fallible and capricious judgment of a single indi-
> vidual—the President of the United States—to determine when
> occasion shall require the employment of force against a State,
> and so invests him with the arbitrary power of initiating civil war.
> To carry out the suggestion of his understanding, (it may be the
> impulse of his resentment or the dictate of his ambition), the bill
> authorizes the President to grasp all the naval and military re-
> sources of the country—the militia as well as the regular services
> —millions of men—and to hurl them in fatal attack upon a mem-
> ber of this Confederacy.
>
> Sir, it signifies nothing, as intimated by the gentleman who
> preceded me, that this measure does not involve an appropriation
> of money. For that defect is all the more portentous, since it allows
> the President to pledge the faith and credit of the country to an
> unlimited amount. Tell me, has all regard for the essential prin-
> ciples of civil liberty, has all solicitude for the blessed reign of
> peace, vanished from among us, that we are willing to arm the
> executive with this enormous power for this flagitious purpose; a
> purpose not only fatal to freedom and shocking to humanity, but
> a purpose plainly prohibited by the principles of the Constitu-
> tion?[32]

He opposed a high tariff bill as a wicked deal. "The importunate
protectionists of Pennsylvania, more clamorous and insatiable than
the daughter of a horse-leech, after higgling successively with every
party for a stipend from the Treasury, at last caught the Republicans
in a moment of exigent need, and from their lust for place, extorted
the promise of a bounty to iron. This bill is the issue of a carnal coali-
tion between the Abolitionists of New England and the protectionists
of Pennsylvania. It is the result of a compact, whereby, at the expense

of public interest, Pennsylvania engaged to support an Abolitionist for the Presidency on the condition that the Abolitionists would repay Pennsylvania by the protection of iron."[33]

Pryor refused to yield the floor for a rebuttal of his attack upon the tariff bill. "No, sir; I cannot yield. 'The galled jade winces'; but she must repress her irrascibility till I conclude my remarks."[34]

During the debate upon the Oregon war debt, the statement was made that General Winfield Scott, general-in-chief of the army, had attested to the worth of a certain proposal. That was no recommendation to Pryor, for "General Scott has organized a military despotism in the capital of the Republic, thus overawing the deliberations of the Representatives of the people with his artillery.

"Not only that, sir, but with a cruelty more unnatural than that of Coriolanus, he contemplates an invasion of his own mother State. I have to tell him, however, that unlike the people of Rome, we of Virginia will not essay to propitiate his pity by an exhibition of the tears of our maidens and our matrons; but will meet him when he comes, as beseems the sons of the Old Dominion."[35]

But in this same bitter month of February, Pryor expressed the hope that reason would prevail. To the House, he declared: "Not for ourselves alone do we deprecate a conflict of arms; but from respect to the memory of our common ancestry; for the sake of a land to be rent by the cruel lacerations of the sword; and in reverence of virtues which a benign religion instructs us to adore. By the persuasion of these pious and persuasive importunities we would soothe in every breast the spirit of strife, and invoke the pacific intervention of reason for the adjustment of our disputes."[36]

He gibed at the preparations for conflict that Lincoln would find in the nation's capital. "Collect the materials of war, so that when your leader descends upon the scene, he may draw the curtain from the bloody drama—so that when he assumes the reins of power, he may precipitate his legions into the bosom of the South. I do not say they will be 'welcomed with bloody hands to hospitable graves'; but this I will adventure, that the people of the South will not surrender their rights without a struggle; and that for whatsoever may be wrested from them by the grasp of superior force, they will indemnify their posterity by bequeathing them the legacy of an untarnished name."[37]

To Pryor was given the opportunity of making to the House the futile report of the Committee of Thirty-three. Actually, his address was as near a thing as there was to an official statement of the South's case. He himself wrote that "the following speech was recognized by my associates as a correct and comprehensive statement of their cause . . ."[38] In part, Pryor stated:

At the epoch of the Revolution, and, indeed, when the Federal Government was organized, slavery prevailed in the North as well as in the South. If not the chief, it was at least conspicuous among the interests for the protection of which our present system of Government was established. The Constitution distinguishes it by express and repeated recognition, in each case fortifying it by particular guarantees.

Now, sir, against this great and vital interest—an interest of which the pecuniary value is indicated by countless millions, and the importance of which, in the more essential aspect of social and political relation, no form of expression can adequately represent; an interest on which subsists the material prosperity of the Southern States, and with which their security and independence are inseparably associated,—this interest, so vast and so vital, is the object of organized and incessant assault by those who are bound by every obligation of written covenant and confederate faith to protect it. They have launched against it the anathemas of moral and legal outlawry, and have canvassed Christendom for recruits in the crusade of Abolitionism. They have burdened it with iniquitous and oppressive impositions. They have denied it the development without which it cannot long endure. They have attacked it in detail by every variety of criminal expedient. And, finally, they have assayed, through the instrumentality of servile insurrection, to involve the South in total and irreparable ruin. . . .

But, sir, we do not rest the vindication of the South on the slavery issue alone, nor mainly. Our adversaries, availing themselves of the present prejudice against slavery, have diligently represented that the secession of the South has no other object than the perpetuation of bondage; and the effect of the mis-statement is visible already in the unfriendly criticism of the foreign press. It is time our cause were placed upon the true grounds of defense; upon principles which, instead of insulating it from the sympathies of the world, will command respect wherever justice rules and the maxims of republican liberty are revered. . . .

Sir, for fifty years the interests of the South reposed and prospered under the sacred safeguards of the Constitution. By that compact the equality of the States was guaranteed, their right of self-government recognized, and each member of the confederacy mutually pledged to the others in a spirit of fraternal alliance. The States of the South acceded to the Union on these conditions; on the conditions that they were to be the peers of their sovereign associates, that their rights were to be inviolable, and their property secure under the provisions of the common Government. This sacred covenant was the bond of union between the confederate Republics. The Constitution imposed reciprocal obligations on the States, and pledged them to mutual offices of good-will. In what manner are these pledges redeemed, and these obligations fulfilled by the Northern States?

Foremost in the catalogue of Southern grievance is the complaint that the fundamental principle of the confederacy, the equality of the States, is subverted by a combination between a majority of States to exclude other States from an equal participation in the common domain, and so to deny them equal advantages of expansion and development under the operation of the Federal Government. Nay, this Government itself is abused to the consummation of that iniquity. . . . But this is not all. In respect of another essential condition of federal union—the guarantee of State sovereignty, the right reserved by each State to administer its own affairs and to develop its own destinies in harmony with the general interests of the confederacy—whatsoever of this right may have survived the systematic encroachment of Federal usurpation has vanished before the threat of military coercion. Already sovereign States are reduced, in contemplation, to the consideration of provincial dependencies; and that doom they would speedily realize but for the indomitable spirit which quails not before all the "pomp and circumstance" of your martial preparation. . . .

An explicit provision of the constitutional compact exacts the the restitution of fugitive slaves; yet that provision—albeit so essential that, without it, the South originally refused to join the confederacy—is shamefully annulled by the Northern States; and by the default millions of Southern property have been confiscated. So flagrantly has the South been cheated of its constitutional rights and denied the advantages of the Union—all the burdens of which, however, it bears in enormous disproportion! . . .

But the defense of the South rests upon still stronger grounds; and her secession from the confederacy is justified by even higher principles than the right to vindicate a violated covenant. Absolute power is the essence of tyranny, whether the power be wielded by a monarch or a multitude. The dominant section in this confederacy claims and exercises absolute power—power without limitation and without responsibility; without limitation, since all the restrictions of the Constitution are broken down; and without responsibility, because in the nature of things, the weaker interest cannot control the majority. Of all species of tyranny, the South is subjected to the most intolerable. . . .

It is against this sectional domination, this rule of the majority without law and without limit—a rule asserted in subversion of the Constitution and established on the ruins of the confederacy—it is in resistance to this despotic and detestable rule, that the people of the South have taken up arms. This, sir, is the cause of the South; and tell me if cause more just ever consecrated revolution? It is the cause of self-government against the domination of foreign power—the very cause for which our fathers fought in 1776. Sooner than submit to the irresponsible rule of alien interests, they tore themselves from the embrace of the mother country and staked all in the triumph of *secession*. . . .

To-day it is slavery which suffers from the overthrow of constitutional guaranties and the irresponsible reign of the majority. But, the principle of absolute power once ascendant in the Government, no interest is secure; and circumstances will determine against what object it may be directed. . . .

And what, I pray you, is the dictate of reason? Not, surely, that a free people should be held in subjection to a government they detest; not that the sword be employed to coerce sovereign States, and constrain them to wear the yoke of an odious and oppressive association; but rather that distinct communities be permitted to follow the bent of their peculiar nationality, and to realize the destiny indicated by their own interests and their own aspirations. . . .[39]

By now the Congressmen of the North were familiar with these arguments, which however, probably never had been couched in such splendid prose on other occasions. "The eloquent R. A. Pryor, of Virginia, . . . submitted a resume of the causes that induced the Southern revolt which deserved an argumentative rather than a bitter, sneering reply."[40]

Although not the motivator of war (he insisted that he was not an antiunionist), Pryor cannot be overestimated as a force with respect to inflaming and to uniting the South. He was recognized as one of the editors who chiefly inflamed the secession movement.[41] "Roger Pryor was an ardent secessionist, and it was due to his influence perhaps as much as to any one man that the War Between the States was precipitated."[42] "[H]e was the man who occasioned the war as much as any single man could precipitate a catastrophe that had been approaching for two decades."[43]

His speeches were no droppings of a disembodied orator, without feeling. Pryor felt what he said, and his sensitively mobile features reflected the depth of his feeling. On February 27, the distinguished artist Thomas Nast visited the House of Representatives and made a sketch in which Pryor appeared prominently in the foreground. Nast did not then know the face but thought it striking.[44]

The original Southern Confederacy was formed by South Carolina, Georgia, Alabama, Mississippi, Louisiana, and Florida in February 1861. On February 4, the delegates chosen by the state conventions assembled in Montgomery. On February 8, a provisional constitution and government were agreed upon by unanimous vote. In general, the constitution was modelled after that of the United States. But the initial words of the preamble, "We the people," were qualified by inserting "Each state acting in its sovereign and independent character." The words "provide for the common defense and promote the general welfare" were omitted.[45]

Pryor's beloved state was not a part of all this. Virginia's pro-Union sentiment was shown by its having given its electoral vote in 1860 to John Bell of the Constitutional Union Party. On January 7, 1861, Governor John Letcher, addressing his legislature, severely criticized South Carolina's attitude. On April 4, a convention voted down a motion to draw up an ordinance of secession, 88-45.[46]

Secession was not regarded as the proper step by many Virginians. On January 23, 1861, Robert E. Lee wrote: "The framers of our constitution never exhausted so much labor, wisdom and forebearance in its formation, and surrounded it with so many guards and securities, if it was intended to be broken by every member of the Confederacy at will. It was intended for 'perpetual union' so expressed in the preamble, and for the establishment of a government, not a compact, which can only be dissolved by revolution, or by the consent of all the people in convention assembled. It is idle to talk of secession. Anarchy would have been established and not a government, by Washington, Hamilton, Jefferson, Madison, and other patriots of the Revolution."[47] At the start of the conflict, the future General George E. Pickett wrote to his fiancée: "I, of course, have always strenuously opposed disunion, not as doubting the right of secession, which was taught in our text-book at West Point, but as gravely questioning its expediency. . . . You know, my little lady, some of those cross-stitched mottoes on the cardboard samplers which used to hang on my nursery wall, such as, 'He who provides not for his own household is worse than an infidel' and 'Charity begins at home,' made a lasting impression on me; and while I love my neighbor, i.e., my country, I love my household, i.e., my state, *more*, and I could not be an infidel and lift my sword against my own kith and kin, even though I do believe, my most wise little counselor and confidante, that the measure of American greatness can be achieved only under one flag, and I fear, alas, there can never reign for either of us the true spirit of personal unity, whether divided under two flags or united under one."[48]

In 1860, John Minor Botts, sometime Congressman from Virginia, wrote of secession: "A more base and cowardly proposition was never submitted to an intelligent people.—It is to run away, not only before we are whipped, but before we are struck a blow.—This is our Government; it all belongs to us. I will not run."[49]

In the opinion of an historian from Virginia, secession was intended as a strategem rather than an objective. "The object was to make terms with the North about slavery, and they thought that probably better terms could be made out of the Union than in it."[50] But this Southern point of view (if such it really was) was not shared elsewhere. An

Englishman wrote in 1863: "The right of secession became thus by force of circumstances the ostensible ground of the war; and with the bulk of the Northern people it must be admitted it was not only the ostensible but the real ground; for it is idle to claim for the North a higher or more generous principle of conduct than that which itself put forward. The one prevailing and overpowering sentiment in the North, as soon as the designs of the South were definitely disclosed, was undoubtedly the determination to uphold the Union, and to crush the traitors who had conspired to dissolve it. In this country we had looked for something higher; we had expected, whether reasonably or not, an anti-slavery crusade. We were disappointed; and the result was . . . a re-action of sentiment which has prevented us from doing justice to that which was really worthy of admiration in the Northern cause."[51]

In his inaugural address on March 4, 1861, Lincoln did not share Pryor's view that the North was the persistent aggressor. The new president addressed a pointed plea to Southerners. "In your hands, my dissatisfied fellow-countrymen, and not in mine, is the momentous issue of civil war. The government will not assail you. You can have no conflict without being yourselves the aggressors. You have no oath registered in heaven to destroy the government, while I shall have the most solemn one to 'preserve, protect, and defend it.' "[52]

Of that momentous day, a Congressman wrote: "Abraham Lincoln takes the oath to support and defend the Constitution of the United States. For the first time in the Republic a Chief Magistrate is installed under the protection of artillery charged with grape and canister. . . . This small but disciplined array, the cold line of infantry with bayonets fixed, the champing of troop horses, the tramp of armed men, the rumbling of cannon, the hoarse command of general officers, the unlimbering of guns trained to sweep the streets; what mean these dreadful preparations? Surely this is a vision of the wrath of war!"[53]

V

Fort Sumter

Pryor had been reelected, to serve in the Thirty-Seventh Congress, but he did not remain in Washington to sit in that body. The climate in the national capital seemed impossible to many legislators from the South. On Inauguration Day (March 4, 1861), a group of Southerners met in Washington: Confederate Commissioner Martin J. Crawford of Georgia; Representatives Muscoe Garnett, Roger Pryor, and Daniel De Jarnetts of Virginia; Senator Louis T. Wigfall of Texas, and L. Q. Washington of Virginia. "We all put the same construction on the inaugural," wrote the last-named individual, "which we carefully went over together. We agreed that it was Lincoln's purpose at once to attempt the collection of the revenue, to re-enforce and hold Fort Sumter and Pickens, and to retake the other places. He is a man of will and firmness. His Cabinet will yield to him with alacrity, I think."[1]

The congressmen of the seceding states, and their sympathizers, did not just disappear, nor did they stalk out of the legislature in righteous anger. The departure, noted a member of that Congress, was in style. "It developed all the graces of eloquence. Fair women from the galleries, warm with Southern blood, gave applause more precious than coronets of gold and jewels to the oratory of their impassioned champions."[2] Another legislator noted of the departing Southern congressmen, "They took leave with no more formality than that with which a private gentleman, aggrieved by discourteous treatment, withdraws from a company in which he feels he can no longer find enjoyment."[3]

Mrs. Roger Pryor took her boys and nurse (Eliza Page) by steamer to Acquia Creek, thence to Petersburg. Her husband followed a few days later, and they made their home with Dr. Theodorick Bland.[4] The Provisional Congress of the Confederate States of America came into existence as of February 4, even though Virginia was still in the Union at that time and Pryor was yet a member of the Congress of the United States; he was designated a member of this body on July 24.[5]

On the night of March 18, Pryor spoke in the African Church in Richmond, a structure better known at the time as "Old Sweat House." Three hundred citizens, headed by a band, came from Petersburg to hear him. He thanked God that the Union had been destroyed and that the Southern States had left, never to come back. He urged Virginia to do her part and said that if she stood firm against the Union there would be no war. Lincoln, he declared, was "a feculent excrescence of Northwestern vulgarity."[6]

Virtually all of the Union forts and arsenals in the South were surrendered to state authorities without incident. The principal exception was Fort Sumter, in Charleston's harbor. But this became a symbol. "All this availeth me nothing, so long as I see Mordecai, the Jew, sitting at the king's gate."[7] Its surrender by the new president would be regarded as weakness; its acquisition by the Confederacy would have the greatest possible effect upon Southern morale. Lincoln realized the gravity of this symbol. In his inaugural address, he announced that "The power confided to me will be used to hold, occupy, and possess the property and places belonging to the Government."[8]

Whether the remaining Southern states would follow the seceding states, no one knew. The Confederacy designated commissioners to deal with the Federal Government in such areas as the status of Federal property physically located in the territory of the self-proclaimed new nation. When the Commissioners asked Lincoln if he would evacuate Fort Sumter in order to preserve peace, he replied, "Why not? If you will guarantee to me the State of Virginia I shall remove the troops. A State for a fort is no bad business."[9]

Fort Sumter was a modern truncated pentagonal structure, which rose abruptly out of the water at the mouth of Charleston Harbor, three and a half miles from the city. Built on an artificial island, the foundations alone cost $500,000 and required ten years to construct. The walls were of solid brick and concrete masonry, sixty feet high and from eight to twelve feet thick. These walls were pierced for three tiers of guns on the northern, eastern, and western exterior sides.[10] But the fort was not yet complete, and its armament and garrison were at only a fraction of their intended strength. There were only three of the largest size guns, 10-inch Columbiads, but there were more 8-inch Columbiads than could be manned. Sixty-five men comprised a garrison that should have numbered 650.[11]

In Charleston, excitement and confusion reigned as troops were assembled to take the fort by force, if necessary. There was more color than order. A journalist recorded: "All night long the roll of the drum and the steady tramp of the military and the gallop of the cavalry, resounding through the city, betokened the progress of preparations for the long-expected hostilities. The Home Guard Corps of old gentlemen, who occupied the position of military exempts, rode through the city, arousing the soldiers and doing other duties required at the moment. Hundreds of the citizens were up all night. A terrible thunderstorm prevailed until a late hour, but in nowise interfered with the ardor of the soldiers."[12]

South Carolina's regiments all had their own distinct uniforms.[13] Included in this contingent was the venerable Edmund Ruffin, 67-year old agricultural expert and hothead, who was a volunteer in the Palmetto Guards.[14]

The daughter of a former governor the state, herself the wife of a United States senator, wrote in her diary of the senior military commander in the city: "Beauregard called. He is the hero of the hour. That is, he is believed to be capable of great things. A heroworshipper was struck dumb because I said that so far he has only been a Captain of artillery or engineers or something."[15] Of General Pierre Beauregard, a Confederate soldier left this description: "In appearance, he was a little Frenchman. His uniform fitted to perfection, he was always punctiliously neat, his manners were faultless and deferential. His voice was pleasant and insinuating, with a perceptible foreign accent. His apprehension was quick, his observation and judgment alert, his expressions tense and vigorous. Like many of our other distinguished soldiers, especially of his race, he was fond of the society of the gentler sex, and at his best when in their company."[16]

There was apprehension in the capital of the Confederacy (which was in Montgomery, Alabama, at this time) that impetuous South Carolina might take an irreversible step against Fort Sumter before the new nation decided upon the best course of action. The Secretary of War, L. P. Walker, ordered Beauregard to demand the fort's surrender or to "reduce it."[17]

In this surcharged atmosphere, only a spark was necessary to trigger an explosion. On April 10, thousands of persons gathered in front of the Charleston Hotel. The crowd (quite festive in mood) reached beyond the Market Place and almost to Secession Hall. A serenade was given to a colorful visitor from Virginia, ex-Congressman Pryor, "a gentleman of the old school with a long coat and longer hair. . . ."[18] His speech was the most frequently quoted one of his career.

"Gentlemen," he declared, "for my part, if Abraham Lincoln and Hannibal Hamlin[19] were to abdicate their office to-morrow and were to give me a blank sheet of paper, whereupon to write the conditions of reannexation to the Union, I would scorn the privilege of putting the terms upon paper." A typesetter interrupted the flow of rhetoric to insert, "Cheers." "And why? Because our grievance has not been with reference to the insufficiency of the guarantees, but the inutterable perfidies of the guarantors; and inasmuch as they would not fulfill the stipulations of the old Constitution, much less will they carry out the guarantees of a better Constitution, looking to the interests of the South. Therefore, I invoke you to give no countenance to any idea of reconstruction."

A voice from the crowd interrupted, "We don't intend to do anything of the kind."

Pryor continued:

It is the fear of that which is embarrassing us in Virginia, for all there say that if we are reduced to the dilemma of an alternative, they will espouse the cause of the South as against the interests of the Northern Confederacy. If you have any ideas of reconstruction, I pray you annihilate them. Give forth to the world that under no circumstances whatever will South Carolina stay in political association.

I understand that since I have been in Charleston that there is some little apprehension of Virginia in this great exigency. Now I am not speaking for Virginia officially. I wish to God I was, for I would put her out of the Union before 12 o'clock to-night. But I bid you dismiss your apprehensions as to the old Mother of Presidents.

Give the old lady time. She cannot move with the agility of some of the younger daughters. She is a little rheumatic. Remember that she must be pardoned for deferring somewhat to the exigencies of opposition. Remember we have opposition in the Pan Handle of Virginia. Remember the *personnel* of the Convention to whom she intrusted her destinies. But making these reservations, I assure you that just as certain as to-morrow's sun will rise upon us, just so certain will Virginia be a member of the Southern Confederation. We will put her in in less time than can be calculated by the clock if you but strike a blow.[20]

According to another reporter, what Pryor said in lieu of that last sentence was, "And I tell you, gentlemen, what will put her in the Southern Confederation in less than an hour by the Shrewsbury clock. Strike a blow! The very moment that blood is shed, Old Virginia will make common cause with her sisters of the South. It is impossible she should do otherwise."[21]

A United States senator noted that "these utterances well expressed the general feeling and sentiments of the leaders who were carrying forward this movement. Pryor's speech was applauded, and telegraphed to Montgomery. . . ."[22]

"Pryor of Virginia spoke from the piazza of the Charleston Hotel," confided a local lady to her diary. "I asked what he said. Louisa [Hamilton], the irreverent woman, replied: "Oh, they all say the same thing, but he made a great play with that long hair of his, which he is always tossing aside.' "[23]

A present-day commentator suggested that Pryor had paraphrased "vainglorious old John Falstaff,"[24] but to a journalist with more distinguished credentials, Horace Greeley, this speech earned the orator a title, "The eloquent tribune of Virgina."[25] "There are many who believe that General Pryor's Charleston speech in April, 1861, was the match that exploded the powder magazine and brought on the war. His audience was ripe for secession, and after his speech they prevailed upon Jefferson Davis to begin firing on Fort Sumter."[26] An editorial expressed the opinion that his "eloquence had much to do with the secession of his native State of Virginia. . . ."[27] This speech, opined another editorial, "stirred his hearers to fire on Fort Sumter. . . ."[28]

"I do not pretend that this consummation was desired or anticipated by the Virginia secessionist," rationalized his wife at a later date, "but affirm only that he 'builded better than he knew,' and that but for his act the nation would not now be free from the reproach of human slavery."[29]

When General Beauregard selected his retinue and advisors, he named both a regular and a volunteer staff. Pryor was appointed to the latter.[30] "Honorables W. Porcher Miles and Roger A. Pryor, having tendered their services to Brigadier-General Beauregard, are hereby appointed volunteer aides-de-camp, and all orders transmitted through them will be obeyed."[31]

On April 12, Beauregard sent four members of his staff to Fort Sumter to demand its surrender, his emissaries being A. R. Chisholm, James Chesnut, Roger A. Pryor, and Stephen D. Lee.[32] Chisholm recorded that Pryor did not actually enter the fort with the others upon this occasion, for his position was somewhat ambiguous: he represented, however unofficially, a state that had not yet left the Union. "Moreover, I believe he was then a member of Congress, and may have been unwilling to compromise himself."[33] Without official status, Pryor did not even have a uniform, but he was easily distinguished from the civilian population by his colored shirt, large spurs (he arrived by rowboat), sword, revolver, and Bowie knives.[34]

Major Robert Anderson of Kentucky, the Union commander at Fort Sumter, refused a demand that he surrender his outpost because "my sense of honor and my obligation to my Government prevent my compliance." He supplemented this written reply with the verbal comment, "I will await the first shot, and, if you do not batter us to pieces, we will be starved out in a few days."[35]

Puzzled by the time significance of this message, Beauregard sent the same four aides back with a second letter, asking when Anderson would evacuate the fort if unmolested by Confederate forces. He replied that he would leave Sumter by April 15, "should I not receive, prior to that time, contrary instructions from my Government, or additional supplies."[36]

Beauregard's four emissaries now held a council of war; and such it truly was, literally and figuratively. Was Anderson's reply one that could be considered a satisfactory response to Beauregard's ultimatum? Decision as to whether to report back that Anderson had refused to accept the ultimatum was a fearsome responsibility. "It is so dramatic

—that scene of the four young men holding in their hands during a moment of absolute destiny, the fate of a people; four young men, in the irresponsible ardor of youth, refusing to wait three days and forcing war at the instant! It is so dramatic that one cannot judge harshly the artistic temper which is unable to reject it."[37]

Of the four men Pryor's responsibility in the making of the decision was the greatest strain upon a participant, for he had no official position as a Confederate. According to John Minor Botts, an ardent Virginia unionist, Pryor "was supposed to have been deputed by his co-adjutors in Richmond, as otherwise he would scarcely have ventured to take such a responsibility upon himself. . . ."[38] But Botts, ever a devotee of legalism, simply could not imagine that any one would act without authority. Pryor had none.

Imminent wars have been stopped even while cannoneers had their eager hands on the gun lanyards. Pryor's personal responsibility for the irrevocable act which started this war has not been noted by historians hitherto, with one conspicuous exception. Beauregard's orders had been to fire on Fort Sumter if that position were not surrendered; was a verbal assurance that it would be relinquished within three days a surrender? A sometime president of the American Historical Association reported that Pryor had stated to him in a conversation on December 30, 1909, that he (Pryor) had ordered the firing at Fort Sumter. "Pryor and his associates did not report back to the General, but, thinking that Davis was trying to reconstruct the Union and negotiate with Seward[39] to that end and that the chance of war was about to slip away forever, they conferred together and decided to give the signal to the gunners to fire—and war began, and such a war!"[40]

At 3:20 A.M. on April 12, Beauregard's aides informed Major Anderson that his reply was unsatisfactory and that he would be fired on in one hour.[41] Then, on the ground that Beauregard's ultimatum had not been accepted, they issued instructions to commence the bombardment. No efforts were made to clear these instructions with President Davis, Secretary of War Walker, or even General Beauregard. The assault was to be started by a battery of sixteen 10-inch mortars on James Island, near Fort Johnson, where a third of the Southern artillery was assembled.[42] The battery commander, Captain George J. James, received the orders to fire. A great admirer of Pryor, the captain said to the Virginia visitor, "You are the only man to whom I would give up the honor of firing the first gun of the war." Pryor, greatly agitated, replied, "I would not fire the first gun of the war."[43] Despite his complicity in the events which made that first shot inevitable, in the opinion of Pryor's wife, had he actually *fired* that first shot, "he certainly would not have become an eminent lawyer in the state of New York and a justice of its Supreme Court."[44]

The opportunity of firing the first shot was then offered to Edmund Ruffin, a hot-headed patriot who was one of America's first distinguished scientific farmers; his study, *An Essay On Calcareous Manures*, had gone through many editions. Pryor, in the *Southside Democrat*, had referred to Ruffin as "this ornament and benefactor of the States . . .," whose monuments were "to be seen in the once barren and wasted but now teeming and verdure-covered fields. . . ."[45] Several writers have bracketed the two men. "Roger Atkinson Pryor, like Edmund Ruffin, is a person known to history, although he awaits a biographer to do justice to his career."[46] Pryor was referred to as "a sort of younger version of Ruffin. . . ."[47] But Ruffin also declined to fire the first shot of the war, and Captain James apparently performed this historic chore.[48]

Major Anderson had been told that the bombardment would begin in an hour. "Punctual to the appointed moment, the roar of a mortar from Sullivan's Island, quickly followed by the rushing shriek of a shell, gave notice to the world that the era of compromise and diplomacy was ended."[49] The first shot burst over the fort, 100 feet in the air.[50] The wife of James Chesnut, one of Beauregard's four Sumter emissaries, heard the discharge. "At half past four, the heavy booming of a cannon! I sprang out of bed and on my knees, prostrate, I prayed as I never prayed before."[51]

Pryor witnessed the opening of the bombardment from a boat midway between Forts Sumter and Johnson.[52]

The bombardment lasted for a day and a half. The living quarters of the fort were set on fire; flames menaced the powder magazine; even the flagstaff was shot down.[53] Beauregard, seeing that Major Anderson was in trouble because of the conflagration, gallantly sent William Porcher Miles, Stephen D. Lee, and Roger A. Pryor to offer assistance, but they were courteously informed that everything was under control.[54]

A reporter painted a vignette of this visitation.

[59]

An incident occured during the cannonading, which for its pecu-
liarity, deserves particular mention. Roger A. Pryor of Virginia,
ex-Member of Congress, was one of the second deputation that
waited upon Major Anderson. He was the very embodiment of
Southern chivalry. Literally dressed to kill, bristling with bowie-
knives and revolvers, like a walking arsenal, he appeared to think
himself individually capable of capturing the fort without any ex-
traneous assistance. Inside the fort he seemed to think himself
master of everything—monarch of all he surveyed—and, in keeping with his pretension, seeing upon the table what appeared to be
a glass of brandy, drank it without ceremony. Surgeon Crawford,
who had witnessed the feat, approached him and said: "Sir, what
you have drank [*sic*] is poison—it was the iodine of potassium—
you are a dead man." The representation of chivalry instantly
collapsed, bowie-knives, revolvers, and all, and passed into the
hands of Surgeon Crawford, who, by purgings, pumpings, and
pukings defeated his own prophecy in regard to his fate. Mr.
Pryor left Fort Sumter "a wiser, if not a better man."[55]

Pryor's chief concern seemed to have been that he would die, not
unnoticed, where, as a Virginian, he had no official right to be in the
first place. To Dr. Crawford he called, "Do something for me, doctor,
right off, for I would not have anything happen to me in this fort for
any consideration."[56]

Captain Abner Doubleday, Union second in command at Fort
Sumter, witnessed the tail end of this episode. "Some of us questioned
the doctor's right to interpose in a case of this kind. It was argued
that if any rebel leader chose to come over to Fort Sumter and poison
himself, the Medical Department had no business to interfere with
such a laudable intention. The doctor, however, claimed, with some
show of reason, that he himself was held responsible to the United
States for the medicine in the hospital, and therefore he could not
permit Pryor to carry any of it away."[57]

After thirty-four hours of bombardment, Fort Sumter was honor-
ably surrendered by Major Anderson, whose command was allowed
to return to New York. On April 17, General Beauregard sent his report to Secretary of War Walker "by Col. R. A. Pryor, one of my
aides (who like the others was quite indefatigable and fearless in con-

veying my orders, in an open boat, from these headquarters to the batteries during the bombardment). . . ."[58] Ten days later, Beauregard sent his official report to Adjutant General Cooper, making reference to several named persons, including Pryor, "for their indefatigable and valuable assistance and night and day during the attack on Fort Sumter, transmitting in open boats my orders when called upon with alacrity and cheerfulness. . . ."[59]

Lincoln immediately responded to the challenge by calling for 75,000 troops on April 15. "I deem it proper," he announced, "to say that the first service assigned to the force hereby called forth will probably be to repossess the forts, places, and property which have been seized from the Union. . . ."[60]

Recorded the soldier son of an ex-governor of Virginia who was a stout unionist: "It has been said that the Southern leaderers fired upon Fort Sumter in order to force these issues, well knowing that Virginia could not be relied upon to withdraw from the Union in any other way. Whether this be so or not, this result was accomplished."[61]

On April 17, the Virginia Secession Convention was held in Richmond, and by a vote of 88-55, an ordinance of secession was adopted.[62] "Virginia could not be restrained," observed a congressman from Maine, "although she was warned and ought to have seen, that if she joined the Rebellion she would inevitably become the battle-ground, and would consign her territory to devastation and her property to destruction."[63]

VI

General Pryor

Roger A. Pryor received a commission from Governor Letcher as colonel in the Third Virginia Regiment, which was mustered into service at Norfolk.[1] He procured a uniform, but there was indecision as to the shoulder-straps. Recorded his wife: "We had not then decided upon the star for our colonels' insignia, and I supposed he would wear the eagle like all the colonels I had ever known. No embroidery bullion was to be had, but I bought heavy bullion fringe, cut it in lengths, and made eagles, probably of some extinct species, for the like were unknown in Audubon's time, and have not since been discovered. However, they were accepted, admired, and, what is worse, worn."[2] Actually, Confederate colonels were supposed to wear three stars of the same size in line.[3] Home needlecraft as practiced by Sara Pryor was likewise resorted to by La Salle Corbell, who at about this time was embroidering the star and wreath of a Confederate general for her fiancée, General George E. Pickett.[4]

Colonel Pryor looked over his men with benevolent despotism. He gave orders that his troops were not be sold liquor; but when one soldier killed another in a drunken camp brawl, the colonel undertook the defendant's case and won an acquittal.[5]

His observation of the Confederate soldiery was perceptive. "They never can stand still in battle; they are willing to yell and charge the most desperate positions, but if they won't move forward, they must move backward. Stand still they cannot."[6] Yet somewhere along the line they must have sat. Colonel Fred G. Skinner of the First Virginians said that his boys were a bit out at the seat, but "The enemy won't see that part of them."[7] Even in the early months of the war, before shortages developed, the Southern troops were indifferently and individually accoutred; a visiting officer of the spit-and-polish Coldstream Guards observed that the only standard piece of Confederate equipment was a tooth-brush, stuck "like a rose in his button-hole."[8]

At the time of Lincoln's inauguration on March 4, 1861, the regular army of the United States by law consisted of two regiments of dragoons, two of cavalry, one of mounted rifles, four of artillery, and ten of infantry, with a total strength of 13,024 officers and men.[9]

The Confederacy as such had no troops at that time, although there was militia of varying quality in each state. Equipment was the big problem. Under the Defense Act of 1850, South Carolina had purchased heavy artillery against the day of ultimate secession.[10] John G. Floyd, while still the Secretary of War of the United States, had caused transfers of arms to Southern arsenals, which well served him when he became a Confederate brigadier-general.[11] Major Caleb Huse, dispatched by the Confederacy to buy arms in Europe, bought vast quantities of Austrian and English rifles and cannon.[12] Early in the war, when the Union armies were consistently put to rout, Confederates merely had to pick equipment off the battlefields where it had been dropped by departing Federals. After the Battle of Bull Run, a whole Confederate brigade was deployed as a skirmish line to salvage Union equipment.[13]

Statistically, the agricultural South should have been hopelessly behind the North in military preparations; but in the judgment of some authorities close to the subject, such was not the case. Even when the imminence of war was obvious to professional soldiers, said one of them, "the Northern people generally paid no attention, took no warning of its coming, and would not realize its existence till Fort Sumter was fired on. . . ."[14] Lincoln wrote to Erastus Corning on June 12, 1863: "The rebellion thus begun soon ran into the present civil war; and, in certain respects, it began on very unequal terms between the parties. The insurgents had been preparing for it for more than thirty years, while the government had been taking no steps to resist them."[15] But the great bulk of the best officers in what began to be referred to as "the old army" (and navy) switched its allegiance to the South. Other officers had less imposing credentials. Pryor admitted at the start of

[63]

the war that he knew nothing of military operations, "for I know no more about the field than a spinster."[16]

Not unnaturally for a trained journalist, Pryor quickly established himself as a trustworthy scout, the role he filled most satisfactorily throughout his military career. Typically, he wrote to the Secretary of War on May 2, 1861: "Reliably reported, enemy will occupy Alexandria. Large force in Washington. Maryland overwhelmed, and reaction there against us. Confusion in our councils in Richmond. Extremely important President Davis be there."[17] To Beauregard he wrote: "My position in command of the forces at this advanced post places me in frequent and full communication with friends within the enemy's lines. They afford me information which I generally find correct. . . . In the New York Times of the 18th, in the local column, is a paragraph to the effect that Banks' expedition of 300 vessels is about to start, with the design of inflicting a destructive blow on the heart of the rebellion. Perhaps it means Charleston."[18] One dispatch from Pryor to the Secretary of War reported not only troop movements at Newport News but the price of gold in New York (161 and rising).[19]

Sara Pryor went to the Blackwater when her husband was assigned there, but he was too busy to see much of her.[20] She made herself useful in camp, aiding the sick and wounded. She prepared as camp equipage a field stove with rotating chimney, ticks for bedding (to be filled with straw, hay, or leaves), and a camp chest of tin utensils, strong blankets, etc.[21] She "gave her hands and heart to her country, ever ready to share, to cheer, to nurse, spending her strength for those who needed. She was capable and ready, whether called to grace a reception, to nurse a wounded soldier, or to comfort one whose hero had fallen. She dismantled her home of all that could be used in camp or hospital."[22] For a time, she had her infant son Theodorick with her at Colonel Pryor's camp near Suffolk; but when life got too rugged, she sent the youngster to the residence of her uncle, Dr. Rice, in Charlotte County.[23]

On one occasion, Sara received word from an orderly that she was to leave Smithfield the next morning before dawn. "Tell the colonel it is impossible!" she exclaimed. "I can't get ready by to-morrow to leave." "Madame," replied the soldier, "it is none of my business, but when Colonel Pryor gives an order, it is wise to be a strict constructionist."[24]

Pryor was described as "a powerful man, and as active as a squirrel.
. . ."[25] The agility of that animal was necessary to combine his roles
of soldier and legislator. He was a member of the House of Representatives of the First Congress of the Confederate States of America.[26] In point of fact, this Congress generally was not characterized by
able men. To seek government service other than in the army was to incur the suspicion of cowardice, and the administrative branches and
the legislature suffered in consequence.[27] Yet the life of a congressman
was not secure. One legislator was whipped on the floor of the House
by a mad woman.[28] Duels were not uncommon, and at least one
congressman was murdered.[29]

Colonel Pryor was a member of the Committee on Military Affairs
of the House.[30] On February 26, 1862, "Mr. Pryor presented a bill to
establish a general staff of the army of the Confederate States of America. Referred to the Committee on Military Affairs."[31] Nothing was
done about this bill, although General Lee was to express a desire for
a staff organization.[32] Pryor also sponsored a bill to create the office
of Judge Advocate General.[33] But most of his time was not spent in
the legislature. On March 12, noted the House Journal, "Mr. Garnett
asked, and obtained, leave of absence for Mr. Pryor during his necessary absence with his regiment."[34]

On January 22, 1862, Colonel Pryor visited Beauregard at his headquarters in Centreville, Virginia. In his own name, and also for the
representative in Congress of the Mississippi Valley states, Pryor urged
Beauregard to consent to be transferred from the Army of the Potomac
(later to be known as the Army of Northern Virginia) to the command
of the Southern forces at Columbus, Kentucky. President Davis wished
the change in command to be made but only would order it if Beauregard consented, which he did.[35] The Secretary of War confirmed the
arrangement. "Colonel Pryor has reported to the President, as the
result of his interview with you, that you would cheerfully accept the
command of the defenses at Columbus, Ky., and that your absence
from the Army would not seriously impair its efficiency."[36]

Pryor acted as confidential contact man on various occasions. On
February 14, Beauregard wrote his regrets that the colonel did not
visit him in Nashville, for "the matter General [Albert] Johnston and
myself had to communicate through you to the Government were of

great importance, being to provide for the very unfortunate contingency now existing here."[37]

Pryor also had time for civilian visitors. Lyman Beecher Stowe recalled that the colonel "told me that it had been the opinion of General Lee and the members of his staff that had it not been for *Uncle Tom's Cabin* and Henry Ward Beecher's[38] speeches in the British Isles the Confederacy could have secured the recognition of Great Britain and France with all this would have meant to them in both moral and material aid."[39]

At the beginning of May, 1862, the Federal army under General George B. McClellan advanced on Richmond via the peninsula between the York and James Rivers. Strong Confederate works at Yorktown had to be turned.[40] Yorktown was powerfully armed and well defended. It was on a little stream known as the Warwick River, which had been dammed in places to form water obstacles to any Federal attack. But when McClellan began to lay down siege lines for an assault in force, the Southern troops were withdrawn on the night of May 3. The retreating Confederates were overtaken and attacked at Williamsburg.[41] Brigadier-General Cadmus M. Wilcox, C.S.A. wrote that "not finding General [A. P.] Hill, Brigadier-General Pryor was called on, and he came up promptly with two battalions."[42] Longstreet reported that "Brig. Gen. Roger A. Pryor had but a small portion of his brigade engaged. He used his small force with effect in making a successful attack, and, toward the close of the conflict, in repelling a vigorous attack of the enemy."[43] Pryor's casualties were 214 men killed, wounded, and missing.[44]

After the Battle of Williamsburg, Pryor was promoted to brigadier-general.[45] Inasmuch as the promotion was announced before the official reports of the battle were written, his exploits prematurely were listed under his new rank. The salary of generals was $301 a month, of which, wrote one officer of that grade, "the $1 was for what they did, the $300 just thrown in to please them."[46]

On May 24, General Irwin McDowell was ordered by Lincoln to lay "aside for the present the movement on Richmond." Actually, the president was concerned lest Washington, denuded of troops, be captured by the Confederate forces. But the order that halted McDowell left the Army of the Potomac divided as two corps had crossed the Chickahominy and three were still on the north side of that river. Gen-

Roger A. Pryor in uniform
Courtesy Sara Dodge Kimbrough

eral Johnston ordered Longstreet to attack. This was the Battle of Seven Pines, sometimes known as Fair Oaks.[47]

Pryor's brigade was under the orders of General D. H. Hill, "a small, delicate man, rather bent, and cursed with dyspepsia, which seemed to give color to his whole being."[48] There were 65,000 Confederate troops to oppose 100,000 blue-coats.[49] Hill's official report stated that "Pickett, Pryor, and Wilcox received their orders to fall back after the firing began, and wisely resolved not to do so until the assault was repulsed."[50] The overall Southern commander, Johnston, wrote that "On the morning of the first of June, the enemy attacked the brigade of Gen. Pickett, which was supported by that of General Pryor. The attack was vigorously repelled by these two brigades, the brunt of the fight falling on General Pickett. This was the last demonstration made by the enemy."[51] Longstreet noted: "I will mention, however, as distinguished for their usual gallantry and ability, Generals R.H. Anderson, C. W. Wilcox, George E. Pickett, R. E. Colston, and Roger A. Pryor."[52]

General Johnston was severly wounded in this battle, and Robert E. Lee was given command of the Army of Northern Virginia. "An unusually handsome man, he has been painted with brush and pen a hundred times, but yet there is always something to say of that noble, unostentatious figure, the perfect poise of head and shoulders and limbs, the strength that lay hidden and the activity that his fifty-five years could not repress. Withal graceful and easy, he was approachable by all; gave attention to all in the simplest manner. His eyes—sad eyes! the saddest it seems to me of all men's—beaming the highest intelligence and with unvarying kindliness, yet with command so firmly set that all knew him for the unquestioned chief."[53]

The Battle of Seven Pines (or Fair Oaks) was so savagely fought over a frequently shifting terrain that the enemy wounded were not always tended with exemplary care. A conspicuous exception was provided by Pryor, who personally saw to it that the injured prisoners received the best possible ministrations. This came to the attention of the Union commander of the Army of the Potomac, who wrote in his memoirs: "I was told, after the battle of Fair Oaks, that when the Confederates were for a time in possession of the camp of Casey's division Gen. Roger A. Pryor went around among the wounded, giving them whiskey and water, and that he told them that it was a repayment of the kindness with which their wounded were treated at Williamsburg."⁵⁴ This chivalrous action came to the attention of an even higher authority than McClellan, with results that were to be highly important to Pryor.

McClellan, hearing that Lee had been greatly reinforced, decided to withdraw to the James, to establish there a new base from which to mount offensive operations. He ordered General Porter to retreat to a prepared position near Gaines's Mill. On June 27, Generals A. P. Hill and Longstreet successively assaulted Porter, who held out with reinforcements from General Slocum. Lee then ordered a general assault, which sustained 8,000 casualties but overran the objective.⁵⁵ Pryor's brigade participated in the battle but did not see major action, its missions being such tasks as safeguarding the prisoners taken by General Hood.⁵⁶

The Seven Days' Battle was a designation given to an almost constant conflict around Richmond from June 24 to July 1. The Confederates lost 19,739 men killed and wounded, while the Northerners had 9,796 casualties and 6,053 men missing. Blunders were numerous on both sides, but Lee succeeded in saving Richmond. "Because it prevented the fall of the capital the Battle of Seven Days, though tactically a blunder, will always be considered as one of the great defensive strategical victories of this war."⁵⁷ Pryor wrote that "In this brilliant fight my brigade bore a not unworthy part."⁵⁸ This was confirmed by Longstreet, who noted as "distinguished among others for gallantry and skill" was General Pryor.⁵⁹

During this battle, Sara Pryor worked at a hospital established in Kent & Paine's warehouse in Richmond. She fainted at her first sight of an amputation. The matron announced, "You are unfit for this work. One of the nurses will conduct you home." Sara refused. In the belief that it was the sickening odor which laid her low, she provided herself with sal volatile and spirits of camphor; and thereafter she conducted herself creditably.⁶⁰ She gave more than her time to the care of the wounded. For bandages, she gave the hospital her linen garments (except for one change) and all of her cotton garments, table linen, bed linen, and even her chintz furniture covers.⁶¹

Lee's army was then divided into two parts. Jackson was sent on a raid to the rear of the Northern invaders. On August 29, he accepted battle (Second Manassas) with General Pope, who was awaiting reinforcements, before Lee could combine his forces again. Jackson drove back the more numerous Union troops, sustaining 10,000 casualties while the Federal army lost 14,000 men.[62] Pryor's brigade was assigned to support the massed Confederate artillery, but when the Northern General Porter's troops broke, Pryor's men dashed forward in pursuit.[63] According to his official report, he had been ordered to intercept the enemy retreat, and his men even charged Union batteries, capturing some field pieces. He advanced ahead of his men and was "detained in my embarrassing position." But he escaped, and his account concluded: "Of the conduct of officers and men in this fight I have to speak in the most complimentary terms."[64]

His "embarrassing position" must have been even more embarrassing to some Union soldiers. Pryor, unaccompanied, found himself in the presence of two Federal troopers, who were sitting at the foot of a hayrick. Their guns were stacked close by. The Confederate general's uniform was covered by a Mexican poncho, and the Northerners obviously assumed he was one of them. They asked him how things were going in the battle, and his vagueness aroused no suspicion, but when he was asked his regiment, brigade, and division, he hesitated. One blue-coat exclaimed, "You are a — Rebel and my prisoner!" Pryor snatched one of the muskets and ran his questionner through twice with the bayonet. The other startled Northerner reached for his gun, but he was likewise stabbed and left helpless on the ground. The general then rejoined his own men. The next day, Pryor sent an aide to the field hospital to find out if there were any persons present with bayonet wounds. One such casualty was found, and Pryor visited him. When he asked the injured man if he recognized him, he was told, "Yes, sir, I do; you're the man who struck me."[65]

After the Second Battle of Manassas, Pryor released numerous wounded and sick Northern soldiers, rather than send them to prison camps.[66]

On September 15, Pryor commanded Anderson's division at Antietam in place of its wounded general.[67] During this battle, he sent a request to Longstreet for more artillery and received this reply: "I am sending you the guns, dear General. This is a hard fight, and we had better all die than lose it."[68] The Confederates were outnumbered, three to one, although the odds were reduced when McClellan failed to get a third of his men into action.[69] On the night of September 18, Lee quietly retreated and successfully crossed the Potomac from Maryland into Virginia without further loss.[70]

On October 10, Pickett was promoted to major-general, his command including Pryor's brigade.[71] Of Pickett, his adjutant left this description: "A singular figure indeed! A medium-sized, well-built man, straight, erect, and in well-fitting uniform, an elegant riding whip in hand, his appearance was distinguished and striking. But the head, the hair were extraordinary. Long ringlets flowed loosely over his shoulders, trimmed and highly perfumed; his beard likewise was curling and giving out the scents of Araby."[72]

On November 1, the division was moved to Fredericksburg, to confront the Army of the Potomac, now commanded by Burnside. The Federal forces were numerically superior to the Confederates; but Lee had his troops impregnably posted on an elevation, with Pickett's division in the center of the line. General Hooker fruitlessly hurled wave after wave of Union troops against the Southerners. He reported that "Finding that I had lost as many men as my orders required, I suspended the attack." His biographer added laconically, "A good reason."[73]

In the autumn of 1862, internal reorganization in the army resulted in the transfer of most of Pryor's troops. His brigade had contained regiments from Alabama, Florida, Mississippi, North Carolina, and Virginia; but under the plan of reorganization, regiments were assigned to general officers from the same state. On November 25, Lee wrote to Pryor and expressed his regrets at not being able to furnish the requested two regiments in order to restore full strength to the brigade. "I regretted at the time, the breaking up of your former brigade, but you are aware that the circumstances which produced it were beyond my control. I hope it will not be long before you are again in the field, that the country might derive the benefit of your zeal and activity."[74]

Pryor was temporarily relieved from duty with the Army of Northern Virginia and assigned to Major-General G. W. Smith in Richmond.[75] One week later, he was transferred back to his original army, for duty with Lieutenant-General Jackson.[76] Lee wrote the Secretary of War to propose leaving Pryor in the Blackwater region, "with which country he is familiar, and he possesses, in addition, the confidence of that community. I still think that his services at this time will be more valuable in that region than elsewhere."[77]

Pryor's military activities in the Blackwater elicited the praise of his fellow generals. After an engagement on January 30, 1863, at Deserted House, or Kelly's Store, near Suffolk, Major-General S. G. French reported: "Col. C. Leventhorpe . . . and General Pryor both deserve commendation for their successful defense of that frontier with their small commands."[78] Brigadier-General R. E. Colston, commanding at Petersburg, declared in a report: "The disposition of the forces along the course of the Blackwater, such as made by General Pryor, seemed to me to be very judicious, and to require no change at present."[79]

But constantly Pryor had to battle for adequate manpower. If he could get a regiment of cavalry and one of infantry, he wrote to General Smith, he could bring up his force to 3,000 men, which would enable him to contain the enemy in Suffolk and to obtain 300,000 pounds of pork (and even more of corn).[80]

The Secretary of War, in a letter to Lee, stated that "there was some force, dignified with the name of a brigade, under the command of General Pryor. . . ."[81] His paucity of troops did not lessen his responsibilities. Lee wrote the Secretary of War on February 15: "I hope Generals French and Pryor have made arrangements by their own scouts to acquire accurate information of the movements of the enemy.[82] Without this, we shall always be at a loss what to do."[83]

For a long time, Pryor chafed at his inability to obtain a command commensurate to his rank. The situation did not go unnoticed. Lee wrote to Major-General Th. H. Holmes, commanding the Department of North Carolina: "With reference to the promotion of Colonel Daniel the Secretary is unwilling to increase the number of brigadiers. There are two now without commands, Generals Wise and Pryor, either of whom can be ordered to you if you desire it."[84]

Pryor wrote directly to President Davis. "If I know myself," he said, "It is not the vanity of command that moves me to this appeal. A single and sincere wish to contribute somewhat to the success of our cause impels me to entreat that I may be assigned to duty." Newspapers noted that he had no command and speculated that he was in the antiadministration group, which he vigorously denied.[85] Davis replied: "Your gratifying letter of the 6th inst. referring to an Article in the 'Examiner' newspaper which seems to associate you with the opposition to the Administration has been received.

"I did not see the article in question; but am glad it has led to an expression so agreeable. The good opinion of one so competent to judge of public affairs, and who has known me so long and closely is a great support in the midst of many and arduous trials."[86]

One speculates in vain about why Pryor was not given an adequate command. His prewar military experience was nil, but so was that of many higher-ranked officers on both sides. His commendations in official reports were many, and when he was given opportunity, "Gen-Pryor's war record was brilliant."[87] "He was a brigadier-general . . . and, wherever it was possible, he was in an engagement."[88] He participated in the Battles of Yorktown, Williamsburg, Seven Pines, Gaines's Mill, Second Manasas, Antietam, as well as the Seven Days' Battle.[89] Perhaps the only explanation was that when army organization was effected along state lines, he was the victim of Virginia's predominance in the field of excellent professional soldiers who were now generals.

When news of the Confederate defeat at Gettysburg reached Richmond, Pryor was in that city, serving on a court-martial. He at once went to the executive mansion to see the president. Mrs. Davis expressed regrets that her husband was not receiving callers, and they chatted. Then the president appeared, "weary, intent, and depressed." He told Pryor that he bore him no ill will despite those stories that the general was now in the opposition clique.[90] (Another general has left this description of Davis at about that time: ". . . I had a good look at that remarkable man. A most interesting study, calm and self-contained, gracious with some sternness; his figure was straight, slim and elegant. A well-poised, ample head was faced with high-bred features and an expression that could be very winning and agreeable.)"[91]

On August 26, 1863, Pryor resigned his commission as brigadier-general.[92] Davis long held up the resignation in the hope that it would be reconsidered,[93] and, in fact, it never was accepted.[94] But Pryor immediately reenlisted as a private in General Fitz Lee's cavalry. Sara begged her husband to stay with her and the children, but he replied: "No; I had something to do with bringing on this war. I must give myself to Virginia. She needs the help of all her sons. If there are too many brigadier-generals in the service,—it may be so,—certain it is that there are not enough private soldiers."[95]

On August 26, Fitz Lee wrote to his new recruit; "Honorable, General, or Mr? How shall I address you? Damn it, there's no difference! Come up to see me. Whilst I regret the causes that induced you to resign your position, I am glad, really, that the country has not lost your active services, and that your choice to serve her has been cast in one of my regiments."[96] Of Fitz Lee, a soldier left this contemporary characterization: "Fitz graduated at West Point in 1856, more distinguished for horsemanship than anything else. . . . He was now [1864], at the age of twenty-nine, a brigadier-general, a bachelor, and gay cavalier of ladies. . . . In appearance, General Lee was short, thickset, already inclined to stockiness; with a square head and a short neck upon broad shoulders, a merry eye, and a joyous voice of great power; ruddy, full-bearded, and overflowing with animal spirits."[97]

As a cavalryman, Pryor had to supply his own horse, and he rode a fine gray named Jubal Early.[98] As a private, he "was assigned the duties of his position, from not one of which did he ever excuse himself."[99] "The record of Roger A. Pryor, who resigned his generalcy and then enlisted in the Third Virginia Cavalry, as a private, is unparalleled in the world's history."[100] That may have been true up to 1924, when this comment was made, but fifteen years later, a deposed Chief of the German General Staff, Colonel-General Fritsch, followed his old regiment in the assault on Warsaw and was killed. "In all probability he sought death deliberately."[101]

The ex-general's fortunes were widely noted. The Head of the Bureau of War noted in his diary on August 16: "Roger A. Pryor has resigned his commission as brigadier general. To the Secretary yesterday, he insisted on a brigade or resignation, was told in frankness he could not get a brigade, then asked 30 days to select the company in which *to serve as a private*, which was granted him. So he is going to serve as a private. I do not think he will do so long."[102] One week later, a War Department clerk wrote in his diary:"Brig.-Gen. Roger A. Pryor, after dancing attendance in the anterooms for six months, waiting assignment to a command, has resigned and his resignation has been accepted. He says he can at least serve in the ranks as a private. The government don't like aspiring political generals."[103] The Confederate War Department must have lost about as much time to compulsive diary-jotting as did President Franklin D. Roosevelt's cabinet.

VII

Private Pryor

Private Pryor served in the Nottoway Cavalry, Company E, Third Virginia Regiment.[1] Most of his services were performed as a scout, under instructions given him by General Robert E. Lee: "Grant knows all about me, and I know too little about Grant. You were a schoolboy here, General[sic], and have hunted in all the bypaths around Petersburg. Knowing the country better than any of us, you are the best man for this important duty."[2]

Sara moved to Petersburg to be near her husband. At first she engaged space in a boarding house; in time, she obtained the use of an overseer's shack owned by a brother-in-law. This was a drab structure with sketchy flooring and no carpets or curtains, but it was home.[3] And she was able to spend some time with her husband. It was here on Christmas Eve, 1863, that she bore Roger, Jr. Not until three weeks later did Private Pryor return from a mission to see his new child in its squalid surroundings. With unaccustomed bitterness, he asked: "Is this the reward my country gives me?"[4]

The infant's grandfather, the Reverend Theodorick Pryor, relinquished his Petersburg church at about this time. At the request of his presbytery, he became an army chaplain, serving in Longstreet's corps in the Army of Northern Virginia.[5] But young Theodorick now left his relatives in Charlotte and came to live with his mother.[6]

Pryor took to his new army duties with vigor. On May 31, 1864, Brigadier-General Bushrod R. Johnson reported of his operations in North Carolina: "For the most reliable information I was indebted to

Roger A. Pryor, who was active, tireless, and daring in reconnaissances."[7] Efforts were made to get him higher rank. Recorded the War Department diarist: "Yesterday a paper was sent to the President by Gen. Pickett, recommending Gen. Roger A. Pryor for a cavalry command in North Carolina. But the President sent it to the Secretary of War with the curt remark that the command had already been disposed of to Col. Dearing, on Gen. Hoke's recommendation. Thus Gen. P. is again whistled down the wind, in spite of the efforts of even Mr. Hunter, and many other leading politicians. It is possible that Gen. P. may have on some occasion criticised Lee."[8]

A day later, this diarist wrote: "The President, in an endorsement, intimates to the Secretary of War that Gen. Pryor might be assigned to a brigade of the Reserve class."[9]

On May 5 began a major Federal advance upon Richmond. Grant, Siegel, Averell, and Butler each commanded one prong of the multiple approach. Butler's troops moved up the James in order to threaten Richmond from the rear and to keep Southern reinforcements from reaching Lee's army that was opposed to Grant's.[10] But Petersburg stood in the way. Pickett was stationed here with a small force: one regiment of infantry, the City Battalion of Petersburg, the militia, and the Washington Artillery, twenty-one guns.[11] General Hagood and part of the Twenty-fifth South Carolina were passing through Petersburg by train when Beauregard, now the overall commander in that city, diverted them to the defense of the community.[12] "Roger A. Pryor, formerly a brigadier of the Confederate Army, but now a private trooper acting as guide and courier to General Pickett, piloted him to the scene of action," recorded the South Carolinian.[13] Beauregard succeeded in defending the city, and Butler withdrew.[14]

In the summer of 1864, Petersburg was under almost constant siege. Shells landed in Sara's very yard. As to the new baby, "The first word she [sic] ever uttered was an attempt to imitate them."[15] A visiting Member of Parliament was impressed with the Pryor household and said: "I am going home and tell the English women what I have seen here: two boys reading Caesar while the shells are thundering, and their mother looking on without fear."[16] Actually, one of her most troublesome problems was the procurement of texts sufficiently advanced for the precocious Theodorick, and Courtenany's *Calculus* was smuggled past the Federal blockade for him.[17]

Later that year, the Pryors obtained the use of a better house. Sara's brother-in-law, Robert McIlwaine, moved to North Carolina and placed at her disposal Cottage Farm, some three miles from Petersburg. This was outside the bombardment area and, perhaps as important to her, there was a piano.[18]

Pryor returned to reconnaisance work and was able to alert the Confederate command to a pending attack upon a key railroad point near Petersburg. General D. H. Hill noted: "The victory at Walthall Junction was greatly due to General Roger A. Pryor. But for him it is probable we might have been surprised and defeated."[10]

When it came to a fight, Pryor was more than an observer. It was reported of an engagement at Reams' Station: "The famous Virginia orator . . . and statesman, Roger A. Pryor, who resigned from the Confederate Congress to take up arms as an independent fighter and scout, appeared on our battle line a-foot and did some sturdy fighting. His imposing figure, finely chiselled face, massive brow and long hair reminded me of our lamented Gen. Tom Cobb, whom he resembled very much. His presence, coolness and courage amid the roar of artillery and the din of battle, were an inspiration to all as he moved and fought with rank and file and gives the lie to the untrue and baseless slander that it was 'the rich man's war and the poor man's fight,' which I have sometimes heard and seen in print."[20]

Pryor's active military service came to an abrupt halt at the end of November. As a journalist, he always sought newspapers as a source of intelligence, even (or especially) about the activities of Federal troops. One day he rode up to a Union picket line and, in accordance with his usual practice, he waved a newspaper to indicate that he would like to exchange periodicals. A Northern officer stepped forward, and papers were transferred. Pryor turned back towards his own lines, reported a contemporary newspaper, "when he was suddenly seized by two or three armed men, who were lying in ambush, and hurried away. The whole transaction, we understand, was witnessed by some of our men, but at too great a distance to render any assistance. Gen. Pryor had frequently exchanged papers with the enemy, and his name and character had, no doubt, been reported to them. They resolved to have him, by fair means or foul, and descended to the basest treachery to accomplish their purpose.

"We trust that some notice may be taken of the matter by our military authorities, and every effort used to secure his early return. During the last few months the general has been acting as an independent scout, in which capacity he has rendered valuable service."[21]

Pryor did not realize that the Federal soldiers were going to seize him until five or six weapons were pointed at him. He clutched at his own pistol but decided that his position was hopeless. At least he could rejoice that his horse, Jubal Early, eluded the Northerners and dashed to safety; Pryor believed that his was the best horse in the Confederacy.[22] The animal found its way, alone, back to Sara at Cottage Farm.[23]

Major-General John G. Parke of the Union army wrote to Brigadier-General John S. Williams on November 27:"I have the honor to forward a prisoner of war, Roger A. Pryor, captured on our lines, in retaliation for the capture of Cap. H. S. Burrage, Thirty-sixth Massachusetts, on the 1st instant."[24] On the same day, Williams replied: "The commanding general desires that you will make a minute report of all the circumstances connected with the capture of Private Roger A. Pryor, Third Virginia Cavalry, giving the names of every officer and soldier taking part in the capture. I am directed to add that the commanding general disapproves of retaliatory acts not directed by himself or a superior authority." But when the commanding general heard the circumstances, he approved of the capture, on the ground that Pryor had visited the Federal lines before, once under an assumed name.[25]

The matter was brought to the attention of Grant by the Confederate Major-General C. M. Wilcox, who requested Pryor's release.[26] Grant referred the question to General Meade, with instructions to handle the affair as he saw fit; the latter refused "sanctioning this irregular and unauthorized intercourse."[27] To Wilcox, Meade wrote that "Private Pryor will have to suffer the consequences of his imprudence. He will be held as a prisoner of war, and with all consideration due to his position,"[28] which, of course, was a private.

Captain Burrage of the Federal army had been captured under similar circumstances, and as General Lee issued an order for his release, Pryor expected that he in turn would be freed. He was not. He was taken to Washington and committed to the Old Capitol Prison.[29]

On November 29, Pryor was sent by train to New York with a military escort commanded by Brigadier-General H. W. Wessels, aided by

[77]

Lieutenant William G. Sheen.[30] The cortege reached New York on the "Owl" at 5:30 A.M. the next morning and went to the Merchants Hotel on Cortlandt Street, where the register was formally signed. The prisoner wrote, "Roger A. Pryor, Fort Lafayette." It was noted that he was cheerful, although by no means pleased with his situation and prospects. "His manner is confident, with a dash of swagger. . . ." He gave his opinions freely. Sherman, he stated, was the ablest of the Union generals and the South had the most to fear from him. He thought that the many Southerners then in New York (estimated by one of his "hosts" to be from 25,000 to 30,000) should be compelled by their own self-respect to return to the South, but one must speculate about how they could have been fed had they done so.

A reporter thus described the prisoner: "In stature he is tall; he wears long black hair, combed towards the back of his head and falling behind his ears; his countenance has a boyish expression, and his age is thirty-five years. He is dressed in a plain though good suit of 'Confederate gray,' including a blouse; he also wears a shawl, which was given him in Washington, a black felt hat, and a pair of ordinary cavalry boots. Altogether, his attire is much better than could have been expected—far superior to that of any other rebel officer who has been brought to this city during the war."[31]

At nine o'clock that morning, Pryor and his two captors walked down Broadway to the Hamilton Ferry, to take the city railroad cars in Brooklyn to Fort Hamilton. Thence the short trip to Fort Lafayette was made. Pryor's Confederate uniform attracted not a little attention on the street and in public conveyances.[32]

According to a contemporary periodical, Fort Lafayette was "the present residence of the traitors who have been arrested by the General Government." The structure was a quadrangular work, detached from the land, standing on a shoal about an acre from the shore of Long Island. Situated in The Narrows, Lafayette was one of the three forts that constituted the main defence of the principal entry to New York harbor. Popularly, it was known as "The American Bastille."[33]

Pryor was confined in a casemate with twelve other prisoners. Straw mats on the floor were their beds. A grate was provided for heating and cooking, but the prisoners had to fetch their own fuel from the coal cellar. Once daily, he was allowed to walk on the ramparts, from which there was a view of New York City. Later his wife was to write retrospectively, "Little did he dream he should administer justice on the supreme bench of the mist-veiled city."[34]

The chief occupational hazard of prisoners—boredom—set in. There was nothing to do except to carve seal rings from coal or to make caricatures of the commandant in coal on the whitewashed walls.[35] Pryor wrote to his wife in December: "In vain I seek some argument of consolation. I see no chance of release. The conditions of my imprisonment cut me off from every source of happiness." Two months later, he wrote her: "I am as contented as is compatible with my condition. My mind is ill at ease from my solicitude for my family and my country. Every disaster pierces my soul like an arrow; and I am afflicted with the thought that I am denied the privilege of contributing even my mite to the deliverance of—. How I envy my old comrades their hardships and privations. I have little hope of an early exchange, and you may be assured my mistrust is not without reason. *Except some special instance be employed to procure my release, my detention here will be indefinite.* I cannot be more explicit. Whilst this is my conviction, I wish it distinctly understood that I would not have my government compromise any scruple for the sake of my liberation. I am prepared for any contingency—am fortified against any reverse of fortune."[36] There was strong reason for his pessimism. His release was strongly opposed by the Secretary of War[37] and by the Lieutenant-General of the Army.[38]

One of Pryor's cell mates was Captain John Y. Beall of the Confederate army, who was suspected of having been involved[39] in a largely unsuccessful plot to burn New York City.[40] Beall asked that Pryor serve as his defense counsel, and Major-General John Dix sent along this request with his own recommendation that it be approved.[41] But approval was not forthcoming, and Beall was defended (without fee) by James T. Brady, an eminent New York attorney.[42]

When Pryor became a prisoner, he was no longer able to draw the rations on which his family had subsisted. Sara emptied out her remaining trunks and sold her belongings, largely the finery worn in her Washington society days: silks, gold brocade, velvet gowns, an opera cloak trimmed with fur, lace. Eventually she was reduced to selling even her handkerchiefs and floral ornaments for hats. Her husband's dress coat was made into gloves to be sold. Her first purchase with her sales' proceeds was a barrel of flour, which, in the war-inflated market, cost $1,300.[43]

Sales of fine clothing from happier days did not hurt her, except, perhaps, emotionally, for women no longer wore such garb in Virginia. The only new dresses were home-woven fabrics colored with home dyes, the buttons being carved peach stones. Trimmings were made from seeds. Hats were made from straw braided at home, or from the lace-like tissue linings of gourds. For ornaments, cotton was shaped into balls and dyed various colors to represent grapes and other articles.[44] Sara's chief need in that day of war shortages was for steel for the front of her stays. An obliging government gunsmith manufactured this commodity for her.[45]

Meanwhile, efforts were being made to obtain Pryor's release from prison. When R. M. T. Hunter was designated as one of the three Confederate commissioners to attend the Hampton Roads peace conference with Lincoln, Sara implored the ex-senator to speak to the president about a release.[46] Washington McLean, the editor of the Cincinnati *Enquirer*, went to see Secretary of War Stanton, who held on his knee his baby daughter Bessie, child of his second marriage. "Well, then, Stanton," began the visitor, "you will understand my errand. There are curly heads down there in old Virginia, weeping out their bright eyes for a father loved just as this pretty baby loves you."

"Yes, yes! Probably so."

"Now—there's Pryor—"

"He shall be hanged! Damn him!" The Secretary's rage doubtless was genuine, for the prisoner's major role in abetting secession was well known. And even the omniscient Stanton could not have known how, eighteen years later, this very baby would be rescued by Pryor.

McLean next went to see Lincoln, armed with a letter from Horace Greeley dated February 6, 1865: "Roger A. Pryor, now a prisoner of war in Fort Lafayette, was captured under circumstances which seem to give him special claims to exchange. My friend Mr. W. McLean of Cincinnati is authorized to offfer any reasonable exchange for Mr Pryor, and I hope it may be effected."[47] What the "special claims" were, Greeley did not specify, but it is known that he did esteem Pryor as a fellow journalist. Moreover, Pryor was captured while exchanging newspapers, life's most precious commodity in the mind of the New York *Tribune's* editor.

On February 15, Joshua F. Speed, a friend of Lincoln's since they rode on the circuit together in Illinois, wrote to the president in a letter that could have used some editing: "Mr McClean of Cincinnati is very anxious to get Roger Pryor . . . now at Fort Lafayette exchanged. He says that he would stake his fortune on Pryors complying with any promise he would make or for the fulfillment of the terms upon which he accepts a parole. . . ."[48]

McLean went to see John W. Forney, Secretary of the United States Senate, who seemed puzzled at the object of this call upon him. "Roger A. Pryor, of Petersburg; Roger A. Pryor, who fired on Sumter; Roger A. Pryor, the hot-spur of Congress?" asked Forney. McLean vouchsafed that this was the same man.[49] They went to see Lincoln. "I think I have a memorandum here that refers to a party of our Pennsylvania boys who were taken prisoners in an attack upon the Petersburg fortifications," declared the president. He drew forth a signed statement of various persons who had shared Pryor's hospitality, food from his own meagre supply. "The man who can do such kindness to an enemy cannot be cruel and revengeful." Lincoln gave McLean a card and said: "I think that will do; at any rate, it is all that I can give you." On the card was written: "To Colonel Burke, Commanding at Fort Lafayette, New York. Please release General Roger A. Pryor, who will report to Colonel Forney on Capitol Hill. A. Lincoln."[50]

Later, Forney wrote to the president: "I do not think that the release of Roger A. Prior [sic] according to your generous card given to Washington McClain [sic] yesterday, would be followed by any but the very best consequences. He has Mr. Greeley's letter to you asking for his deliverance. A fair and honorable exchange is offered by his friends. I am full of sorrow that Mr. Stanton should object to the fulfillment of your promise in his behalf, and I now write this note in the hope that you will permit your own wishes to be carried out."[51]

Lincoln had several reasons for paroling Pryor. As a division commander, the Virginian had in turn paroled 5,000 persons in the Federal General Pope's hospital camp and sent them to Washington instead of to Confederate prison camps.[52] General George B. McClellan also had acknowledged Pryor's conspicuous care of Union prisoners.[53]

There was the incident at Petersburg about which the president had spoken to Forney and McLean. Lincoln, furthermore, must have been favorably impressed by Pryor the journalist, whose editorials were the admitted source of two of Lincoln's most famous speeches: "a house divided" and "the irrepressible conflict."[54]

On the evening of March 2, Forney and Pryor reached Washington and immediately went to call upon Lincoln. The president declared that the release order was attributable to Pryor's kindness to prisoners in Richmond. Grant, continued Lincoln, was "not altogether favorable to the passing his lines upon a return to Virginia."[55]

Forney took Pryor to his own home in Washington for a week, although he patriotically disliked the Southern leaders and resented the presence of his guest.[56] It was no secret. The reluctant host was highly indignant when the vitriolic Representative Thad Stevens asked him each morning, "How is your Democratic friend, General Pryor? I hope you are both well."[57] Innumerable persons came to visit Pryor. A reporter learned that his family had been having meat once a week; tea and coffee were out of the question. He did not think the Secessionist cause was *in extremis*, for a victory over Sherman could turn the tide.[58]

At this point the president apparently learned that Grant was something less than overjoyed at the prospect of returning to the Confederacy the man who had done so much to foment the war (but for which, the lieutenant-general might well have remained a penurious tanner). Grant had written to the Commissary-General of Prisoners: "I think Pryor and a Sergeant Waterbury, now at Point Lookout, should not be exchanged so long as we hold a prisoner."[59] Grant's reluctance to effect this exchange led the embarrassed president to send this apologetic communication to his senior commander: "I am in a little perplexity. I was induced to bring R. A. Pryor here, with a view of effecting an exchange of him. But since then I have seen a dispatch of yours showing that you specially object to his exchange. Meanwhile he has reached here and reported to me. It is an ungracious thing for me to send him back to prison, and yet inadmissible for him to remain here long. Cannot you help me out with it? I am conscious that there may be difference to you in days, and I can keep him a few days to accommodate on that point." Grant replied from City Point, Virginia: "Send

Pryor on here, and we will exchange him. He can do us no harm now."[60]

Then the Virginian was sent home under parole. Under date of February 25, he was given this safe-conduct: "Pass for Roger A. Pryor. Allow the bearer, Roger A. Pryor, to pass to Gen. Grant, and report to him for exchange. A. Lincoln."[61]

On February 27, the United States Assistant Agent for Exchange wrote to Grant: "Pryor arrived this evening. Shall I hold him, and inform Mr. Ould how and why? He has a pass from the President. . . ."[62] Grant replied the next day: "You may send Pryor through with the first prisoners sent off. Speak to him, however, about John Dent, and say to him that he has been promised his freedom so often that I had thought of detaining him until Dent was released. On reflection, however, I thought it better to trust and wait."[63]

The news reached Richmond promptly, and the War Department diarist noted: "Roger A. Pryor is to be exchanged. He was the guest of Forney in Washington, and had interviews with President Lincoln."[64]

Pryor returned to Sara and their temporary home on the outskirts of Petersburg. He was under parole and, of course, could do nothing to help the Confederacy's faltering war efforts. Perhaps unnecessarily, he was reminded of this fact. When the Southern troops were preparing to retreat from Petersburg, Pryor's father mentioned to General Lee that the ex-general expected to move if his division did. "That would be violation of his parole, Doctor," was the reply. "Your son surely knows he cannot march with the army until he is exchanged."[65] Lee's counsel was not to be taken lightly. "Every man in that army," said one of them, "believed that Robert E. Lee was the greatest man alive, and their faith in him alone kept that army together during the last six months of its existence."[66]

When the Union army approached Petersburg, Mayor Townes asked if Pryor would go under a flag of truce to surrender the city. Sara refused on behalf of her sleeping husband.[67]

On April 2, Federal troops occupied Petersburg, and Pryor was arrested. Taken to army headquarters, he was at once released when he showed Lincoln's pass, but this performance was repeated any time a new contingent of Union soldiers took over the position.[68] The follow-

[83]

ing day, Major-General H. G. Wright entered the city with the VI Corps and discussed the situation with Pryor. Brigadier-General Hamblin of the Second Brigade also met him and then asked Major-General Alex S. Wright, "Would it not be well to have Pryor examined by some competent person?"[69]

When Lincoln arried in Richmond, he sent for Pryor, who declined to come, saying that as a paroled prisoner, he could hold no conference with the commander-in-chief of the opposing army while Lee was still in the field.[70]

General Sheridan commandeered the Pryor house for his adjutant's office. Pryor felt that he could not remain under these circumstances and received permission to leave the city in order to visit his sisters in Nottoway County.[71] Because of his vaguely defined status, he tried to keep apart from both armies. "His bearing was courterous but dignified; he could not be less than a perfect gentleman, even to the enemy."[72]

VIII

Picking up the Pieces

After the Union troops occupied Petersburg and Richmond, the late wartime economy of short rations gave way to near starvation. Food no longer could enter these cities from the countryside. The Federal army gave out pickled pork and cornmeal to all who would come for it; but after a few days of this easy system, a method was devised whereby a specified amount of food was rationed to each house. The Secretary of the Relief Committee reported that from April 8 to 15, 1865, there were 86,555 rations thus issued.[1]

But much of this food had accompanied the Northern forces on their long campaigning. After finding caterpillars wriggling through the meal, Sara Pryor wrote to the senior officer present: "Is the commanding general aware of the nature of the ration issued this day to the destitute women of Petersburg?" An orderly brought her the reply: "Mayor-General Hartsuff is sorry he cannot make *right* all that seems so wrong. He sends the enclosed. Some day General Pryor will repay." Enclosed was this slip: "The Quartermaster and Commissary of the Army of the Potomac are hereby ordered to furnish Mrs. Roger A. Pryor with all she may demand or require, charging the same to the private account of

GEORGE L. HARTSUFF
Mayor-General Commanding.

Sara at once sent this response: "Mrs. Roger A. Pryor is not insensible to the generous offer of Major-General Hartsuff, but *he ought to*

[85]

have known that the ration allowed to the destitute women of Petersburg must be enough for

MRS. ROGER A. PRYOR[2]

But that was not enough for General Hartsuff's wife, who came to visit Mrs. Pryor, bearing a basket of coffee, sugar and crackers, which she implored her startled hostess to accept.[3]

On April 17, word of Lincoln's assassination reached Petersburg. The following day, the people of that city adopted resolutions, deploring this untimely death and denouncing the assassination. Pryor drew up these resolutions.[4] "Roger A. Pryor stated in Petersburg that he believed Mr. Lincoln was indispensable to the restoration of peace, and regretted his death more than any other mishap of the South. He and the Mayor placed themselves at the head of a movement for a town meeting to deplore the loss on both private and public grounds."[5]

During the course of the war, Pryor's opinion of Lincoln had shifted radically to admiration. The president's ability to withstand the buffetings of adversity particularly impressed the Virginian. "I thought he never would stop getting up."[6]

After Lee's surrender at Appomattox Court House, the Pryors returned to their home in Petersburg. The house had been looted of everything it contained.[7] "A comfortable fortune had disappeared."[8] From a New England officer came this letter: "A very fine mare belonging to you came into my camp near Richmond and is now with me. It would add much to her value if I could get her pedigree. Kindly send it at your earliest convenience, and oblige. . . ." Pryor did not send the requested pedigree but he dispatched a photograph of the animal, with himself on her back.[9]

Soldiers or others looking for buried treasure dropped chains down the wells as grappling irons. The water became poisoned, and, in turn, each of the Pryor children got malaria. So did Sara. The ex-general was the nurse.[10]

Pryor could find no work in Richmond. His wife later recalled that "He had no profession. He had forgotten all the little law he had learned at the university. He had been an editor, diplomat, politician, and soldier, and distinguished himself in all four. They were now closed to him forever! There seemed to be no room for a rebel in all the world."[11]

That Pryor could not find employment in that day was scarcely surprising. There was now realized the apocalypse which he had prophesied in a speech in the House of Representatives in 1861, just before the war erupted: "Imagine, then, for a moment the complete subjugation of the South after every spark of vitality is extinguished, and her inanimate form lies prostrate before you, tell me, what recompense do you gain for all your sacrifice, or what consolation in the tormenting memory of your fratricidal deed?"[12]

A few months after Appomattox, a traveller noted: "The South has had enough of war for a long time to come; it has supped full of horrors. The habiliments of mourning, which one sees everywhere in its towns and cities, will cast their dark shadows upon any future attempt at secession, long after they have been put away in the silent wardrobes of the past. Only in the case of a foreign war might we expect to see a party of malignant malcontents go over to the side of the enemy."[13]

Immediately after the conflict ground to a halt, a Richmond editor recorded: "That war was closed on a spectacle of ruin, the greatest of modern times. There were eleven great States lying prostrate; their capital all absorbed; the fields desolate; their towns and cities ruined; their public works torn to pieces by armies; their system of labour overturned; the fruits of the toil of generations all swept into a chaos of destruction; their slave property taken away by a stroke of the pen; a pecuniary loss of two thousand millions of dollars involved in one single measure of spoliation—a penalty embraced in one edict, in magnitude such as had seldom been exacted unless in wars synonymous with robberies."[14]

The worst of the South's blows had not been physical. "The greatest loss that a people can suffer, greater than any material destruction, is their spirit."[15] But "The spirit of the South seemed dead in the dreary summer of 1865. It was beyond the power of comprehension to realize that everything the South represented had suddenly become unfit for future life."[16]

Many soldiers really died as of the date of surrender. "They all lived, of course, in a way, as the Greeks pictured the dead as living in Tartarus, but for all great things the lives of most of them was over."[17] Recorded one Virginia soldier of his return to civilian life: "I was dead. Everything that I had ever believed in politically was dead. Everybody that I had ever trusted and relied upon politically was dead. My beloved State of Virginia was dismembered, and a new State had been erected out of a part of her,[18] against her will. Every hope that I had ever indulged in was dead."[19] A diarist wrote on May 18, 1865: "Frank Ravenel, in his quiet grave on Malvern Hill, has the best of it."[20]

"It is difficult for us at this day," observed a woman who had lived through the South's agony, "ro realize what little promise life held for the young American of the South; difficult even for the South of the present to appreciate the irritations and humiliations that vexed and chafed him. Many felt that they no longer had a country. . . . But the old people of the South never reacted. Many simply sat down and died, succumbing to bereavement, hardships and heartbreak. They felt that their country was dead."[21]

All of this Pryor must have realized and felt. In addition, he was a marked man. After Appomattox, the United States Circuit Court at Norfolk indicted for treason Robert E. Lee and other prominent Southerners, including Pryor.[22] General Hartsuff, the Federal commander at Petersburg, sent him word to leave Virginia, for men in power were hinting at punishment and retribution. Hartsuff's Commissary General, Captain Gregory, told Sara that "there is a future before your husband. New York is the place for him. . . . Only *send* him—and speedily."[23]

At length the Pryors decided that he would go to New York to seek to earn that bread which seemed impossible to earn in the South. Sara raised funds for his passage by selling her watch and a diamond-encrusted cameo ring that he had given her before marriage. With the proceeds and a $300 loan, she bought the tickets, quinine, and a suit to replace his threadbare Confederate uniform.[24]

Pryor did not believe in a policy of resistance or revenge. "We have been fairly whipped," he declared shortly after Appomattox, "and I think that such men in LEE'S and JOHNSTON'S armies as do not lay down their arms and return at once to their duties as law-abiding citizens should be treated as outlaws. For myself, I yield that the cause is hopeless, and if I am only left two old mules to work a few acres of land with, in part pay for those that SHERIDAN'S men took from me, I will go back to the plough and my duty as a loyal citizen."[25] His last political act before heading North was to address a letter to his former constituents, urging them to accept gracefully the inevitable issues of the war, to accord at once the right of suffrage to the Negro citizens of the South, and to enter heartily upon the work of reconciliation and reconstruction.[26] Then he set out for New York, in his wife's words, "into the arms of the enemy." She added, "and the enemy was always good to us."[27] "Undaunted, he tilted at life anew."[28]

Many Southerners were shocked at Pryor's going to the North, but not all. "After the war," wrote an old neighbor, "true to his combative and courageous instincts, he sought the fields of the enemy for forage . . . though handicapped by poverty and regarded as an alien, and by many as a traitor to the old flag. . . ."[29] New York was the logical place to go, as that city "welcomed Southerners, for they made it easier for the city to recapture its old-time Southern business."[30]

Pryor expected to be in New York only long enough to make a reconnaissance of the job situation. But a week after his arrival, he wrote to Sara: "What will you think when I tell you that several gentlemen suggest to me to settle here? Dare I 'then, to beard the lion in his den— the Douglas in his hall!' Not in his 'hall,' certainly, unless I am very specially invited by him, but I might in time wrestle with him, in a court-room. I have a mind to try it. 'The world is all before us where to choose.' I shouldn't like the Douglas to find out I have forgotten all the law I ever knew. Neither would I like my good friend Professor Minor (if he reads the N.Y. reports) to make a similar discovery." In a few days, he wrote: "I am not yet determined when to return. I was to leave this morning, but Mr. Ben Wood of the *News* has requested me to remain a day or two that he might have a talk with me. What this means I am not sure."[31]

Benjamin Wood, who was born in 1820, had purchased the New York *Daily News* in 1860, acting as editor and publisher.[32] He was strongly pro-Southern and opposed New York's participation in the Civil War. On January 1, 1861, he recommended that New York secede from the Union.[33] On April 14, his paper proclaimed: "The wealthy will not supply the means to depreciate the rest of their property by prolonging this unnatural war."[34] His attitude incurred the hostility of the administration in Washington, and the privileges of the mails were denied to his newspaper by Postmaster-General Blair, an action approved by Congress.[35] But he was elected as a Democrat to the Thirty-seventh and Thirty-eighth Congresses, serving from 1861 to 1865.[36] Much more famed was Ben's brother Fernando, who was mayor of

New York City. The brothers also owned several New York lotteries, which had charters from Southern states.[37]

In 1863, Ben had written a novel, *Fort Lafayette; or, Love and Secession*, which suggested that Pryor's career was of more than passing interest to him. At any rate, Wood hired Pryor secretly, and the Virginian agreed to write incognito. "The wounds of the war were still too fresh to permit a Confederate general to mold public opinion in a Northern city."[38]

Pryor wrote to his wife of his new position.

> I have accepted Mr. Wood's proposition *for the present.* The only difficulty I see is the fact that they refuse me a pardon. If they learn that I am writing for the *News*, they may send me to keep company with John Mitchell. I understand that charges are constantly made against me in Washington. Whatever they are, they are false, trumped up to serve some sinister purpose. Yet I am resolved never to degrade myself by an abject submission. I have never solicited "pardon," and I mean to approach them with no further overture.
>
>   . . . I am going to work like a beaver and with no other purpose than to earn a living for my dear wife and children. Ambition! The ambition of my life is to have my darlings settled in comfort. May God assist me in that endeavor!
>
>   My room is at 47 West 12th Street. There you must send my winter clothes—and we must try, whatever is left undone, to send the boys to school.[39]

The newspaper position paid Pryor twenty-five dollars a week, but meanwhile he devoted every possible moment to the study of law. To Sara he wrote: "Sometimes I sink in despair; but then I rally and press on. Don't you think heaven will prosper me for *your* sake? The obstacles to the success of 'a rebel' in this city are almost insurmountable."[40]

By December, 1865, Pryor was admitted to the New York bar. The event did not go unnoticed, and the Brooklyn *Daily News* observed: "Roger A. Pryor has opened a law office in Nassau Street. More fortunate than his English predecessor of the same name, who was imprisoned for treason, Pryor is permitted to live among the Yankees, whom he formerly held in such contempt."[41]

Even his wife did not know that Pryor had been studying law, until his admission to the bar was a *fait accompli*. Perhaps he did not want her to be worried about how intensively he was working; perhaps he did not want to find himself in a position where he would have to confess failure. It had been contemplated by the Pryors that some day he would practice law, but no consideration had been given as to when. Early in December, however, he sent to her the glad tidings with illy disguised exultation.

> Sitting late one night with Mr. Ben Woods in the *News* office, he turned to me and said rather abruptly, "General, why don't you practice law?" I answered, "For the best of all possible reasons— I am not a lawyer." He replied, "Neither is C, nor T; yet 1they make $10,000 a year."
>
> Of course the idea of my ever making so great a sum was too preposterous for a moment's though. . . . But just then I received an invitation from Mr. Luke Cozzens for temporary desk room in his office and the use of his library. I have really borrowed books and been studying law in my leisure hours ever since I came to this city, and I now resolved to made application to the Bar! The application was made by James T. Brady, the most eminent of our forensic orators. . . . Thereupon the Hon. John B. Haskins—my former associate in Congress—was appointed to examine me as to my knowledge of Law. . . . We returned to the Court, and he reported in favor of my application!"[42]

Mr. Hughes, identified only as "an English sympathizer," rented Pryor a room for one dollar a month in Tyron Row, "an undesirable locality." "I have commenced attending the Courts regularly and have heard the leading lawyers. I am not vain, as you know, but—*I am not afraid of them*! But when, when shall I have a chance? The great difficulty in my way is the prejudice against 'rebels'; and that I am sorry to see is not diminishing. I hope to wear it away after a while if, meanwhile, I do not starve. It is my last cast—and I am resolved to succeed or perish in the attempt. . . . Look now for uninteresting letters. It will be study, *study, study,* ever after this!"[43]

Benjamin Wood sent Pryor his first law case.[44] Mr. France, of Baltimore, sought an attorney to argue for his discharge in a bankruptcy motion. Pryor won the case and the judge's encomium, "It is a great privilege to hear a good argument from an able lawyer!" He also won a $1,000 fee, for, fearful lest the client consider his intended $50 charge exorbitant, Pryor insisted that Mr. France name the amount.[45]

On December 28, Pryor wrote to Sara: "My prospects have brightened a little with the promise of a case that would, in time, have yielded me two hundred dollars, but a friendly priest (and he was wise) persuaded the parties to settle out of Court, and so my hopes were dashed to the ground. . . . My thoughts at Christmas in my lonely office were with my precious household at Cottage Farm. How I regretted my want of money would not permit me to send some holiday presents, but we must bear these privations till happier days. . . . If only you can feel happy, I can bear my portion of the burden."[46]

In 1866, Pryor moved to a house on Waverly Place, near New York University. His office was at 95 Liberty Street.[47] He became a member of the New York Law Institute.[48] But fees came slowly. In February, he wrote his wife: "I have some little money owing me and some doubtful claims, and the Court and lawyers treat me with marked courtesy. I study intensely and am as diligent as possible in my attention to my duties. I mean at least to deserve success—which is the surest way to realize it."[49]

In his next letter, he confided that "I am convinced the chief obstacle to my success is the prejudice against 'rebels.' That is fearful, and I feel its effects every day. I was lately employed as a referee to report the facts in an application for the discharge of a prisoner by the process of *habeas corpus*. When my name as referee was announced, one of the counsel arose and protested to the Court that he would not appear before a rebel whose hands were yet red with loyal blood. Thereupon, of course, I declined the appointment. Still, I must toil on, nothing disheartened. The memory of the little household at Cottage Farm animates and substains me in my troubles. May God bless and prosper us!"[50]

"Did you ever know any one who lived honestly, worked hard, and exerted competent talent to fail in any enterprise of life?" he asked rhetorically in another letter. "I think we have competent ability; as for the rest I am certain; my health is perfect."[51]

Pryor's most promising client proved to be just that: it promised but made no payment of fees, and bankruptcy ended the matter before his

$3,000 bill could be settled. To Sara he wrote: "I am not dismayed, however, *au contraire*! My present impulse is to retrieve the loss by extraordinary efforts. Work, *work*, *work*, is my duty and destiny; your welfare the goal that beckons me on. I contemplate nothing else—I desire nothing else."[52]

Sara, meanwhile, was struggling at Cottage Farm to keep the family together. She had hoped to return to a once-promising literary career, but darning hosiery had a debilitating effect upon her aspirations with the pen.[53] She gave piano lessons to seven children.[54] Her husband wrote to congratulate her upon her success in keeping the children together. "Beg Gordon to apply herself diligently to my books—or what is left of them. . . . I wish her to be the most brilliant girl of the day." As for himself, "*here I mean to stay*! It is my last cast in the game of life, and if I fail now, all is lost. I am writing again for the *News*. I need the money to support us."[55]

In his first year and a half in New York, Pryor did not leave his room for any recreation whatsoever except for one visit to Virginia and an occasional visit to his former fellow congressman, John B. Haskins, who lived in Fordham.[56] That first visit to his family was a memorable occasion. On January 24, 1868, Sara bore a fourth daughter, Fanny.[57]

Back in New York, Pryor applied himself to his work with renewed vigor. He had no helpers and even served his own papers.[58] To his wife on January 23, 1867 he sent a check for $200, "with one hundred and ninety-seven of which you must take up a note due Ashwell, the Northern sutler. This is what remains of money due him to redeem the silver tray[59] from which you parted to purchase shoes for the prisoners. . . . Next spring you *must* join me. Do let us make the experiment. By hard work and strict economy we may contrive to tide over our difficulties. We must remember that we are poor, and must act accordingly. We must be content to live humbly. *Anything* is more tolerable than the life we now live."[60] On March 5 he added to this invitation: "May we not live here humbly, but content in one another's presence? . . . We can at least be sustained by our mutual love and admiration. What care we for the world?"[61]

For a short time, Pryor had the pleasure of knowing that his highly gifted son, Theodorick, was in New York, although not under the same roof. The lad attended school at the College of St. Francis Xavier; but when he became disenchanted with the program, his father sent him to the school of John Christian in Petersburg. At the classical school run by Professor Gordon W. McCabe, Theodorick won the Pegram Prize for the best scholarship in the senior class.[62] In April, 1867, Pryor wrote to his son: "I am pleased to hear that you are reading 'Boswell's Johnson.' It was the book that first gave me a taste for literature, and the habit of reading—a taste which I have found not only the chief agency in the development of my intellect, but the most unfailing source of happiness. While a prisoner of war, my love of letters sustained and cheered me; and I find it now the best solace in weary and unhappy moments. . . . My observation is, that the chief difference between men, in an intellectual sense, is the superior love of letters which distinguishes one above another. Besides, it is the rarest thing in the world to see a bad man addicted to literature."[63]

A month later, he wrote to Theodorick: "Make it a rule *always to do your best*, and never to be content with a slovenly or imperfect performance. Avoid fine writing, however, by which I mean the use of big words and an artificial mode of thinking. . . . Press forward in your studies. We'll see what can be done toward sending you to College; so be prepared."[64]

Pryor was now living at 5 Great Jones Street, and his office was at 39 Nassau Street.[65]

In July, he received a $2,000 contingency fee for a trial that he had won. This was the windfall the family had been awaiting so eagerly. In two weeks' time, his wife closed up their Virginia home and sailed for New York with five children and her Negro laundress; the oldest child, Gordon, remained in Charlotte County for the summer. Baggage was not much of a problem. Sara could bring from "the melancholy wreckage of a home" only a few damaged books, a box of silver, and one trunk.[66]

After much hunting, Pryor rented a furnished house for $1,800 far out in Brooklyn,[67] which at that time was not embraced in New York City. Their first Northern home was unsubstantial and unattractive, but soon they moved to Brooklyn Heights, close to the New York ferry.[68] Their home was at 127 Willow Street, on the left side going from Poplar southwest to Amity Street, between Clark and Pierpont Streets.[69]

Little Willy encountered difficulties with the neighbors' children because his terrier was named Rebel. So the dog was called Prince on the street, Rebel in the privacy of their home. One of the Pryor girls was told by her new associates that she would not be allowed to live on that street, as they were "Rebels, and slave-drivers, and *awful* people." To her father she exclaimed: "Momma told me that God loves us. Will everybody else hate us?"[70]

Gordon entered the senior class at the Packer Institute, from which she was graduated the following year (aged 18) with first honors.[71]

There were few Southerners in New York when the Pryors set up house, and they had no friends among their first neighbors, "to whom, of course, we made no advances."[72] That seemed to be inevitable at the time. "Our extreme poverty forbade any expectation of indulgence in social life, even had we felt we had the smallest right to recognition."[73] Pryor was "regarded as an alien, and by many as a traitor to the old flag. . . ."[74] He was not helped by untrue rumors.

On August 16, 1867, the Secretary of the Navy noted in his diary: "At the close of the Cabinet session to-day, Mr. Binckley, the Acting Attorney-General, submitted a copy of the *New York Times* of yesterday, containing a statement and sundry affadavits of parties who swear they had been bribed, or suborned by Roger A. Pryor, Ben Wood, and others, to destroy the character of Attorney-General Joseph Holt. These affadavits, it is said, are filed in the office of the Attorney-General or War Department and office of Military Justice." Three days later, he noted: "The affadavits which have been published implicating Pryor and Ben Wood are undoubtedly false and fraudulent."[75] But as long-time journalists, Pryor and Secretary Welles might well have remembered that old aphorism that no one reads retractions.

The family troubles seemed to continue. Sara's Aunt Mary became incurably ill, and the silver presented to Pryor by the Virginia Democrats in 1856 had to be pawned once more to procure funds.[76]

Pryor's merciless dedication to his mastery of the law affected the entire family. Recalled his wife: "Not one moment's recreation did we allow ourselves—our 'destiny was work, work, work'—and patiently we fulfilled it. Hard study filled my husband's every working hour, and few were his hours of sleep. Excessive use of his eyes night and day so injured them that at one time he found reading impossible. Gordon read his law aloud to him for many weeks. I once copied a book of law forms for him as we had no money to buy the book—the hardest work I have ever done!"[77] But her husband did not accept this as a matter of course. "What a wonderful woman you are—so content, so cheery in spite of all our privations," he exclaimed.[78] His writings (even legal arguments) were read aloud and copied at home, for he wanted to know Gordon's layman reaction.[79]

Many Virginians resented Pryor's having left his ancestral home. When he stated that Southerners' salvation was conditioned upon their acquiescence in the inevitable, with justice to the Negro, their outrage was mighty. Hearing of this resentment, he wrote a lengthy letter to the Richmond *Whig* on October 5, in which he said in part:

> When I renewed my oath of allegiance to the Union, I did so in good faith and without reservation; and as I understand that oath, it not only restrains me from acts of positive hostility to the government, but pledges me to do my utmost for its welfare and stability. Hence, while I am more immediately concerned to see the South restored to its former prosperity, I am anxious that the whole country, and all classes, may be reunited on the basis of common interest and fraternal regard. And this object, it appears to me, can only be attained by conceding to all classes the unrestricted rights guaranteed them by the laws and by obliterating as speedily and as entirely as possible the distinctions which have separated the North and South into hostile sections. . . .
>
> With this conviction, while I pretend to no part in politics, I have not hesitated, in private discourse, to advise my friends in the South frankly to "accept the situation"; to adjust their ideas to the altered state of affairs; to recognize and respect the rights of the colored race; . . . it is absolutely essential to the peace, repose, and prosperity of the South that the emancipated class should be undisturbed in the enjoyment of their rights under the law and should be enlightened to understand the duties and interests of social order and well-being. . . .
>
> And thus, leaving to others the ostensible part in the work of reconstruction, and abstaining studiously from all political connection and activity, I have hoped in some measure, and in a quiet way, to repair the evil I contributed to bring upon the South by availing myself of every appropriate opportunity to suggest these counsels of moderation and magnanimity. . . .[80]

In September, 1868, Theodorick was accepted by Princeton College as a junior, rather than as a sophomore, as had been hoped. (His father would have preferred the University of Virginia, but that institution had not yet recovered from the war.) Funds had been a great worry;[81] the young man, however, won a scholarship by reason of his excellent entrance examination.[82] In June, 1870, he was graduated as First Honor man of his class, with the second highest average that ever had been attained at Princeton: only Aaron Burr, ninety-nine years earlier, had posted a higher figure.[83]

Theodorick (now known as Theo) then returned to the Pryor home in Brooklyn, where he was included in the census tabulation made that June:[84]

Roger	41	Lawyer	Virginia
Sara	39	'Keeping House'	Virginia
Theodoric [*sic*]	18	Student	Virginia
M. Gordon	20		Virginia
Roger A.	16	In school	Virginia
Mary	14	In school	Virginia
William R.	12	In school	Virginia
Lucy	10	In school	Virginia
Fanny	7	In school	Virginia

Theo was hired by the Reverend S. W. Plumer, professor of the Theological Seminary at Columbia, South Carolina, as a proof reader of a commentary on the Epistle to the Romans.[85] In September, Theo went to the Theological Seminary at Princeton and began a joint study of theology and mathematics. In a few months, he went to England as a Mathematical Fellow, to study at St. Peter's College at Cambridge University. But finding the climate and English students uncongenial, he returned to Brooklyn after one year.[86] He entered the Columbia University Law School, at the same time studying German literature and philosophy; he wavered meanwhile between law and theology. Not wishing to be a financial drain upon the family, he helped out in his father's law office and became a tutor.[87] He became disillusioned by the corruption of the times and frequently was depressed.[88] He drove himself precisely as his father had done with himself, but apparently he did not have his father's stamina and that terrible will to win.

On Sunday, October 15, 1871, Theo seemed to be ill and complained of chills. But he chose to go out for a walk, alone. He never returned. Early the next morning, the police were notified of his disappearance; later that day, his body was found floating in the East River. His coat, watch and purse were missing, but there were no signs of violence upon his body. It was believed that he had had a temporary derangement of his reason and had walked off a dock. Burial was at Princeton, the scene of his greatest triumph and the place where he had started such a promising career.[89]

IX

Law and Politics

Burial in his work was Pryor's solace as well as his economic necessity. Added to the other buffetings of fate, the loss of his highly gifted son might have undone a man who had nothing on which to lean. Pryor's conception of religion as a source of strength was stated in an address he made two years after Theo's death. On June 12, 1873, Pryor addressed the alumni of Hampden-Sydney College. Barely eight years after the war, virtually all of the persons in his audience must have been experiencing dark days.

"Gentlemen," declared Pryor, "though amid the blackness of the gathering gloom we need not, *we must not*, abandon ourselves to despair. The present darkness is but the shadow of a passing eclipse; from which, be assured, truth will emerge with undiminished lustre."[1] He viewed with misgivings the seeming triumph of the burgeoning sciences, as revealed by Charles Darwin and others. "Yet again, as science knows of nothing beyond the finite and phenomenal; and as all experience proves the universality and uniformity of law; then every impulse of volition is determined by its antecedents: and with the freedom of his will man loses his moral responsibility."[2] The source of his own responsibility, Pryor recognized. "Man alone is conscious of the God within, who instructs him in the nature of good and evil: man alone links this his present life with the hopes of an unending hereafter. Consider, too, how paltry and perishing are all the gratifications of sense; how sterile and insufficient are all the resources of the intellect even; and then mark the infallible guidance of conscience in steering us away from evil, ponder the great problems of the infinite and eternal, of which faith, and faith only, vouchsafe us a solution . . . then say by what an imperial ascendancy the spiritual faculties of men predominate over the carnal and the intellectual: and by what urgency of momentous interest it behooves him not to leave in abeyance the culture of his religious nature."[3]

Gradually Pryor's law practice began to increase in volume and in importance. He moved to a new office at 22 Pine Street in New York.[4] He began a lengthy and profitable association with General Benjamin F. Butler, one of the greatest lawyers in the nation,[5] who, long before most other men, was willing to consort with the late enemy. Butler, who had been the senior major-general in the Federal army during a large part of the Civil War, was a "loner" in his legal career, but he frequently selected an associate for a particular piece of litigation; with increasing frequence, he turned to Pryor.

Late in October, 1873, a month after the failure of the great banking firm of Jay Cooke & Co., A. & W. Sprague Manufacturing Company of Providence, Rhode Island, suspended operations. Assets were appraised at $19,495,000 and liabilities at $11,475,000, but payments could not be met. The business interests of the prominent Sprague family were widely extended.[6] Pryor was affiliated with General Butler in the maze of lawsuits that followed this major insolvency.[7] Pryor's work here commended him to the family, and he was counsel in the divorce suit of Governor Sprague of Rhode Island and in the various litigations respecting the Sprague estate.[8]

Butler was described in that year by an observer:

BENJAMIN F. BUTLER, of Massachusetts, is a burly, heavy man, who waddles as he walks, and carries his head slightly bent forward. He is the best abused, best hated man in the House. It suits some persons to imagine that Ben Butler, as he is popularly called, is simply a blustering, swaggering politician without much ability of any kind. The truth is that Butler's big head contains a good share of the brains of the House, and he possesses qualities that would make him a leader in any cause he might espouse. . . . Butler is much of a philosopher. He is a man of strong feelings, but he has learned to control them, and, when it suits him, he can pocket his grievances, and work with a smiling face by the side of the men whom he hates with all the intensity of his nature.[9]

Later, Butler himself engaged Pryor for a delicate piece of work which (the wily Butler realized) needed not only an able lawyer but a highly regarded Southern personage with good connections. Butler's son-in-law, Adelbert Ames, was the carpetbagger Military Governor of Mississippi. Subsequently, as a Republican, he became Governor of that state, with a Negro lieutenant-governor. "The darkest days of Mississippi had dawned. . . ." In time, the Negroes controlled the entire state government; stripped of his powers, Ames fruitlessly asked President Grant for Federal troops, which were, however, denied him. When Ames organized his own Negro militia, Federal soldiers were sent into Mississippi to prevent bloodshed, while impeachment proceedings were started against the ineffectual governor on various charges, including bribery.[10]

At this point, Pryor was retained. "I opened negotiations with the leading men against us, with many of whom I had old and intimate associations," he wrote to Butler, as if that crafty attorney had not been fully aware of these connections all the time. "[I]t was arranged that they would dismiss the charges, and then the Governor would resign."[11] Ames advised his father-in-law that "Conviction was certain. . . . A conflict could have resulted in no good to any one."[12] Pryor wrote to his client: "Appreciating the sensibility which restrains you from resigning while charges are pending against you, we are, nevertheless, clearly of the opinion that in the event the charges are withdrawn, you may retire without the least compromise of your reputation."[13] The deal was accepted: the articles of impeachment were dropped and Ames resigned.[14]

In 1874-1875 the case which firmly put Pryor among the foremost attorneys in New York occurred. This was the sensational, highly publicized adultery suit of the prominent editor, Theodore Tilton, against Henry Ward Beecher, one of the most eminent clergymen in the land and brother of Harriet Beecher Stowe.

Tilton and Beecher were close friends as well as associates on the *Independent*, a Congregationalist journal. Dr. Beecher had married the Tiltons and remained on intimate terms with both of them, terms which were, in fact, too intimate, Mrs. Tilton confessed to her husband in 1870. The story did not become public until 1872, when it appeared in a little-noticed periodical, *Woodhull and Clafin's Weekly.* Another two years elapsed before Tilton lodged a formal complaint against Beecher in church. Mrs. Tilton stood by the clergyman.

The trial began in Brooklyn City Court in August, 1874, and was the sensation of the newspapers for months. In addition to an adultery trial involving prominent figures, the high calibre of the attorneys served notice that this was no ordinary lawsuit. Morris & Pearsall represented Tilton, with William A. Beach serving as chief counsel and Pryor as an associate. Shearman & Sterling represented the minister, with the distinguished William M. Evarts as chief counsel. The complaint stated that Beecher sought to alienate the affections of Elizabeth M. Richards Tilton and asked for $100,000 and costs. Beecher denied everything except that Elizabeth was Tilton's wife and that she had lived with Tilton as man and wife until 1874.

In the lengthy court proceedings, Pryor had the responsibility of presenting two propositions: (1) that the defendant (Beecher) should not be granted a bill of particulars and (2) that Tilton was competent to appear as a witness, even though his wife's alleged activities with the defendant were the heart of the proceeding. Upon these two questions the case of Tilton largely depended.[15] Pryor argued that he did not wish to be bound by a bill of particulars, for a date or an address could be wrong. "This defendant," he insisted, "if he be innocent, is entitled to a vindication; he is entitled to an absolute and complete vindication—not a vindication which finds that he did not commit the act of adultery in Livingston-street, that he did not commit the act of adultery on the 19th of August, 1868, but a vindication which ascertains and proclaims that he never committed this act (in his own language), at any time or at any place . . . [A]llowing the order will be a practical denial of justice to the plaintiff as well as to the defendant, for that matter: that it will exclude all consideration of the real question in controversy."[16]

As to Tilton's competency to appear as a witness, Pryor argued: "Now, sir, this witness does not offer to take the stand and testify in this case in legal sense, for or against his wife. He presents himself to testify against the wife's alleged seducer." She could not be convicted of adultery by his testimony. "By the Levitical law, as your Honor is aware, both man and woman were denounced to death for the act of adultery. . . ." Such was the law in England under the Puritans. "But upon the return of reason and the Stuarts, that law was repealed; and it never was the law in New York . . . that adultery was a crime."[17]

Pryor was successful in both of these motions, although he was opposed by the mighty William M. Evarts, a strikingly handsome man with highly intellectual appearance, carelessly falling hair, hawk-like nose, and gray glittering eyes, who bore a remarkable resemblance to Cicero.[18]

The Court of Appeals held on December 7, 1874, that no bill of particulars had to be filed.[19] In these proceedings, Pryor represented Tilton; Evarts, Beecher.

Technical matters now being disposed of, the trial of Beecher was begun in the City Court of Brooklyn on January 5, 1875. On January 11, the jury now being acceptable, the actual trial began.

"Nor has anything been wanting to lend dramatic interest to the trial itself. The counsel employed are among the most eminent at the American bar. On the one side Mr. Pryor, a man of large erudition and of a marvelously alert mind; . . . [and] Mr. Beach, a pungent and powerful speaker. On the other side . . . Mr. Evarts, who to a reputation already established as an acute and learned lawyer, has by his conduct of this case added that of a master of the entirely distinct art of advocacy before a jury."[20]

An attorney who observed the trial recalled: "There was also Roger A. Pryor, who had come out of the South to display his learning and his fiery oratory. . . . Among all the lawyers who represented the plaintiff there was none, in my estimation, who in discussion of the relevancy of testimony reached greater heights than those reached by Mr. Pryor. He was a dramatic figure, with his long black hair and high cheek bones, and seemed almost the counterpart of an Indian Chief on the warpath, or, again, a martial member of the staff of Lee in the Confederate Army. When there was a question that required learning or the apt quotation of the legal principle from the reported case, the chapter and page were on the tip of his tongue."[21]

The trial lasted for 112 days and ended in an anticlimatic hung jury.[22] But Pryor, at least, should not have been disappointed by the results of the trial. He was now a marked man. "It is by far the most celebrated jury trial in America for the past half century, and every part of it could be studied with profit and advantage."[23]

Pryor had come a long way in a short time. It was less then ten years since he had left Virginia to try to rebuild his life in New York. "He came to a strange city 35 years of age, with a large family, and broken in health from imprisonment and exposure—without a dollar —with no influential friends, and unlearned in the law of the state he had chosen. His indomitable courage did not forsake him. . . ."[24]

In this month, the census-taker found the Pryors still living at 157 Willow Street in Brooklyn. Roger's age was shown as 41, as was Sara's,[25] although actually they were 46 and 44, respectively. At about that time, a visitor thus described the household: "I never saw a more cheerful circle of hearts nestling in a lovelier home. During the four or five days that I spent under their roof I was the object of a thousand attentions, without feeling any of that embarrassment which so often results from over-notice."[26]

Pryor prosecuted the first of the damage suits against the elevated railroad companies, the structures of which deprived property owners, along the right of way, of light and air. He obtained a permanent injunction to restrain an elevated railroad company from erecting its structure in front of 170-174 Greenwich Street without the consent of the owner of that property.[27] The principle thus established by Pryor was affirmed by higher courts, where property owners were represented by lawyers of greater recognized professional stature than he possessed at the time. Thus, William M. Evarts was the successful counsel in one such case[28] and the renowned Joseph H. Choate represented the property owners in another Court of Appeals case.[29] Pryor's position ultimately was sustained by the United States Supreme Court, which held that an abutter on a street in New York may recover, against a company constructing an elevated railroad in front of his building, damages for discomfort and inconvenience.[30]

Pryor won a woman an alimony settlement on his argument that the husband's threats of violence were of a character sufficient to induce a reasonable apprehension of bodily injury. Threats, plus charges of infidelity, plus an allegation shortly after the birth of her child that some one else had sired it, were enough (he maintained) to constitute "cruel and inhuman treatment" within the meaning of the statute authorizing limited divorce; and the court agreed.[31]

He established that a representative in the Congress of the United States held a "public office" within the provisions of the Brooklyn City Charter, which prohibited an alderman from holding "any public office." Hence the congressman's post as alderman was automatically vacant.[32] Pryor's authorities were not only United States cases and legal authorities; also cited were Henry E. Brougham on the British constitution and De Tocqueville's *Democracy in America*.

Pryor now had the legal assistance of his son, Roger, Jr., and at this time they moved to a new office at 74 William Street.[33]

Ever since the close of the Civil War, Pryor had been concerned about the strained relations between North and South. The harsh results of Reconstruction and the continued presence of Federal troops in the South made reconciliation difficult. The Compromise of 1877 between Republicans and the onetime rebel-slaveholder group resulted in Hayes' election to the presidency and withdrawal of the troops; in return for Southern support in the disputed Hayes-Tilden election, the restoration of home rule in the South had been promised.[34] "It was not until 1877 that the mass of Southerners could take pride in being called Americans, look upon the American flag with joy, or feel that they were a part of the United States."[35]

Pryor felt that the new president had a splendid opportunity to effect a reconciliation. The day before the inaugural, he declared:

> Should Mr. Hayes recognize Hampton and Nicholls,[36] and otherwise show a sense of fairness to the South, they will support his Administration. He can take the Southern people into camp in one week. I am satisfied, from private advices, that Mr. Hayes's single, sincere, and earnest desire is to repair and restore the South. Whether he will be able to act on the volition of his own will remains to be seen. He has a great opportunity, such as is rarely given to the rulers of men. I can see a policy before President Hayes by which he will destroy the Democracy in the South, and consequently in the country; and that by calling into existence and activity the old-line Whig element of the South, which, having been originally opposed to secession, has, since the war, been yoked angrily and unevenly in a Democratic alliance. By the policy of calling to his succor and support the old-line Whigs he would build up a legitimate native white Republican party in the South.[37]

Pryor felt the need for reconciliation more than did most persons, for as a prominent Southerner now living in the North, he had been made to *feel* the impact of hatred and prejudice. He was pleased to

[105]

accept an invitation to give a Decoration Day address at the Academy
of Music in Brooklyn in 1877, but he declined the bid when veterans of
the Grand Army of the Republic registered protests. He reconsidered
and finally accepted, however.[38] This was the first combined reunion
in the country of both Northern and Southern veterans. The Academy
charged a twenty-five-cent admission fee, for the erection of a Soldiers'
Home at Bath, New York. Within, boxes were draped with American
flags, and from the proscenium were suspended red, white, and blue
bunting, while from the flies to the wings were stretched streamers of
the same colors. The Thirteenth Regiment Band provided the music.[39]

"The Confederate General Roger A. Pryor was the speaker of the
evening. He was received with hearty applause."[40] Alluding to the
Civil War, he declared in part:

> From the vantage ground of a larger observation, with a more
> calm and considerable meditation on the causes and conditions
> of national prosperity, I, for one, cannot resist the conclusion
> that, after all, Providence wisely ordered the event, and that it is
> well for the South itself that it was disappointed in its endeavor
> to establish a separate government. Plain is it that, if once es-
> tablished, such a government could not have long endured. It
> was founded on principles that must have proved its downfall.
> It must soon have fallen a victim to foreign aggression or
> domestic anarchy. Nor to the reestablishment of the Union is the
> Confederate soldier any the less reconciled by the destruction of
> slavery. People of the North, history will record that slavery fell,
> not by any efforts of man's will, but by the immediate interven-
> tion and act of the Almighty Heaven. And in the anthem of praise
> ascending to heaven for the emancipation of four million human
> beings, the voice of the Confederate soldier mingles its note of
> devout congratulation. And now in the unconquerable strength
> of freedom we hope that the existence of our blessed Union is
> limited only by the mortality that measures the duration of all
> human institutions.[41]

This speech was very well received. "Such were his large and states-
man-like views of what the status of the North and South really should
be, that his speech has gone very far toward healing the dissensions
between the two sections of the country."[42] A local editorial com-

mented that Decoration Day speeches were flooding the country, but most were mere rantings. "The propriety of this distinction will be appreciated by such of our readers as compare the vast volume of swash poured out in our cemeteries yesterday with the admirable address delivered by General Pryor in the Academy of Music last night. . . ."[43] The Richmond *Whig* observed: "The address of Gen. Roger A. Pryor delivered on Decoration Day at Brooklyn, N.Y., is a brilliant production. Like everything emanating from him, it is full of fine thought and fine sentiment, with a sweeping array of glowing genius, all clothed in a diction simple, pure, and as apposite as if the idea and language had been born together from a brain original and independent in its conceptions. The spirit of the address, too, is national, catholic, patriotic, and grandly American from beginning to end. Pryor is a man of splendid parts, and Virginia has reason to be proud of him."[44] Pryor's proud but practical wife sounded the only discordant note. "But, unhappily, honor does not fill the basket, nor warm the body, nor pay the rent, nor satisfy the tax gatherer. It is a nice, nice thing to have,—there's no use denying it,—but I think my dear general would have given it all, every bit, for one good, remunerative law case."[45]

His law practice did not keep up with his professional reputation. A few months after the widely noted Brooklyn Academy speech, the Springfield (Massachusetts) *Republican* declared: "Roger Pryor is pegging away very quietly in his law office, with increasing business, although it is not of a very conspicuous character nor very remunerative, I imagine, for he does a great deal of work for poor people; but he sticks so closely to his business that comparatively few people know that he is here. . . ."[46]

As so many other lawyers without profitable clienteles have done, Pryor turned to politics. There were two points of distinction from the usual situation, however. Firstly, he had been a practicing politician *before* he had been a practicing lawyer (that is, a lawyer with a practice). Secondly, to him politics was a crusade for good government. There was now a real impediment, however. By the 1870s, no white Southerner was deprived of the right to vote, but he was still forbidden to hold office.[47] All his life he was to remain a Democrat;[48] but now he could not be elected or appointed to anything. He could be a king-maker but not a king.

In 1872, Pryor reentered politics on a small scale. Horace Greeley,

editor of the New York *Tribune,* was running for the presidency on the
Democratic ticket against Grant, and as one journalist to another,
he appealed to Pryor for help in getting the Southern vote. Pryor
agreed. John Russell Young, a Republican friend of Grant's, wrote
unbelievingly to Pryor:

> . . . The idea of R. A. P.—the representative fire-eater, the
> Robespierre, or Danton, or, if you like it better, the Harry Hot-
> spur of the Southern Revolution,—the one orator who clamored
> so impatiently for the Shrewsbury clock to strike,—oh, my
> friend! The spectacle of *this* leader championing Horace Greeley!
> . . . But there is no honest reconstruction possible under Mr.
> Greeley and the men who would accompany him in power. The
> South has its future in its own hands. If the men who led it as you
> did had followed your example when the war was over, there
> would be no trouble. But that required courage—a higher cour-
> age than ever rebellion demanded; and if the South has not re-
> asserted itself, it is the fault of the Southern men themselves.[49]

In 1876, Pryor was a delegate to the Democratic National Convention in St. Louis.[50] He was obliged to hear Robert G. Ingersoll characterize the Democrats: "Recollect the men who starved our soldiers
and shot them down are all for Tilden and Hendricks. All the hands
dipped in Union blood were in the Democratic party."[51]

How seriously Pryor considered reentry into active politics is not
known; it seems unlikely that he would have gone through what he
had to become a lawyer if he were not determined to practice law. He
was not eligible to hold public office under the terms of a general law,
but perhaps he merely wanted to be freed of this disability as a matter
of principle. On June 7, 1865, District Judge John C. Underwood had
a Norfolk Grand Jury indict the Confederate leaders,[52] including
Pryor. President Johnson's proclamation of May 29 had amnested
and pardoned all except fourteen classes of Confederates upon their
taking a prescribed oath, and others could make specific applications.[53] Johnson bestowed his pardons liberally, and on Christmas
Day in 1868 he extended it as far as was within his power.[54] This
proclamation stopped any treason prosecutions, and the Norfolk
indictments were *nolle prossed* on February 13, 1869.[55] But the

Fourteenth Amendment and acts of Congress provided impediments to the Confederate leaders. In 1872, a general amnesty was extended to all but about 500 Confederates,[56] including Pryor. On March 8, 1880, at about the time he was becoming active in politics again, he wrote to the Senate and to the House of Representatives: "Your petitioner, Roger A. Pryor, citizen of the State of New York, respectfully represents that by reason of the provisions of section 3, article 14, of the amendments to the Constitution of the United States he is under political disabilities; that he is and has been since the close of the war of the rebellion a peaceable and quiet citizen of the United States; that he submits to and obeys the Constitution of the United States and the laws of Congress in all respects. Therefore, your petitioner prays that his said disabilities incurred by reason of his participation in the said war may be removed."[57] His petition was sent to the Committee on the Judiciary,[58] and on March 27 a bill for the removal of his political disabilities was presented in the form of H.R. 5935.[59] The Senate enacted a similar bill, which was passed by the House on April 16.[60] Ten days later, the President of the United States signed S. 1489, which removed the political disabilities of Pryor "of New York."[61]

At about this time, Pryor was offered the support of Tammany Hall for the Democratic nomination as a United States congressman. This was tantamount to election, "but," his wife asked rhetorically, "how could he pay the assessment demanded by that organization?"[62]

The 1880 census recorded the Pryors as occupants of their house on Willow Street. Roger's years were now correctly listed at 51, although one year had been added to Sara's true age. Gordon and Mary had married and moved away to the homes of their respective husbands.[63]

That summer, Pryor participated in the presidential campaign of General Winfield Scott Hancock, the Democratic nominee; the candidate and Pryor had opposed each other as generals at the Battle of Antietam.[64] Pryor campaigned vigorously, emphasizing the point that even if his candidate were a general, he was anything but power-mad. Noted an editorial in the New York *Tribune*:

> General Pryor is an impulsive sort of person. Being so we can understand why he gushes over the nomination of Hancock, and

plunges into top-lofty high-daddy on account of it. It is not strange, perhaps, that after he gets fairly warmed up in a speech he should represent Hancock as having unlimited power offered him, which he spurned, and gave the people freedom when he might have enslaved them. He exaggerates just a trifle; but they all do that . . . That is all very well, but when he challenges the New York City Democracy to "search the annals of classic republics and tell him if such conduct be not unparalleled in the patriotism of Greece or Rome," he is laying out too much literary work for his audience. The men whom General Pryor was addressing have no time to "search out the annals of classic republics" for parallels; it's all occupied with searching the kennels of the modern republic for repeaters.[65]

Hancock was defeated for the presidency by James A. Garfield. Right after Election Day, it was reported that a black flag flew from Pryor's Brooklyn home, and reporters went to investigate. A neighbor (a Republican) had displayed an American flag on his house when the election results were announced, explained Pryor, while an unidentified member of his own household hung out a black shawl. "I don't suppose," he said, "there is a Democrat in the State who, wishing the election of Hancock, took the results more philosophically than I did. I anticipated and therefore discounted the result. A man at my age is not likely to explode in that way, and besides I consider General Garfield is conservative for his party."[66] But it had been "understood" that if Hancock were elected president, he was going to name Pryor as Attorney-General of the United States.[67]

X

Recognition

Late in 1880, Pryor was called to act as attorney in a matter of grave national political import. Congressman James Garfield of Ohio, the Republican nominee for President of the United States, was claimed to be an advocate of the importation of cheap Chinese laborers. The story appeared first in *Truth*, a New York City penny newspaper, and Garfield did not bother to issue a denial. Meanwhile, outraged labor sympathizers and the increasingly important unions demanded retraction of this advocacy of a measure that would force down the salaries of unskilled men. Garfield's campaign managers belatedly got their man to deny the story.[1] On October 20, *Truth* published a letter that Garfield allegedly had written in January to Henry L. Morey of the Employers' Union in Lynn, Massachusetts, which stated that the United States should adhere to its treaty commitments with China, allowing unlimited immigration.[2] The exuberant Democratic party widely circulated copies of the Morey letter as evidence of what labor could expect from a Garfield administration. Frightened Republicans set out to prove that the letter was a forgery, and on October 27, Kenward Philp was arrested in Brooklyn and brought before Judge Davis in New York Supreme Court. Assistant District Attorney Joseph Bell and Colonel George Bliss represented the people, while Charles W. Brooke and Roger A. Pryor represented Philp.[3]

Because of the national significance of the matter, the trial dragged out for weeks. On November 13, two of the witnesses against Philp were arrested for forgery, but early in December a grand jury brought in an indictment against him for writing the letter and against the publishers of *Truth* for printing it. The publishers of that newspaper apologized to Garfield, conceding the letter was a forgery,[4] and on May 19, 1881, the district attorney dropped the indictment against Philp on the ground that he had not been proven to have been the writer.[5] The Democratic Party clearly lost face for having circulated a forged letter. Whether Pryor really had been engaged by the party to defend its name cannot be said, but he certainly fulfilled his obligation in getting a dismissal of the indictment against his client of record, Kenward Philp.

Law and politics each drew on Pryor's time and talents. He served as Chairman of the Committee on Resolutions at the Democratic State Convention, which opened its sessions at Syracuse on September 21, 1882.[6] His platform of thirteen planks was widely applauded. The first plank called for "economy and honesty" in the government of the state. The second plank urged the relief of "an overtaxed people from all unnecessary burdens." The third protested against "the dangerous power of public patronage," insisting upon Civil Service reform. The fourth referred to "the unredeemed outrages on our foreign-born citizens." The fifth lamented the lowering of the "standard of public service." The sixth demanded "the restoration of the National Guard to the efficiency of which it has been deprived." The tenth declared that "the laws should be revised that taxation may be reduced so far as possible and that personal and corporate property may pay their fair proportion of taxes." The twelfth was aimed principally at the convict labor system. The thirteenth avowed the fidelity of the Democratic Party "to those tenets of economy, simplicity and respect for the liberty of the individual which characterized the administration of Government in the primitive days of the Republic."[7]

Pryor participated in one of the most celebrated will cases of the day. Jesse Hoyt died on August 14, 1882, leaving a $7 million estate. A life income was provided for his daughter, Mary, the bulk of the estate going to her uncles and cousins. Mary claimed that her uncles had put her in an asylum just before her father's death and that he had been under his brother's influence unduly. For more than a year and a half, the proceedings were heard in the surrogate's court; appeals took several additional years. A brilliant galaxy of attorneys handled the proceedings. The executors were represented by Elihu Root, William M. Evarts, and Joseph Choate. The daughter was represented by Roscoe Conkling until his death, when General Butler and Pryor were retained. The surrogate ultimately accepted the will, and his findings were upheld by the New York Supreme Court[8] and the Court of Appeals.[9] In a separate action involving a phase of the legal skirmishing, Butler and Pryor teamed up to defeat a motion made by Evarts and Root.[10]

Butler and Pryor worked together frequently. The latter wrote to the general about a brief: "I have framed it in conformity with my conception of the case. But undoubtedly you will reinforce the argument by many cogent considerations."[11] The two lawyers were associated in a suit in the United States Circuit Court of Appeals to recover the New York & New England Railroad for its original stockholders.[12] Pryor suggested to Butler that he could be a candidate who would win the labor vote.[13]

In 1883, Pryor received an international assignment. Serious disorders occurred in Ireland as a result of the Coercion Bills and the Land Act. Lord Frederick Cavendish, England's Chief Secretary for Ireland, and Thomas Burke, Permanent Irish Under-Secretary, were assassinated in Phoenix Park, Dublin, on May 6, 1882, by the Invincibles, a fanatical patriotic society.[14] Twenty men were arrested, but the Crown's case looked tenuous until James Carey, "prince of informers,"[15] placed the blame upon the actual murderers, although it was he who had given the execution signal with a handkerchief.[16] Five men were hanged, and Carey was given his freedom as part of the deal. Prudently, he slipped out of England for the Cape of Good Hope, under the alias of Power, but Patrick O'Donnell pierced his identity and shot him aboard ship.[17] Extremists' sources in the United States were blamed for this shooting, for O'Donnell had been a teamster in the Northern army during the Civil War.[18] Perhaps this feeling was not dispelled when Irish patriots in the United States engaged Pryor to go to England for the purpose of assisting O'Donnell (an American citizen) in any way possible.

Just what Pryor was expected to accomplish is obscure; probably the persons who had engaged him wanted to assure themselves that everything possible was being done for the man who had dispatched a despised informer. An editorial observed: "When Mr. ROGER A.

PRYOR went over to London post-haste to act as counsel for O'DONNELL, the slayer of CAREY, it was remarked that the selection, while it was an admirable one for the accused, was unfortunate, inasmuch as Mr. PRYOR could not appear publicly at a British bar. . . . It is very likely that the visit of Mr. PRYOR, the debate to which his peculiar employment has given rise, and the kindly exchange of international courtesies of which Chief-Justice COLERIDGE was one of the latest recipients, may eventually result in amending in one important particular the procedure of British and American courts."[19]

Pryor himself was not certain whether he could appear in a British court when he embarked for England, but an Irish barrister aboard ship assured him that only members of the British bar could make appearances. "This does not surprise me," he wrote to Sara. "I can be usefully employed in consultation and suggestion. I have industriously read in the law of homicide, and on those topics I consider myself an expert."[20]

He was cordially received in England, for his romantic career as a soldier and lawyer was well known.[21] He refused to ask that he be given special consideration. "I will not allow a motion to be made that I be heard in the case," he wrote Sara, "for I do not choose to solicit a favor, nor to incur the hazard of a rebuff, nor to expose the American bar to the incivility which would be involved in rejecting such an application from one of its members. My presence, however, is not without good effect, nor have my services been unimportant."[22] O'Donnell's barrister "pays me every possible attention, and I can see relies upon me in the conduct of the case."[23] But O'Donnell went to the gallows.[24]

Before leaving England, Pryor attended a number of important dinners and met prominent personages, whom he had avoided during the trial so that "My clients cannot suspect me of yielding to British blandishments!"[25] In London one day he saw a band of ruffians molesting a young woman, whom he unhesitatingly rescued without regard to his fifty-five years. She proved to be Bessie Stanton, the daughter of Lincoln's Secretary of War. Eighteen years earlier, she had been the baby in Stanton's arms when he had refused the plea of Washington McLean to release the Confederate soldier from prison with the words, "He shall be hanged! Damn him!"[26] The veteran duellist and fighter had lost none of his ardor. Writing at about that time, a congressman noted: "He is a hale, manly, courageous man."[27]

Pryor's law work was only one of his interests. He lectured. He wrote. At this period, it was recorded: "His contributions to the literature of the day have largely enriched it, and we may well say of him that now, in the midst of a large and increasing practice, with an iron energy, with all the instincts and ambitions of the student and scholar, he has still a brilliant future before him."[28] And he kept up his active participation in politics, remaining steadfastly aloof from political machines that might have advanced his career. At the Democratic state convention at Saratoga in 1884, he indignantly denied any affiliation with Boss Kelly, chieftain of New York City's Tammany Hall. To the New York *Times* he wired: "The telegram in your paper to-day is altogether inaccurate. I support Cleveland, and I have not seen Mr. Kelly."[29] A celebrated enemy of Tammany had other views on the subject. One magazine ran a Thomas Nast cartoon that showed three portraits, surmounted by vultures, with the legend: " 'Exactly So. Butler, Kelly, and Pryor meet'—of course, *to nominate men above suspicion.*"[30]

With his increasing activity, Pryor found it advisable to have his home nearer his office. The family moved to 38 East 33 Street in New York City.[31] His wife missed the relative peace and quiet of their Brooklyn location; writing of their new home, she noted that on one side was the rear of a great hotel, with kitchens and servants' quarters overlooking the house. Behind was a sash and blind factory of much noise and dirt. On the other side was a garden where the householder pitched an awning and "holds his revels—his card and wine parties."[32]

It was at this new home that the Pryors gave a reception immediately after the wedding of their daughter Lucy to Arthur Page Brown, a New York architect, on February 25, 1886. After the ceremony at the Church of the Transfiguration, the guests were received at the bride's former house. Included were Augustus St. Gaudens, the distinguished sculptor; Cyrus W. Field, inventor of the Atlantic cable; and Colonel Washington Roebling, great bridge builder.[33]

Pryor's next big case was a sensational murder trial. This appeared to be an almost impossible assignment for any defense counsel. A Texan adventurer, well armed, had come to New York with the avowed intention of making some fast money. He made contact with a pair of well-known confidence men (he knew what they were up to all the time); and when they tried to outsmart him, he deliberately killed one of the swindlers in cold blood. A witness saw it all, and the police made a very prompt arrest. The gunman denied nothing; he freely described what he had done.

Tom Davis and his brother Theodore ("The") had an office at Reade Street and West Broadway in New York. They were prominent confidence men, specializing in a "switch game" known as "sawdust." James T. Holland, newly arrived from Texas, was seeking persons with whom to match wits, and he was taken to the office of the Brothers Davis on August 31, 1885. He agreed to pay $500 in cash for $10,000 in other notes, which were guaranteed to be of such superior workmanship that he himself could not distinguish the bills from his own. Genuine notes in the amount of $10,000 were shown to Holland for his scrutiny, then were placed in a bag before his eyes. Later, when his attention was supposed to be diverted momentarily by "The" Davis, a panel in the wall slid back and brother Tom, in an adjoining room, tried to substitute another bag for the one containing the true currency. But Holland was expecting this to happen, and as the panel slid back, he drew a revolver and fired one shot, which killed Tom.[34]

Holland's trial for murder bordered upon the sensational. He engaged Pryor as his lawyer; and numerous transplanted Confederates thronged the court room, for the assistant district attorney prosecuting the case also was a former Southern officer, John Randolph Fellows. Actually Fellows was born in Troy, New York, but he went to Arkansas as a young man and later enlisted in the Confederate army. He rose to colonel before his capture at Fort Fisher. After the war, he went into practice of the law in Little Rock before moving to New York.[35] Numerous "short card men" and other swindlers crowded the court room to see justice administered to the slayer of one of their own.

Little Holland seemed harmless enough to the spectators, who thought the desperado was the burly man next to him (actually, this was Deputy Sheriff McCloskey, his guard).[36] Attention also was focussed on a mysterious, black-draped woman who, throughout the trial, hovered around the prisoner. She was suspected of being (1) a devoted woman whose husband Holland had filled with a peck of bullets or (2) a man in disguise who was out to kill (the victim varied according to the version of the tale heard). Actually, she was the jailer's wife, who was assigned to minister to the prisoner's needs.[37]

"The historical figure of General Roger A. Pryor formed the centre of a picturesque gathering in the Court of Oyer and Terminer yesterday when the crier called for the trial of James T. Holland," recorded an eye-witness. Holland was represented by the leading barrister of Abilene, Texas, and several other lawyers from that state;[38] but "First and foremost was General Roger A. Pryor, turning his aboriginal countenance upon his associates and eying the empty witness stand with a hungry, hawk-like look that boded ill for whoever might be called to fill it." As soon as a witness appeared, "General Pryor's inky locks were at once floating in the air."[39]

The state's chief witness was "The" Davis, who described emotionally how Holland had shot down an unarmed businessman in his own office. He swore that no deception had been planned, that he and his late brother always had been men of rectitude, unblemished by any contact with evil. When it was Pryor's turn to cross-examine Davis, the lawyer "turned his hawk-like profile upon the witness as though to rend his staements to shreds." He got "The" to recall that he had been a bounty jumper in the Civil War, that he had been in the liquor business, that he had been arrested for robbing a bank messenger. That disposed of the character of the witness. But that was not all. "How," demanded Pryor, "did you get your picture out of the Rogues' Gallery?"

"I did not know it was there."

"Didn't you beg an official to remove it, as you had reformed?"

"I don't remember."

"You had been in the sawdust business [switching worthless goods for valuable] for some time?"

"Since 1871."

"How many people have you swindled?"

"I don't know."

"Don't you keep books?"

"No."

"Only their cash, I suppose," persisted Pryor.

When "The" testified that after the shooting he had asked the way to the police station, the relentless attorney cried, "You were four years there. Did you not know where the police station was?"

"No, I didn't."

"Doubtless you didn't want to."[40]

Holland explained that there was nothing criminal about the business deal as far as he was concerned, for the only money he saw was genuine. But when the Davis brothers tried to switch bags, the aura of complete honesty suddenly vanished through no act of his. "I believed Davis was going to kill me at the time and I shot him to save my life and property."[41] Holland completely won the sympathy of the crowd with his innocent story of how nothing had protected his savings from swindlers except his own quick reflexes. He demonstrated his fast draw to a delighted court room.[42]

The case was drawing to a close, and "General Pryor plunged into an argument touching the indictment, which, drawn as it was under the old common law, he deemed defective. The action of a man who is suddenly called upon to slay another in defense of his life or property, he contended, could not be premeditated and malicious." And premeditation and malice could not be proven by the testimony of a thoroughly discredited witness. Look at "The" Davis. "Such a man sullied the Scriptures by his putrefying salutation. Can you trust this malefactor, fresh from skulking in his den and lying in wait for his victims—this thwarted rascal, who comes not for justice—no, no—but for vengeance, vengeance?" Here the reporter switched from Pryor's words to his own. "And General Pryor shook his snaky tresses till they whirled about his aboriginal profile, and stamped on the floor like a Tuscarora brave in the throes of a war dance."[43]

The summation was tremendous. "General Pryor began his harangue before noon, and had a fair start up and up with the eight-day ticker on the wall. For four hours he held his own with it. Then he pulled out of the race with a peroration to which Victor Hugo and various other eminent personages contributed, and with a toss of his tresses, sat down." The applause, slow at first, became so tumultuous that Judge Van Brunt (irreverently known to the bar as Old Iron Pants) ordered the court room to be cleared.[44]

While the jury was out, the displaced spectators were suffered to return. The numerous gambler friends of Davis were active, and odds of five to one for acquittal were freely quoted. But there was not much opportunity for this sort of thing. Although the jury had listened to the case from February 25 to March 5, only ten minutes were required to bring in a verdict of Not Guilty. The exuberant Holland wildly shook hands with everyone within reach, including the startled Judge Van Brunt.[45]

Pryor's law work covered a wide spectrum. One type of work that he handled was, in that day, spurned as not entirely "respectable" by many other prominent lawyers who wished to retain a proper clientele: labor. "As a lawyer he advocated on several occasions the rights of labor unions, and was supposed to be a favorite among the laboring classes."[46] In the Spring of 1886, a demand for a revolutionary eight-hour day was gaining some supporters, and 5,000 men went out on strike in New York City. To some newspapers, the villains in the piece were the unions and not the workers, who, after all, were but the slaves of the unions. Yet it was the strikers who were arrested, on the ground that they had conspired by collective action to deprive their whilom employers of the opportunity to do business. Under the head "Upholding Slavery Again," one editorial declared:

> The boycotters are to be defended by General Pryor. That is their right; the question whether it is or is not a violation of law to conspire for the purpose of breaking up a man's business ought to be fairly and fully tested in the courts. The labor union has determined to bear the expense of employing the General, and it is to be hoped that he will do his best on their behalf. If the law does not reach this offense, it is high time to have another law that does. . . . The slavery of labor to trades-unionism, and to the minority who have chosen to organize, is the precise issue here, and Mr. Pryor is fitly chosen as the champion of slavery, as in other days he was one of the most eloquent defenders of the slavery of black labor to white capital.
>
> He states, it is reported, that he means to demand for the men tried a jury of their peers; that is, a jury not composed of business men or employers, but of workers. . . . In the old days Mr. Pryor would not have allowed a slave, or one whose slavery was in question, to sit on a jury to decide whether another man was rightfully held as a slave. He may naturally conclude that the unorganized laborers are not proper persons to try a question whether organized labor has a right to drive unorganized labor out of employment.[47]

Pryor's sympathy for labor, coupled with his reputation as a lawyer and as a champion of the rights of the individual, presumably were responsible for his participation in one of the most controversial incidents in the postbellum nineteenth century: the Haymarket bomb explosion.

There was serious labor unrest in Chicago (and elsewhere) in 1886. This was of particular concern to members of a revolutionary society which for years had advocated the overthrow of the social order by violent methods. On May 3, a meeting was held to discuss the shooting of workmen by police. Bombs made by Louis Lingg were distributed judiciously, as were inflammatory handbills. A general mass meeting was called for the following evening, to be held in The Haymarket on Randolph Street. This proved to be too small, and the meeting was held nearby in Des Plaines Street, with an excited audience of perhaps 1,500 workmen. (The name "Haymarket Affair" persists, but it is a geographical inaccuracy.) Police were massed to cope with any disorders. As the meeting gathered momentum and heat, the police advanced upon a wagon on which the speakers stood. One of the members of the revolutionary society cried, "We are peaceful." Most of the conspirators were Germans, and the German word for "peace," *ruhe*, was the prearranged signal for violence. Whether it was intended to have started at this moment is not known. At any rate, an unidentified person hurled one of the bombs that Lingg had constructed, and there was a tremendous explosion. Seven policemen were killed, while sixty other bluecoats were seriously wounded. A number of members of the society was arrested and tried for the murder of Matthias J. Degan, one of the slain policemen.

On August 20, a Cook County jury brought in a verdict of Guilty against eight men. Public feeling ran high. Foreign-style anarchism was virtually unknown in the United States of that day, and it was felt widely that strong steps had to be taken to stamp out the evil before it became deeply rooted. Admittedly, however, none of the prisoners could be related to the actual throwing of the bomb.

On September 14, 1887, the Illinois Supreme Court upheld the decision of the lower tribunal on the ground that the defendants were members of an unlawful conspiracy involving the use of force and violence; murder had resulted as the natural outcome of that conspiracy, and hence each conspirator was deemed guilty of the murder.[48]

Funds for an appeal to the United States Supreme Court were solicited by the Anarchist "Defense Committee" of Chicago. Captain W. P. Black, who had been one of the prisoners' lawyers in the unsuccessful litigation to date, now sought "the most noted Constitutional expounders in the Union" and went to see Pryor.[49] More than $50,000 had been collected for the appeal.[50]

Emerging after a two-hour meeting with Pryor in the latter's office, Black announced to reporters: "I have won him to our side." "I have not the least doubt that our application for a writ of error will be granted." added Pryor. "Indeed, the records show so many errors in the ruling and in the trial that I cannot see how our application can be denied."[51] Many persons, who believed that public hysteria had condemned the defendants in the two trials to date, applauded Pryor's action. William Dean Howells, the leading man of letters in the United States, wrote to Pryor: "I am glad you have taken the case . . . for I have never believed them guilty of murder, or of anything but their opinions, and I do not think they were justly convicted."[52]

On the morning of October 21, counsel appeared before the Supreme Court in Washington. Noted was "angular General Pryor with massive, granite-like jaw, coal black eyes and long, black hair."[53] Arguments were held on October 27, three hours being alloted to each side.[54] General Butler, once again associated with Pryor, declared that if prisoners could be sentenced in their absence and that of their counsel, and if there could be unreasonable search and seizure, it might be better if the nation were overturned into an anarchy. "I have no fear of being misunderstood upon this question," he explained. "I have the individuality of being the only man in the United States that condemned and executed men for undertaking to overturn the law.[55] There were thousands of them."[56]

Pryor argued that the Illinois statute under which the men were condemned was not "due process of law" within the meaning of that provision of the Constitution of the United States. Due process, he maintained, implied and required a trial by an impartial jury, which was not the situation here. The Illinois statute, he claimed, made competent a juror with a preconceived and present opinion as to the guilt of the accused. Some of the accused were, by the production in evidence of papers and property unlawfully seized and taken, compelled to be witnesses against themselves. The nation, through its congress and its courts, can afford to its citizens at home complete protection against the discriminatory legislation of states which may attempt to invade their privileges and immunities.

Morrison Remick Waite, Chief Justice of the United States, refused to allow a writ of error. As to Pryor's arguments, Waite declared that the bill of rights was not intended to limit the process of the states in respect of their own people. Partial jurors could be challenged. Under the Illinois law, preconceived opinions did not disqualify prospective jurors. When a person offered himself on his trial for examination as a witness on his own behalf, he must submit to cross-examination under the law of the jurisdiction where he is tried.[57]

Pryor was not convinced. After the Supreme Court had spoken, he asked: "If there were a plot in existence, do you suppose that they [the accused anarchists] would have had their wives and children there?"[58]

XI

Reconciliation and Acceptance

"Perhaps one of the most curious facts concerning . . . Pryor is that his legal; political and military record have overshadowed the position to which his scholastic training entitles him."[1] But as his legal career brought him ever increasing stature, he became in great demand as a speaker and writer. He addressed college societies on literary themes; he wrote for the *North American Review*, the *Forum*, the *Encyclopedia Britannica*,[2] *Johnson's Encyclopedia*.[3] In 1884, he received the honorary degree of doctor of laws from his undergraduate college, Hampden-Sydney.[4]

A favorite strain of Pryor's in his speeches was that despite the memorable glories of the past, the present, too, was memorable—especially in the United States. To the graduating class at the Albany Law School he said in June, 1888: "Nor need we travel abroad for examples and illustrations of forensic oratory in its highest perfection; for in the sublime passion of Patrick Henry, in the gorgeous vehemence of Choate, in the brilliant and abounding fancy of Prentiss, and in the magnetic simplicity of Webster, we find at home every beauty and every power of eloquence displayed with an effect not inferior to the achievements of the mighty masters of antiquity."[5] In speaking of the postbellum constitutional amendments, which were so odious to most Southerners, he declared: "Along with Magna Charta and the Declaration of Independence, these ordinances will descend to the remotest posterity as monuments of human freedom and progress."[6]

At the annual banquet of the New York State Bar Association in

Albany on January 15, 1889, President Martin W. Cooke announced: "The next in order is the benediction. There is no poetical sentiment accompanying this toast, but if you will bear with me I promise you learning, poetry and eloquence. To that end I call upon General Roger A. Pryor."[7]

Pryor then spoke about Virginia's part in American history and her reconciliation.

> [N]ever more will you see from Virginia any intimations of hostil-
> ity to the Union; she has weighed the alternative of success, and
> she sees now, every sensible man in the South sees, that the greatest
> calamity that could have befallen the South would have been the
> ascendency of this ill-starred Confederacy. . . . And, moreover,
> we see now, you will be surprised at what I say, I voice the senti-
> ment of every reflecting man in Virginia, and woman, too, we see
> now that slavery was a material and a moral evil, and we exult
> that the black man is emancipated and stands as our equal under
> the law.
>
> Why didn't we see it before? You know the story of the view of
> the opposite sides of the shield. We had been educated under
> slavery, our preachers had taught us that it had the sanction of
> Divine Scripture, we never saw any other aspect of the question,
> but now since it is changed, we look at it and we perceive that
> slavery is not only incompatible with the moral principles of gov-
> ernment, but is hostile to the material interests of the country, and
> I repeat that today, if the people of the South were permitted to
> vote upon the question to re-establish African slavery, there would
> not be a hundred votes in the entire South, in favor of reshackling
> the limbs of the liberated negro.[8]

A month later, he spoke in the same vein at the fourth annual dinner of the Ohio Society of New York at Delmonico's. There was no raised dais here, but a reporter had no trouble in locating "the poetically luxuriant locks of Roger Pryor. . . ." That worthy asked his audience and himself, "What has Virginia done since the War? There is not a man in Virginia to-day that would, if he could, reshackle the slaves who have been emancipated. We have come back, or rather, we have

Pencil sketch, 1889, of Roger A. Pryor, Esq., drawn
by his son-in-law, William de Leftwich Dodge
Courtesy Sara Dodge Kimbrough

been brought back, into the Union, and we are here to stay, and don't you forget it. Do not confound Virginia, I implore you, with other Southern States. Virginia looks to an indestructible Union of Indestructible States."[9]

Pryor's position apparently was not contrary to the sentiments of his native state; for on the following March 9, he was elected Governor of the Society of the Virginians.[10]

He addressed an annual meeting of the Virginia State Bar Association on the subject, "The Influence of Virginia in The Foundation of the Federal Constitution." Apparently he felt obliged to explain the presence of a New Yorker before this body. "Although I live under another sky, remote from my native state, my heart, unchanged, is still true to the Commonwealth of Virginia. Her renown I cherish as a priceless heritage, and any derogation from her glory I feel as a filial bereavement."[11]

On April 27, 1893, Pryor was a speaker at a birthday dinner tendered to General Grant at the Hotel Waldorf. Introducing Pryor, Horace Porter (a former Union general) declared: "Gentlemen, we have a distinguished general here to-night who fought with us in the war—but not on the same side. It has been said that it is astounding how you like a man after you fight him! That is the reason we have him here to-night to give him a warm reception. He always gave us a warm reception. He used to take us, and provide for us, and was willing to keep us out of harm's way while hostilities lasted—unless sooner exchanged. He was always in the front, and his further appearance in the front to-night is a reflection upon the accuracy of our marksmanship. Not knowing how to punish him there, we brought him up to New York, and sentenced him to fourteen years' [sic] hard labor on the bench"[12]

Pryor rose to eulogize Grant. "Laying aside, however, all his other titles to renown, this remains unquestioned and unquestionable—that this strong arm upheld the Union in the instant of imminent overthrow, and assured it an endless duration of grandeur and glory; and I, a Confederate soldier, proclaim that by the preservation of the Union Grant rendered to the cause of liberty and civilization as transcendent a service as any recorded in the annals of human achievement."[13]

Ever a loyal Democrat, he nonetheless gave his opinion on how the incoming Republican President of the United States, Benjamin Harrison, could bring Southern votes back into the Republican column. It was similar to his unheeded advice to President Hayes twelve years earlier.

> If he will conduct his Administration upon these lines, laid down in his Inaugural, and will appoint respectable characters to office in the Southern States, in my judgment he will break up what is called the Solid South, and attach a very large proportion of the Southern vote to the Republican party. . . . While my paramount duty as a citizen is to the whole country, I own that my views of public policy are largely colored and directed by my regard for the interests of the South. With the extinction of slavery the recasting of the Federal Constitution by the recent amendments, my own political faith underwent modification. There is no room now in our system for the doctrine of Secession. And while I still think as an economic question the principle of free trade is a demonstrable doctrine, yet other than mere economic interests must operate in the conception of a scheme of public policy.[14]

Such a "modification" of "political faith" startled the New York *Tribune*, an editorial in which declared: "This distinguished Democrat has come to believe so nearly in Republican principles that he is liable to be called a traitor by his hot-headed Democrat friends."[15] Actually, no one familiar with Pryor would have been startled by his refusal to accept a party line categorically.

Pryor's yearning for reconciliation of North and South reached fulfillment upon a very personal basis. His home in New York was visited by a veritable *Who's Who* of former Union generals: Grant, McClellan, Sherman, Sheridan, Hancock, Fitz-John Porter, Butterfield, Slocum, and others.[16] Grant, who once had stated that the prisoner Pryor should not be exchanged whilst there remained another captive in the cells, [17] dropped in on the Pryors without even an invitation, and so did his wife.[18] Sheridan, who had requisitioned the Pryor home in Petersburg for his adjutant, said to Sara: ". . . I am grateful to Mrs. Grant for giving me this opportunity to tell you that no man in this country more cordially rejoices at General Pryor's success than I do."[19] When Sara exclaimed to Sherman, "*Never* did I think I should find myself in the same boat with you!", he replied, "Now see here! I'm not so black as painted."[20] Veterans of the two armies well might have noted this *rapprochement* of the generals; Pryor had said in his famous Academy of Music speech in 1877 that politicians were responsible for the war while "officers and soldiers who took part on both sides were men of peace."[21]

Pryor must have derived considerable satisfaction from the professional development of his youngest son, William. After being graduated from the College of Physicians and Surgeons in New York in 1881, he became professor of gynecology at New York Polyclinic Hospital, as well as visiting gynecologist at St. Elizabeth's Hospital. He wrote three textbooks in the field. On June 5, 1888, he married Louise Allan in Fredericksburg, Virginia.[22]

A blow came to Pryor in the form of the death of his father in 1890. He was buried under the pulpit of the Presbyterian Brick Church in Nottoway with his third wife, Frances Fitzgerald Pryor.[23]

At the height of his legal career, Pryor shared his talents with the public service. He acted as prosecution counsel for the New York Senate Trust Investigating Committee. Chairman Frank B. Arnold was very much interested in the affairs of the Standard Oil Company.[24] On February 28, 1888, the company's dominant figure, John D. Rockefeller, appeared before the committee with a legal staff headed by Joseph H. Choate. The committee's lawyers, Colonel George Bliss and Pryor (who had been opposing counsel in the *Philp* case), were not able to see eye to eye now. Bliss stated that it was not necessary for Standard Oil to produce its books; Pryor demanded that they be produced. With understatement, a reporter noted, "This decidedly made a sensation."[25] Pryor persisted: "Will you produce the record books of the trustees?"

Choate arose hurriedly and stated, "I don't believe General Pryor will press his demand for those books."

"Yes, I will," shot back his adversary. He held firm over the protests of his opponents and of his own co-counsel. Later, Bliss said he would call more trustees as witnesses. "I prefer not to examine any more witnesses within the trust," interposed Pryor. "I believe in going outside for witnesses who are hostile."[26]

Not surprisingly, the divided counsel did not fare well against the oil company. Senator Raines endeavored to have both of the committee's disputatious lawyers dismissed.[27]

But Pryor continued to maintain his conviction that a trust could be inimical to the public interest, and he was sought again by the state when a matter of outstanding significance was to be prosecuted. "General Pryor's career as a member of the bench is best remembered by his initiation of the first litigation in which the validity of a trust combination was challenged—a litigation which culminated in a decision by the New York Court of Appeals that such a combination was repugnant to the principles of the common law and was sufficient cause for the forfeiture of corporate charters.[28] He argued the case of *People of the State of New York v. The North River Sugar Refining Company,* the first effort to break up a trust combination that was successful.[29] As special counsel for the state, he appeared with Attorney-General Charles F. Tabor, and the New York Supreme Court held that dissolution of the corporation was justified.[30]

The company appealed to the highest court in the state. Pryor's argument there declared in part: "[C]orporate franchises are granted in trust, and upon condition; in trust, on the one hand, that they be excited to the attainment of the object for which they are conceded, and on the other that they be not abused to the public detriment; upon the condition that for *nonuser* or *misuser* they may be reclaimed by the State in the appropriate judicial proceeding. . . .[31] Any act of corporation, in violation of law and to the public detriment, forfeits its franchises[32] . . . The etymological is neither the scientific nor legal sense of monopoly, but both political economists and judges recognize and reprobate *partial* and *temporary* monopolies, operating respectively partial and temporary detriment to the public interest."[33] He traced the evils of monopoly and deliberate withholding of rights throughout the earlier forms of government known to history. "Much more in a republic is the free circulation of property the life-blood of the commonwealth. . . ."[34] His brief bristled with quotations from the great economists, from Adam Smith to John Stuart Mill.

The Court of Appeals sustained this position.[35] This was regarded as a great personal triumph for Pryor. "[H]is most important professional fight was against the Sugar Trust."[36] He had reached the pinnacle of the New York Bar without sponsors, powerful friends, or political organizations. His own rise in his profession was well characterized in a book that he wrote for the guidance of young attorneys: "It is possible that by sheer force of audacity, and the tricks of a ready wit and the persuasions of a facile and fluent oratory, one may masquerade a while as a lawyer, and attract to himself a profitable clientele; but without solid and extensive learning in the profession one cannot achieve a real and enduring eminence at the bar, nor long impose a fictitious reputation upon the public. For soon the pretensions of the charlatan will by exploded by his misleading advice and the miscarriage of his causes; and his deceived and ruined clients will apply, perhaps too late, to some competent lawyer for the reparation of their fortunes."[37]

In the Fall of 1890, Chief Judge Richard L. Larremore of the New York Court of Common Pleas resigned. Daniel E. Sickles, who had served with Pryor as a member of the Thirty-sixth Congress before entering service in the Union army (he became a major-general), mentioned to Governor David B. Hill that Pryor was the man to fill this vacancy. The Virginian received a cryptic note asking him to meet Hill during the intermission between acts at a certain theatre one evening. The meeting took place. "One gets the impression of physical strength from Hill; almost a physical ferocity. With black eyes and black hair—what fringe there is to hold its desperate ground behind his ears—and a black coat, Hill offers a somber effect. And, with a face pale to sallowness, finishing below on a shirt-front of dead white, this somberness becomes sinister. These, added to a lawlessness of soul which lurks in the man, confer an outlaw atmosphere that repels."[38] But the interview must have been satisfactory to both parties, for the governor offered Pryor an appointment to fill out Larremore's unexpired term on the bench.[39]

Although the position was one within the bailiwick of Tammany Hall, the governor did not wait to clear the appointment with Boss Richard Croker. Possible the mysterious theatre meeting was to prevent the boss from suspecting that Pryor was under consideration at all. Croker, in fact, had thrown the full weight of Tammany in support of the candidacy of ex-Judge Henry A. Gildersleeve of the Court of General Sessions. On September 20, Hill merely announced his intention of appointing Pryor.[40] "Gen. Pryor is a typical Southerner," observed the New York *Times*, "one of a large class who were leaders of Southern thought in the days preceding the Rebellion, but who, when the judgment of war went against them, accepted the situation in good faith, urged their compatriots to acquiesce in the results, and turn their energies to the pursuit of peace."[41]

Pryor received his appointment on October 1. "Gen. Pryor is so well

[129]

known that extended mention of his career is unnecessary. . . .Gen. Pryor was one of those Southern leaders who gracefully accepted the inevitable."[42]

To honor the new judge, a dinner at the Astor House was given him on October 9 by John Russell Young, journalist and onetime minister to China. The host sent hand-written invitations to forty distinguished guests, adding a phrase that should have made the request irresistible: "no speeches." Three persons were obliged to decline: the Duke of Marlborough, the great actor Edwin Booth, and the prominent lecturer and agnostic Robert G. Ingersoll. The invitees who did come included the President of the United States (Grover Cleveland), Chauncey M. Depew (President of the New York Central Railroad), Henry George (distinguished economist), John S. Wise (lawyer and politician), General William T. Sherman, Senator Arthur P. Gorman (who was known as the Bismarck of the Democratic Party), Senator George Hearst (who was believed to have been wealthier than the Count of Monte Cristo), General Daniel Sickles, Mark Twain, Joseph Jefferson (an actor most famed for his interpretation of Rip van Winkle), George Jones (proprietor of the New York *Times*), Thomas Nast (the great political cartoonist), Dr. A. P. Martin (President of the University of Peking), Augustin Daly (well-known comedian), F. B. Carpenter (the painter of "Lincoln And His Cabinet"), A. K. McClure (editor, lawyer, and politician). McClure told the diners: "Such an assemblage was impossible prior to the rebellion, and there has been none since, and it is not likely that any man at this table will ever look upon its like again." A Philadelphia newspaper did not exaggerate in its heading of the story: "A Fabulous Dinner."[43] It was "a magnificent testimonial to the position in New York which Judge Pryor had reached in the face of the most pronounced obstacles, and while combating conditions which might reasonable have defeated his ambition and his hope."[44] General Sherman declared that "We would have done all this for him long ago, but he had to be such a rebel!"[45]

"So this duelist in field and forum, this secessionist fore and aft, went to New York, direct from the field of battle, and the fire of the elements in him consumed opposition, burned away barriers and opened to him the position of [judge] . . . in the metropolis of the Empire State. . . ."[46]

XII

The Bench: I

It was a great time to be a judge in the New York courts, for there were legal giants practicing there in those days: Joseph H. Choate, Charles Evans Hughes, Elbridge T. Gerry, Elihu Root, Francis Wellman, Paul D. Cravath, Samuel Untermeyer, Max D. Steuer, Benjamin Cardozo, David Dudley Field, Louis Marshall, William M. Evarts, the legendary Hummell & Howe.

Judge Pryor heard his first arguments on November 3, 1890.[1] His first decision was handed down on November 20. The action was brought by Sarah B. Brush and others for an injunction restraining the operation of an elevated railroad in front of their property and to recover for past damage caused by the maintenance of the road. He dismissed the complaint, citing statistics which showed how rentals actually had increased since the elevated structure had been built. "And the undisputed evidence," he declared, "demonstrates that this vast improvement and enormous increase in the value of plaintiff's property are due chiefly, if not exclusively, to the operation of defendants' railroad in immediate proximity to the property; and yet I am asked to award plaintiffs thousands of dollars for injuries inflicted on this property by defendants' railroad. To my mind the claim is untenable and unjust."[2]

The new judge was not reluctant to admit his inexperience. In a case a few weeks later, he declared: "I am of opinion that upon the whole the defendant's railway is a substantial injury to plaintiffs' property, and that accordingly an injunction should issue; but I must avow the greatest perplexity in measuring that injury by a money standard."[3]

An observer noted that "To the surprise even of his friends the political debater became a learned justice, the passionate Virginian an American."[4] His recipe was the same he had used as a lawyer. "He brought to the bench the habits of self-denial and unremitting study he had practised for twenty years," recorded Sara. "During all that time, and after, nobody ever saw him at a place of amusement, theatre, ball, or opera, and very rarely at a dinner-party. He knew no part of New York except the streets he traversed to and from his office or court room. His brief summer holidays were spent at the White Sulphur Springs in Virginia, where his studies continued."[5]

Of Pryor, a reporter declared that "His appearance was as picturesque as his career. His hair, which he wore long, was raven black . . . and his cut of features and swarthy skin might have suggested an Indian brave."[6] One who had heard and seen him wrote that "a rejected Irish applicant before his court spoke of him as 'that confounded Injun of a Pryor.'"[7]

After about a year, Pryor was nominated to succeed himself on the Court of Common Pleas;[8] and he was elected to serve a full term. On Election Day, he had a 60,000 majority, which was even more than that received by the governor who headed the ticket.[9] To one reporter, this life seemed quite different from the Virginian's earlier years. "Judge Roger A. Pryor, of the Court of Common Pleas, is enjoying the comparative quiet of a judicial office after an unusually varied career. He has been in turn editor, duellist, Congressman, soldier, prisoner of war and practising lawyer, and was no mean adversary in any of these varied fields of conflict."[10]

In 1895, the state constitution was modified, and the Court of Common Pleas was merged into the New York Supreme Court,[11] on which Pryor began service in 1896. On February 7 of that year, he underwent a dangerous surgical operation, which was performed at his home by Dr. Afrad G. Gerster, assisted by Dr. O. G. T. Killani and by the justice's son, Dr. William R. Pryor. Despite intensive suffering, Pryor had deferred his operation until the completion of the January term of his court. "Judge Pryor's sturdy constitution had stood him in good stead through it all. He is sixty-seven years old, but is well preserved and does not show his years."[12]

As a judge, Pryor showed that depth of research which had characterized him as a lawyer. At times he manifested greater familiarity with an issue than the attorneys who were presenting the case. "We have discovered, however, an adjudication, not cited by counsel, which expressly affirms the validity of this action," he announced on one occasion. "The decision was in the reign of James II. . . ."[13]

He did not, however, blindly take English decisions as authority in the courts of New York. "But, be the reason and justice of the case as it may, it is answered that the law is settled otherwise by authoritative adjudication. In England, doubtless; but upon a principle peculiar to the domestic and social economy of that country."[14] He rejected an argument that parties could not verbally release an agreement which bore their signatures with specialty (that is, under seal). "The rule that a specialty cannot be discharged by parol is a relic of a barbarous age," he ruled, "is a purely arbitrary and conventional regulation; stands upon no substantial reason or assignment of policy; and is opposed, as we see it, to the strong current of American authority."[15]

Pryor was thorough. "True, the first decision . . . was without an opinion; and hence respondents argue that it was not an adjudication of the point in controversy. But the headnote states otherwise. . . ."[16] "A ruling by the learned trial judge, not noticed in appellant's argument, should be indicated, that it may be avoided on the new trial."[17] In one case on appeal, after many citations, Pryor declared: "In deference to the elaborate and able arguments of the learned trial judge we have been at pains to collect the foregoing authorities; but in truth, the question in controversy is decisively determined against respondent by the adjudication of the court of appeals in *Hume v. Mayor*, 74 N.Y. 264. . . ."[18]

Pryor was clear-minded and refused to be ensnared by verbiage. "Notwithstanding the elaborate briefs of counsel, and the absence of authority on the point, I think the question thus presented is susceptible of easy solution by the application of familiar principles."[19] "After all the elaborate discussion expended on this appeal, the questions involved are extremely simple and of easy solution."[20]

At times he must have infuriated trial counsel by his didactic manner. "A complaint must contain a statement of the facts constituting the cause of action."[21] "This is elementary law."[22] But if Pryor acted as a teacher, he was as ready to bestow praise as is any good instructor. He commented upon "the thoroughness of the able and exhaustive briefs with which we are favored."[23] "We are invited by the interesting arguments of counsel to the consideration of important problems. . . ."[24] He was just as quick to rebuke sloppiness. "We see no excuse for this appeal."[25]

Pryor's courtesy was legendary. "Gentlemen, I have carefully considered the very interesting and able briefs with which you have favored me on this motion to dismiss the complaint, and I proceed to announce my decision."[26] "The courtesy of his manner and the fine diction of his judicial opinions have made him especially marked among the judges in the superior city courts. Some of his opinions have been among the most eloquent and forcible in expression which have recently appeared in the volumes of reports. He has unfailing politeness toward the members of the bar who appear before him. . . ."[27]

His judicial neutrality did not always conceal his feelings. In finding against a defendant who was wrong morally, he said: "Happily, for the interests of justice, the defendant's escape from liability is no more consistent with law than with morals.[28] "We fully share the anxiety avowed by the learned trial judge to annul this assignment [for] the benefit of creditors], but we are more fortunate than he is in assuring ourselves of sufficient legal grounds for the gratification of our common desire."[29] "Between two such claimants, I am happy to be able to award the benefit to the defendant."[30] "Happily, the well-settled principles of our law are of sufficient energy to arrest the evil in its incipiency."[31]

But he was not always able to experience such poetic justice. "Whatever our reprobation of the plaintiffs, and sympathy with the defendant, our decision must still be in conformity with the rules of law."[32] "To this conclusion I am compelled, but I am not forbidden to say that my reason revolts against it. . . . The absurd and mischievous consequences of the present judgment do not relieve me from the necessity of pronouncing it. . . ."[33]

He was not a slave to verbiage. "In reason, no formula of words can effectually alter the nature of things, and transmute the actual agent of one party to a negotiation into the agent of the other."[34] The real meaning was what counted. "Is the defendant's building a 'tenement house'? The question is to be solved, not by the definitions of real-estate brokers, but by the true interpretation of the terms of the covenant."[35] One case involved the right to recover for an injury caused by an awning, on the grounds that it was a nuisance. "But, argues the appellant, he had a license from the city to maintain the awning, and hence it was not a nuisance. The awning simply, no. But its delapidated and unsafe condition was the nuisance, and for that the defendant neither had, nor could have, a municipal license."[36]

An insurance policy provided that its terms could not be enforced against the insurance company; attorneys in fact were to bear any liability. Pryor disagreed, holding that "a provision in a contract that the party breaking it shall not be answerable in an action is a stipulation for ousting the courts of jurisdiction, and, as such, is void, upon grounds of public policy. . . . Who shall be defendant in an action the law prescribes, and it is not competent to parties, by private convention, to supersede the legal provision."[37] Nor could a steamship company limit its liability for lost baggage by the language of a claim check given to a passenger after the vessel had been at sea for several days. "When a party has no freedom to reject a proposed stipulation because then unable to reinstate himself (here to reclaim his baggage and to decline the carriage by the defendant), an inference of his assent to the stipulation would be simply preposterous."[38]

Pryor objected to excessive legalism. A physician who had registered his license with the board of health rather than with the county clerk, as required, could not be penalized if he corrected this error before the present action. He *was* licensed. "Why, then, should he be chastised by a penalty denounced against imposture only?"[39] An insurance policy provided for a death payment of a stipulated amount if death were occasioned by disease, with double indemnity if death were other than by disease. The insured died of pneumonia, which an "expert" (the quotation marks were Pryor's) and a lower court held was not a disease. Reversing this decision, Pryor declared: "It hardly consists with judicial gravity to argue against a propostion of which the absurdity is self-evident, which involves at once an affront to common sense, a misconception of the plain sense of a plain word, and a contempt for the uniform and universal signification of scientific nomenclature. That pneumonia is a disease is a notorious fact, and so a fact of judicial cognizance."[40]

He was not impressed by the title of "expert." "The testimony of experts is not evidence which courts are disposed to accredit beyond the strict sanction of the law."[41] "Such an egregious discrepancy of estimate affords a striking illustration of the untrustworthiness of expert testimony. But of the two witnesses plaintiffs' seems entitled to the greater confidence, because of his larger experience, and his better opportunities of information."[42]

That a requirement was technical did not disturb Pryor. "Legal procedure is a system of technicalities, the observance of which, especially upon points of jurisdiction, is indispensable to the orderly administration of justice."[43] But the proposition must work both ways. "Since plaintiffs seek to stand upon the extreme technicality of the law, a failure on their part to observe that same technicality suffices for their overthrow."[44] Technicalities could not be used for purposes of subterfuge. A statute prohibited saloons from being located within two hundred feet of a school-house. This did not mean that a saloon was safely placed where its door was two hundred feet from a school, if part of the structure were closer than the legal limit. "In view of its obvious policy in protecting the school against the evil influences of the saloon," ruled Pryor, "the statute should be so expounded as to accomplish its benign intent, and to that end accorded a literal or a liberal interpretation as may most effectively avert the apprehended mischief."[45]

Pryor ordered a retrial where a lower court had brought in a cash verdict against a man who had sold the plaintiff's horse by day, instead of at night as required by the contract. "The only proof of damage is the general evidence that horses bring better prices on a sale by electric light than in the daytime; but how much more is nowhere indicated in the case."[46]

The doctrine of precedents was duly noted by Pryor. He refused to allow a reargument after judgment had been affirmed by a higher tribunal. "Why allow the chance of a verdict which the court would be bound to set aside?"[47] "The cases cited by plaintiff sustain his contention," agreed Pryor before giving judgement to the defendant, "but they are contrary to . . . the adjudication of this court in [previous cases]."[48] Yet he did not regard a citation as binding upon him if it, "In my opinion, is supported neither by principle nor authority."[49]

XIII

The Bench: II

The rights of the individual were of particular concern to Pryor, but he had the misfortune of hearing one of his more widely cited phrases quoted against him after an unpopular decision. "The liberty of the citizen," he had declared, "is not the sport of judicial discretion."[1] When a membership corporation is created in New York, its certificate of incorporation must be approved by a justice of the New York Supreme Court. Members of the Agudath Hakehiloth of New York, a Jewish organization, applied to Pryor for approval of their articles of incorporation, which he refused to grant, on the ground that its annual meetings were stipulated for the second Sunday of each January. "The law which scrupulously protects them in the observance of this ceremonial," he explained, "gives them no license, as I am sure they have no desire, to affront the religious susceptibilities of others. . . . Because the holding of corporate meetings on Sunday is contrary to the public policy of the state, if not to the letter of its law, I decline to approve this certificate."[2]

On December 27, 1896, representatives of thirty-six Jewish congregations in New York City attended the annual meeting of Zion Lodge of the Independent Order of Free Sons of Israel at Odd Fellows Hall. A speaker denounced the action of Justice Pryor, reminding the audience that only a year ago, Pryor had said that the liberty of the citizen must not be made the sport of judicial discretion. "The audience was very much aroused," noted a reporter, who quoted a rabbi as saying that a certificate of incorporation really was not necessary "and the meetings can be held on Sunday in spite of all the Justices in the United States."[3] Proclaimed an editorial in the New York *Times:* "We have no doubt that the Justice has kept strictly within his view of the law, has used only the discretion derived therefrom, and used it as he believed it to be his duty. . . . If that is "good law," it is hardly good policy. . . . Moreover, Sabbath observance of the strict sort imposed by Justice PRYOR is as a matter of cold fact accepted formally only by a small minority of professing Christians and practiced by only a minority of those who accept it."[4]

Aside from this controversy, Pryor's interpretations of the rights of the individual were widely applauded. Ruling on a contempt action, he declared: "In compliance with the genius of the American institutions, every intendment and implication, not manifestly inadmissible, must be indulged in favor of the liberty of the citizen; and we are unwilling, upon a strained construction of a statute, to detain the defendant in jail for an indefinite time, in order that, by such constraint, he may be compelled to discharge a civil liability."[5] Even a malefactor's rights must be safeguarded. "It may be that the defendant is a criminal, and, by the vacatur of the attachment, will escape with his spoil; still, whatever my desire to frustrate his villainy, I may not withhold even from him "the equal protection of the law.' "[6] He reinstated a celebrated police captain who had been dismissed for failure to show up at a hearing when allegedly he had been ill. That he had been dismissed without a hearing disturbed Pryor. "Assuming the guilt of the relator, still, better his escape than the overthrow of the only safeguard of innocence."[7] In a similar action, he stated: "But we had supposed that even on the trial of a policeman, he is entitled to the presumption of innocence. . . ."[8]

Justice was the sought-for key to Pryor's decisions; he returned to this theme constantly. "What decision of the motion is the dictate of justice?"[9] He explained an action with his simple motivation: "We are satisfied that the interests of justice will be promoted by sending the case to another jury."[10] "We are entirely satisfied that the interests of justice require the submission of the case to a jury."[11] "Of scarcely greater moment is it to do justice than, if possible, to satisfy suitors that justice has been done."[12] As he did in the case of jurors, Pryor thus endeavored to demonstrate to litigants that their position in his court was of concern to him.

Justice was not something with which to trifle. A document ac-

cepted by a lower court for one purpose and specifically repudiated for any other purpose could not later be used as evidence for
that repudiated end. "To do so would be a juggle upon justice."[13]
Where a director breached a trust to vote himself into office and control, "The spectacle is revolting to the sense of justice."[14]

Pryor closely studied the persons who came before him. He could
not believe that a certain failure to act was attributable only to ignor-
ance, for the alleged oversight "evinces a stupidity which she did not
display as a witness. Though an illiterate woman, she is not blind in the
perception of her own interests. . . ."[15] In reducing a jury award,
he commented that "These consequences, if they exist, (which is
doubtful), may be attributable to her morbid condition, rather than
to the injury inflicted by the defendant."[16] "The case is of first impression."[17]

Pryor distinguished himself in his humane treatment of marital
problems, particularly where children were involved. Divorce on the
ground of adultery was denied, where the husband (the plaintiff) permitted the act to be performed in his presence before he stepped from
concealment to confront the lovers. "The inference is irresistible that
the plaintiff was willing that the defendant should commit the act in
order that he might obtain a divorce." Furthermore, husband and
wife still lived with their young children after this act, which showed
that the husband did not consider her an unworthy companion for his
children and himself. "In the interest, therefore, of the parties concerned, and of the state, which cherishes the stability of the marriage
relation, I am happy to find legal ground for denying the divorce."[18]

An adulterous mother was allowed to visit her children. "Surely,
the signal reformation shown by the petitioner deserves the reward of
an occasional visit to her infant offspring. Perpetual banishment from
their presence—an indelible mark of disgrace—tends to render her
desperate of a good repute. Association with them will fortify and
confirm her in the resolution for a better life. What harm can come to
these children from an interview with their mother? . . . Indulgence
of the filial instinct is not only a source of happiness, but is the spring
as well of the finest social virtues,—obedience, love, sympathy, and
reverance. Whether, therefore, we regard the interests of the children,
the mother, or of society, it is equally evident that the petition should
be granted."[19]

He refused to find adultery in the case of a man where the only

[139]

alleged witness was his frankly hostile mother-in-law. "An infant child is issue of this marriage, and we cannot tolerate that its character shall be sullied, and its career clouded, by a judicial conviction of the father on such evidence of infidelity to the most sacred of obligations. Since the 'common-law-marriage,' so-called,—another name for concubinage,—is obtrusively prevalent in the community, and our calendars are crowded with applications for divorce, it behooves us not to relax the stringency of the rules which, in the interest of good morals and social security, have been presented by law for the safeguard of the sanctity and stability of the marriage relation."[20]

Pryor would not permit a husband to have his marriage annulled on the ground that his wife had a past and an illegitimate child. The evidence was that the husband had known all about it. As to the wife's oath concerning this, "upon the essential facts her testimony was candid, unequivocal, and credible."[21] In a divorce action, he brushed aside the plea of the husband that he never had been married to the plaintiff on the ground of a previous marriage, a relationship which the "second" wife had not disproven. Declared Pryor: "To conclusively [sic] disprove the allegation would require of her evidence that defendant was not married to any of the millions of women on the habitable globe—, a preposterous undertaking."[22]

A life insurance policy could not be assigned to a third party (a woman) at the expense of the stated beneficiary, the assignor's wife. "For 30 years the defendant in the present action was the faithful wife of Charles Gern. She has borne him many children, and doubtless, by her industry and self-denial, she has assisted him in the accumulation of the means for the purchase of the endowment in question. Upon the evidence, it is apparent that, her youth and beauty gone, his affection departed with them, and that, by the destination of this bounty to the plaintiff, he intended a recompense of services odious in law and abhorrent to a society, of which the praiseworthy mission is the succor of the widow and the orphan."[23]

De Lancy Nichol, attempting to have one of Pryor's decisions reversed by a higher court, complained: "While we have perfect confidence in the rectitude of his intentions, we cannot escape the conclusion that his chivalric nature and almost reverential tenderness for the gentler sex led him unconsciously away from the paths of strict justice and impelled him to acts and impressions which had no place in the calm atmosphere of a court."[24] Lawyers selected Pryor as the justice before whom divorce suits by women would get the kindest treatment. He had no sympathy with the custom of concealing facts in the case of wealthy divorce litigants. On one occasion, a lawyer spoke to him: "Your Honor, there are reporters present. We would request you to have them excluded from the hearing." "Not so," he replied. "I am now sitting as a court, and I am going to hold open court."[25] He startled a court room by announcing that he would not believe the confession of a corespondent, backed by the statement of a private detective, against the unsupported denial of the wife. Husbands who sought divorces from wealthy wives aroused his scorn, and one time he exclaimed impulsively, "It is infamous to marry a woman just for her money!"[26]

But Pryor did not always decide marital suits in favor of the wife. Refusing separation to a woman who claimed that her husband was brutal in his intimacies, he explained: "It is a delicate topic, to be touched with delicacy, and I must be content to say that the peculiar injury inflicted by the husband falls short of the *saevitia* [brutality] necessary to a decree of separation."[27] In a breach of promise suit against a wealthy and very prominent philanthropist, he denied a woman's request to strike out a portion of the man's answer as irrelevant and scandalous. The defendant had claimed that despite her allegation that she had been chaste, the woman had been committed repeatedly by police magistrates for profligacy. Ruled Pryor: "The matter objected to, being relevant upon the question of damages, cannot be scandalous."[28]

He felt that a law properly could be used to protect persons against their own weaknesses. An act authorizing lotteries he voided as being contrary to state laws against gambling, which sought to end the evil. "That evil consists in the temptation and facilities afforded by the lottery for the indulgence of the passion of gambling—an indulgence, by all experience, as inimical to the well-being of the state as of the individual."[29]

But as a man who ruggedly had stood on his own two feet throughout life, he would have no truck with the concept of a welfare state, even if it assured the creature comforts of its citizens. More broadly, the individual would disappear if his rights were surrendered to a state agency. In holding unconstitutional a law requiring tenement house owners to supply water at places on each floor to be designated by the board of health, he declared: "The postulate upon which the legislation in question proceeds is the duty of government to exercise a paternal protectorate over the people, whereas the distinguishing characteristic of the American commonwealth is that it restricts the operation of government to the narrowest possible sphere, and reposes upon individual intelligence and effort for the development of a free and fruitful civilization. A conclusion contrary to the present decision would involve the essential principle of that species of socialism under the *regime* of which the individual disappears, and is absorbed by a collective being called the 'state'—a principle utterly repugnant to the spirit of our political system, and necessarily fatal to our form of liberty."[30]

Pryor insisted upon proper court room manners and decorum in his chambers. On one occasion, an acrimonious and wordy dispute erupted between opposing counsel. The judge tapped gently on the floor. When the disputants stopped their angry exchange, he said in the most gentle of tones: "Please to remember, gentlemen, when you practice law in this part of the court and when I am on the bench, that it is as important to study Chesterfield as Blackstone."[31]

In his court room he was the supreme arbiter in all things; any other interpretation would tend to degrade the position of the judge. In a malpractice case, a physician placed the accent of *paresis* upon the second syllable. Pryor was not a physician, but he was well versed in classic tongues. Presumably he was aware that the word was a compound of Greek words, the first of which was *para*. He interrupted: "Excuse me—the word you mean is possibly par'esis?" "Now, your Honor," protested the doctor, "I concede all wisdom to the bench in legal matters, but I am a physician, and in the profession the word is pare' sis." Pryor yielded nothing. "It is par' esis in my court."[32]

He spurned hyphenism. The application of a Hungarian social club for incorporation was rejected because of the proposed title. "When a man leaves his native land his love for it becomes merely a sentiment," he explained. "When he has declared his intention to become a citizen he must realize that it is to this country he owes his duty in peace and war."[33] Certainly the judge did not consider himself to be a Southerner-American.

His professional standing with his fellow judges was enviable. When one of his decisions was appealed to a higher court, that review body affirmed his verdict and declared: "We need add but little to the satisfactory opinion of Pryor . . . upon the demurrer to the original complaint."[34] Observed Mr. Justice Giegerich of Pryor: "His knowledge of the law was profound and he had mastered its principles so well and was so accurate in his applications of them that he was seldom reversed."[35]

Pryor frequently was called upon to expound his theories of law and justice. At the annual dinner of the New York University Law School on April 18, 1895, he responded to the toast, "The Bench," with these words: "[W]ealth is not the reward of the lawyer, but by noble endeavor he may attain a better prize—a name of renown and an influence for good." He then developed his concept of the bench. "The dispensing of justice, the righting of wrong, the protection of innocence, the punishment of guilt—these are its functions; and what prudence, what labor, what vigilance, what learning, what courage, what probity, are indispensable to their faithful fulfillment! . . . Over the infirmities of the upright judge charity will cast its veil; and the worth of the magistrate may atone for the weakness of the man."[36]

To a graduating class of the Albany Law School he gave this counsel: "Gentlemen, the calling with which you have chosen to link the destinies of your life is indeed a noble vocation. Charged with the conservation of the highest and dearest interests of humanity,—the property, the character, the happiness, the liberty, the life of the citizen,—the consciousness of so lofty a commission cannot but impart to the profession a commensurate elevation of thought and expansion of sympathies."[37]

Pryor was now seventy, and he was required by law to relinquish his judgeship by the end of the year. On December 10, he and another justice, William N. Cohen, were given a dinner by their associates of the bench at the Manhattan Club. There were no addresses or even toasts.[38]

On December 23, Pryor sat for the last time in the Supreme Court. He presided in Special Term, Part VI, and disposed of a number of motions.[39] Then he stepped down, to be succeeded on January 1 by James M. Fitzgerald.

The press thought that it would miss this colorful figure. "The Justice has furnished here a whiff of the old chivalry of the South before the war," a reporter noted.[40] He was remembered for his courtesies and unfailing good manners.[41] "For himself as the representative of the law, Justice Pryor has always commanded the utmost respect."[42]

XIV

The Late Years

On March 31, 1897, the Pryors' youngest daughter, Fanny, married
William de Leftwich Dodge, who had been born in Virginia a year
before her birth there. Dodge was one of the most famous and honored
of American painters of that day. He won numerous European medals
and also the 1893 medal of the Chicago World's Fair. He painted the
mural "Ambition" in the Northwest Corner Pavillion of the Library
of Congress, as well as murals for the Brooklyn Academy of Music,
banks, theatres, court houses, ships, and palatial private homes.[1]
At one time he was the national fencing champion,[2] a proficiency he
had acquired, perhaps, during the many years he lived in Munich
and Paris during his youth. Five weeks before the wedding, he sold
106 of his paintings and drawings at auction at the Fifth Avenue Art
Galleries.[3]

Fewer than one hundred persons attended the wedding itself,
which was held at the Pryor home on 69th Street. The ceremony was
conducted by the Reverend Dr. David H. Greer, rector of St. Bartholo-
mew's Church, in the drawing room. The bride wore a gown of white
satin, trimmed with point and duchesse lace and orange blossoms.
There was no maid of honor or bridesmaids, but Fanny's three small
nieces served as flower girls, carrying large bouquets of pink roses that
matched their pink frocks. The best man was the bride's brother,
Roger, Jr. One of the ushers was Dr. Bolling Lee, a grandson of
Robert E. Lee. After the ceremony was a reception and wedding

breakfast. The guests here included President Seth Low of Columbia University and his wife, Mr. and Mrs. John D. Rockefeller, and Colonel and Mrs. Frederick D. Grant (he was the general's son).[4]

The wedding, recorded an enthusiastic society news reporter, "was one of the prettiest of the Lenten nuptial celebrations." Conspicuously displayed was a portrait of the bride, which had been painted by the groom-to-be.[5] After the wedding, the couple made a leisurely tour through southern Europe before taking up residence in Paris, where Dodge had his studio.[6]

Pryor was beside himself with happiness when, the following year, the Dodges had a son, who was named Roger after his grandfather. On February 6, 1898, Pryor wrote to Fanny:

> No incident of my life ever gave me greater pleasure than I derived from your letter. I read it with tears of joy. My delight was not only from the honor you did me in giving my name to the little boy, but as much from the affection that prompted you to write in such critical circumstances. Ever since I heard of your condition my heart has been full of anxiety for you; and un-speakable was my relief on the announcement of the happy birth. . . . I long to see him, and to caress him for his dear mother's sake. For, Fan, you are the idol of my heart, and I love you all the more for your faraway absence. I beg that you will not suffer other interests to detach you from your old father, but will believe that he is, as ever, with the utmost devotion,
>
> Your Father
> Roger A. Pryor[7]

Upon their fiftieth wedding anniversary on November 8, 1898, the Pryors gave a reception at their home. The rooms were handsomely decorated with a profusion of American Beauty roses and chrysanthe-mums. In the fireplace, surrounded by growing plants and a wreath of roses, were paintings (made from fifty-year old miniatures) of how the celebrants had looked in 1848. Sara wore a gown of black satin veiled with the same lace which had been on her wedding dress, and her coiffure was ornamented with the same jewelled comb which she had worn as a bride. More than 1,500 invitations were issued for the after-noon and evening reception.[8] "My observation is," announced Mr. Justice Pryor, "that disagreements are most frequent at first in married life; with time the yoke wears easier, and the true honeymoon is from the twenty-fifth to the fiftieth year."[9]

At the beginning of 1899, Pryor reentered the private practice of law. As an associate he had Chauncey S. Truax, an experienced practitioner who once had been professor of international law at Roberts College in Constantinople. Their office was in the Exchange Court Building, at 52 Broadway in New York City.[10] To those who knew Pryor, his refusal to be "retired" by the mandatory age limit for judges was logical.

When her children were married and her husband no longer needed her help on his professional problems, Sara turned her energies to external matters. She was First Regent of the New York Chapter of the Daughters of the American Revolution when it was established in 1891.[11] She was a charter member of the Colonial Dames of America in the State of Virginia, vice-president of the Mary Washington Association, incorporator and honorary vice-president of the Association for the Preservation of Virginia Antiquities,[12] honary vice-president of the Daughters of the American Revolution.[13] Charity claimed much of her time, and she was president of The Ladies' Jacksonville Relief Society; she organized relief parties for the benefit of victims of major disasters, such as the Galveston flood and the San Francisco earthquake.[14]

In literature particularly she made herself a niche. Sara was seventy-two when she wrote her first book, *The Mother of Washington and Her Times*, which was published in 1903. The following year there was published *Reminiscences of Peace and War*. "The two biographical volumes have the freshness of youth. . . ."[15] In a critique of the latter volume in *The American Historical Review*, Professor William E. Dodd declared: "It is a proof that despite many facts of a contrary nature, we are not so vindictive as some have thought."[16] Later she was to write *The Birth of the Nation* (1907) and *My Day* (1909).

Sara's first book was dedicated:

> *To The Hon. Roger A. Pryor, LL.D.*
> *In Whom Lives All That Was Best*
> *In Old Virginia.*[18]

Her husband was not able to reciprocate for nine years; his book, *Essays and Addresses*, was published shortly after Sara's death in 1912, with this dedication:

TO THE MEMORY OF
HER
WHOSE INFLUENCE IS
THE INSPIRATION OF THIS BOOK.[19]

The Birth Of The Nation was illustrated by Sara's famous son-in-law, William de Leftwich Dodge. It was dedicated to the Pryors' first child, Gordon:

To M. Gordon Pryor Rice
in Token of
Her Mother's Love and Admiration.[20]

In 1902, Sara was innocently involved in what must have been one of New York City's first recorded automobile accidents. On June 26, the vehicle of Spencer Trask, a banker, ran down Mrs. Henry Stauf at Sixth Avenue and 59th Street. The chauffeur-driven car was occupied by "a handsome, well-dressed woman and a pretty little girl of eight years. . . ." Continued the newsman: "The woman is reported to be the wife of a New York Justice." But the chauffeur refused to say who owned the car. "Pull her out and find out who she is!" demanded some one in the gathering crowd of passersby. "What right have you got to know who she is?" persisted the driver. A desperate situation was avoided when members of the New York Athletic Club, near which the accident took place, rescued the passenger from an irate crowd.[21] A day later, Captain Lantry of the East 51st Street precinct identified the woman as Mrs. Pryor.[22]

Pryor's days on the bench were over, but a ghost threatened to return with unpleasant implications. The city's Democratic Party headquarters, Tammany Hall, was being investigated by the Mazet Committee, a legislative agency. Many persons who had been appointed or nominated for political office were questioned about the mechanics of obtaining this distinction; and Pryor was one of those invited to testify. "On the 14th of October, 1891," he began, "—I had been nominated for the bench—I contributed $10,000 and also $500 to the County Democracy. It seemed that a particular friend of mine had contributed $500 to that organization, and I felt it my duty to reimburse him."

"Would you be willing to state who requested you to do so?"

"I have no objection."

"Will you kindly do so?"

"Richard Croker."[23] The Mazet Committee members doubtless were overjoyed by this revelation, for Croker was the chieftain of Tammany Hall. (Subsequently Abraham Smaulhed, an attorney known as "one of the keepers of King Croker's 'conscience,'" suggested to the boss "that he should say to the Committee that he never asks anything from Judges relating to decisions of cases and all that." But Croker only walked away.[24]

Pryor calmly explained that his check had been written to the order of Croker as chairman of the finance committee of Tammany Hall; the check was then returned by an emissary, "who said that he preferred to have the check payable to bearer. That he himself would collect it and turn the money into Tammany Hall."

"Do you not think, Judge, that the judiciary would be more elevated in the eyes of the people and made more independent in the performance of their duty if they were relieved by law from the payment of political assessment?"

"Decidedly," Pryor replied. "I am on record as being of that opinion long ago."

When asked if actions such as his might not put judges in an embarrassing posture, he replied: "No member of Tammany Hall, from Mr. Croker down, has ever suggested to me any decision, how I should decide."

The admission by a candidate for elective office that he had given $10,000 to a political party looked serious indeed, particularly in the case of a person with Pryor's reputation for integrity. But he was completely unembarrassed and saw no sinister overtones in his contribution; his check "was not only for my own election, but was also a contribution to the general canvass of the party. I had been in the habit before that time of distributing according to my means what I could."[25] That put a new slant upon the situation. No one ever doubted his veracity. And inasmuch as he had been an outstandingly successful lawyer at the time of his nomination, a substantial gift in the pattern of his precandidature habit did not seem to be suspicion-breeding. He was questioned no further.

The Pryors' son, William, a physician, who lived at 6 West 84 Street in New York, died in 1904.[26] Later that same year, Sara dedicated a book to him:

I DEDICATE THIS BOOK TO THE MEMORY OF
MY SON
WILLIAM RICE PRYOR, M.D.
WHO GAVE TO SUFFERING HUMANITY ALL THAT
GOD HAD GIVEN HIM[27]

Another book she dedicated to her departed first son:

To The Memory of
My Son
Theodorick Bland Pryor.[28]

As he approached the age of four score years, Pryor maintained a prominent place in New York. "Among the Southern citizens of this city, Roger A. Pryor has for many years occupied a conspicuous place."[29] Many of his old comrades-in-arms he saw to their graves. As the organizer of the Confederate Veterans' Camp of New York, he served as honorary pallbearer at the funeral of Colonel Andrew Glassel Dickinson, who had been chief of staff for General J. B. Magruder, C.S.A.[30] He induced the owner of a pistol used by the Southern General Robert Hatton (killed at the Battle of Seven Pines in 1862) to return the weapon to the Hatton family as a memorial.[31]

In his eightieth year, Pryor's name still made news. It was noted that he and General Daniel Sickles were the only survivors of the Thirty-sixth Congress. Pryor expressed the opinion that Charles A. Culbertson of Texas should have been nominated for the presidency by the Democrats, rather than William Jennings Bryan. Culbertson, he declared, had ability, reputation, and experience. "Besides that, he is a Southern man, and it is time the Democrats gave the South a nominee again."[32] In the next presidential election year, the Democrats did nominate Virginia-born Woodrow Wilson.

Pryor spent his eightieth birthday at his home at 3 West 69 Street, and a reporter observed that the ex-general, his wife, and his canary grew old gracefully together. "His eyes are bright, and his sight is very good. His hair, which falls to his shoulders, is only tinged. He is not at all thin or worn; his face is as healthily brown as a seashore youngster's. His voice is still strong and resonant, and his philosophy of life, mellowed by numerous and well-filled years, is gentle and true."[33] He objected to the statement of the eminent physician, Dr. William Osler, that men are old at forty. "Some men at eighty are really young," proclaimed Pryor, "that is, more efficient than others at fifty. It is obvious therefore that in his prescription of the so-called 'old man' Dr. Osler talks simple nonsense."[34]

On November 8, 1908, the Pryors celebrated their sixtieth wedding anniversary. Lucy and Arthur Davis of Petersburg penned "A Greeting from Virginia":

Not yours a paltry lustrum—
No petty decade tame:
Nor quarter—nor half-century,
    Your wedded life could frame. . . .

He turned from war's loud turmoil,
From days with danger fraught,
To great forensic pleading,
To calm judicial thought. . . .[35]

As befitting an old soldier, Pryor discoursed freely on the subject of *his* war. "Davis didn't want to fight," he explained. "There were a number of reasons why that was natural. He had been educated at West Point, and it was hard to take up arms against the United States Army. He had many friends in the North. He had been Secretary of War also. He stood a chance for the Presidency of the entire country[36] and besides all that he had too much sense not to know that the odds were overwhelmingly against the South."[37] On another occasion, he declared: "I cannot forget the Civil War, but in generations to come people will think of those differences less and less. The words North and South are simply geographical expressions now and have no political significance whatever. You need not ask me why; the word 'union' simply expresses everything."[38]

Alluding to the Civil War, he stated: "Oh, it was a good thing after all that the Union was saved—good for the North, good for the South, good for Republican Government. I've come to feel glad that the result was what it was.

"But the States had every right under the sun at that time to secede if they so desired, according to the organic law of the land. Since the war that had been universally admitted. There is not a law professor in any institution, North or South, who does not admit that without hesitation. It wasn't a question of law; it was a question of self-preservation with the North, and they fought for that preservation."[39]

Pryor was in great demand as a banquet speaker. Noted an observer: "His repartees, always appropriate and in place, are heightened in effect by his almost preternatural counternance, in which the smile seems fairly weird-like."[40] Presumably that comment was intended to be a compliment.

He resigned his regular membership in the New York County Lawyers Association in order to accept honorary membership in that body,[41] and on December 8, 1909, the secretary of that organization advised him that "you are the first person selected for honorary membership under the provision of our by-laws (Article VI, Section 3) that the honorary members of the Association shall be 'such persons distinguished for public service and eminence in the law as the Directors shall elect.' "[42] On January 24, 1911, the association accepted his picture with these words: "The portrait will hang where it will be a constant reminder to the members of the Association that the qualities of instant courage and unsullied honor characterize the upright Judge not less than the true soldier.[43]

This was not Pryor's first honorary membership, for on November 7, 1908, he was given the following engrossed certificate:

> The Governors of the Lawyers' Club have in mind the long and distinguished career of Judge Roger A. Pryor replete with elements which go to make it unique.
>
> They recall his early activities, which through the Press, and in Congress, made him an influence at the very outset of his career, in that old South which has passed away after great stress and struggle, to give place to a new and greater South.
>
> They remember the distinction he won in the profession of the law, the universal recognition of which placed him upon the Bench, and won wide approval of his work as a Judge.
>
> But above all, they appreciate the broad and high views of American citizenship which have been his standard, and the charming and genial courtesy which has endeared him to his fellows in this Club.
>
> With this record before them the Governors of the Lawyers'

Club, by virtue of the powers conferred upon them, hereby appoint Judge Pryor the first Honorary Member of the Lawyers' Club, expressing their earnest wish that he and they and the fellow-members of the Club may long enjoy his continued association.[44]

Among his other honors, the University of Virginia made Pryor a member of its Board of Visitors.[45]

His combative spirit and physical courage did not lessen with the years. When he was eighty-one, as he was leaving an elevated railway train in New York, a young man forced himself into the car, deliberately ramming into the octogenarian. Pryor followed him back into the train and assaulted his attacker with an umbrella. When the conductor left his position between the cars in order to intervene, Pryor demanded: "Go back to your place on the platform and hold this train two minutes for me." The voice of authority was heeded. "Not until Judge Pryor wielded his umbrella repeatedly on the offender's head and shoulders, tucked the weapon under his arm, glanced at his watch, and stalked out, did the conductor ring the bell to start the train."[46] This was not the act of an aged eccentric or an old man who was relying upon the protection of his years. It was merely a continuation of what he had done on the duelling field as a young man, what he had done with a bayonet at the Second Battle of Manassas when endangered. No one harms me with impunity!

In 1912, Pryor issued *Essays and Addresses*, a collection of eight of his works, including his address to the Committee of Thirty-three his argument in *People of the State of New York v. The North River Sugar Refining Company*, and various speeches. He stated in the very brief introduction: "In my declining days, when 'Whether for thought or for action my career is at an end,' my mind naturally reverts to the past, and in retrospect quite as naturally lingers on events in which I myself bore a part, of more or less consequence. To these events the following collection of Essays and Addresses refers; and while intrinsically they are doubtless of little interest, they may be not without attraction to students who find instruction even in the ephermeral effusions of the passing day."[47]

In that year, Sara, to whom his book had been dedicated, died at their home on 69th Street. This was on February 15, four days before what would have been her eighty-second birthday.[48] It was the heaviest blow to Pryor in a life which had experienced more than its allotment of crushing blows. "I have lost the sweetheart of my life,"[49] he stated with deceptive simplicity. "The romance of General Pryor's life was his marriage. They were married when he was twenty and she was eighteen years old and it is said they were sweethearts until she died on February 15, 1912, more than sixty-three years later."[50] Certainly she was one woman who could not have complained that her husband regarded her with diffidence. Typically, he said to her two score years after the wedding, when Madison Square Garden was being constructed: "Here in New York . . . a great hot theatre is to be called a garden and crowned by Diana of the Ephesians! St. Gaudens is making the goddess. But *you'll* not need gardens or goddesses to make you happy! Ah! What a wonderful woman you are— so content, so cheery in spite of all our privations."[51] "Mrs. Pryor," declared a eulogy, "was known in literary circles as an author, but more on account of the sweetness of her disposition and the charming story of her domestic life. . . ."[52]

There seems to have been some sort of transference of Pryor's love for his wife Sara to their little granddaughter, Sara Dodge. To her Pryor wrote seven months after the death of his wife: "A thousand thanks for the photograph! No other present could have been so acceptable to me. A beautiful picture, but not so beautiful as the little girl herself. It shall be finely framed; and put beside your grandmother in the parlor."[53] On June 8, 1914, after his granddaughter had visited his home on 69th Street, Pryor wrote to her: "You owe me no thanks for what you suppose I have done for you. On the contrary, the pleasure of your presence—suggestive every moment of your Angel Grandmother—more than compensates me for any service I may have rendered you."[54] On June 20, 1917, he wrote to her from Atlantic City: "Far from 'stupid' is your letter. Nothing from 'Miss Dodge's' pen can be otherwise than brilliant; but its intrinsic defects, if any, would be redeemed by your Grandmother's name."[55]

On April 19, 1912, the state legislature passed a special act, which was approved by the governor, appointing Pryor an official referee of the State of New York. He made his office at 37 Wall Street.[56]

In his retirement, Pryor liked to attend trials, such as that of Harry K. Thaw for murder. He watched with critical eyes. Virginia's "unwritten law," he opined, could well be followed elsewhere. Under this law, a husband on trial for murder "would only have to say, "That man debauched my wife and I shot him,' and the jury would have said, "Good for you," and let him go. That unwritten law, let me tell you, has a very salutary effect. If the community knows an offense against a woman can be reckoned with directly, a man inclined to such offence will be more careful."[57] "More careful," however, is scarcely synonymous with "more moral."

But the courtroom was only one of Pryor's interests. When a newspaper queried various distinguished persons about their favorite Shakespearean quotations, on the bard's 350th birthday, Pryor quoted from *Measure For Measure*, Act II, Scene 2:

> No ceremony that to great ones longs,
> Not the King's crown, nor the deputed sword
> The Marshall's truncheon, nor the Judge's robe,
> Become them with one-half so good a grace
> As Mercy does.[58]

In World War I, his sympathies were with the Allies, especially France. "I am a Virginian and my stock is English. I must say, however, that I am deeply depressed by the showing the English have made. It is cowardice."[59] He predicted with uncanny foresight that the Germans would make a separate peace with the Russians.[60] "As an old soldier," he announced, "I can say there is nothing in war. I have seen enough of it. The world is not at a stage now where constant killing of men by their fellows can go on. This war will be the great lesson."[61]

He approved of President Wilson's stern *Lusitania* note. "After reading and studying the note . . . both as a former Justice of the Supreme Court and as an American-born American, I can truthfully say that I unqualifiedly indorse it both as to style and substance."[62]

The substance of any writing, of course, was what had meaning for him. Replying to a gift, he wrote the donor: "While thanking you for Lincoln's Gettysburg Address, candor compels me to say that I do not esteem it is masterpiece: but consider his Second Inaugural altogether and far superior."[63] It is easy to see why Pryor was attracted to the Second Inaugural Address, which so well stated his own beliefs: "With malice toward none, with charity to all, with firmness in the right as

God gives us to see the right, let us finish the work we are in, to bind up the nation's wounds, to care for him who shall have borne the battle and for his widow and orphans, to do all which may achieve and cherish a just and lasting peace among ourselves, and with all nations."[64]

On his eighty-seventh birthday on July 19, 1915, Pryor took his daily walk in Central Park, despite the heat. He read; he received callers. He liked to sit at the open window of his library, which jutted into the street. His hair was not yet entirely gray. "He is very vigorous," noted an observer, "does not even use glasses except for reading, and has no difficulty in hearing ordinary conversational tones."[65]

Early in 1919, Pryor was ill for several weeks, and pneumonia developed. On the night of March 14, he died at his home.[66] Thus quietly perished "the last survivor of the firing on Fort Sumter. He outlived the thousands of participants on both sides of the historic conflict."[67]

Funeral services were held at the Pryor home on March 17. Then he was interred in the family plot at Princeton, New Jersey, where his wife and two sons were buried. He was survived by five children: Mrs. Frank T. Walker (Gordon), Mrs. Henry E. Rice (Mary), Mrs. Arthur Page Brown (Lucy), Mrs. William Leftwich Dodge (Fanny), and Roger A. Pryor, Jr. There were thirteen grandchildren and eight great-grandchildren.[68]

Pryor's estate was estimated for probate purposes to be $20,000 in realty and $2,000 in personal property, including that much-pawned silver service, which was bequeathed to the Confederate Literary Society of Richmond.[69] But what he really left behind was not susceptible to valuation by any surrogate.

Business in the New York courts was suspended for the funeral services. In Trial Term, Part XV, of the State Supreme Court, John Bogart arose and said: "It is true that we are busily engaged in our vocations of everyday life and the time of the courts is necessarily taken up with litigation, but it also should be true that when a judge has rendered the services that Judge Pryor did in his lifetime as a great lawyer and as a great judge, it would be amiss if recognition was not made of it on the minutes of the court."[70] Declared Mr. Justice John Ford: "I venture to say that no man who has sat upon the Bench of the Supreme Court left it in the enjoyment of higher respect from the Bar and the esteem of his colleagues. . . . In brief, he was an honor to the Bench that he graced. He lived and died a great man and a fearless, upright and just judge."[71] Court was then adjourned.

Mr. Justice Leonard A. Geigerich in Trial Term, Part XVI, stated: "His ability was exceptional. Indeed, in my opinion, he was one of the ablest men that ever sat on the bench in this country."[72] He adjourned his court.

One obituary noted that "It is given to few men to crowd as many varied incidents into life as did Judge Pryor, even into a long life such as his."[73] An editorial observed that "here was the man who had made at Charleston the great speech which stirred his hearers to fire on Fort Sumter. . . . the man who, stronger than any other Virginian of prominence, had stood for secession."[74]

His most moving "obituaries" actually were written while Pryor was still alive, by persons who knew whereof they spoke. "A country boy of the poor lands of Dinwiddie and the old fields and simple homes of Nottoway," recalled a kinsman, "editor, politician, special ambassador, member of Congress of the United States and of the Confederate States, General in the Southern Army, private soldier, prisoner, penniless and countryless man, lawyer, judge, justice; in the retrospect of this chequered career, the thing he recalls with most satisfaction is, that instead of succumbing under the ruin in which the war involved him at the age of thirty-seven, in middle life, he equipped himself for a new profession, and although poor and with a large family, he struggled with such patience and industry, that in a strange and then hostile community, he has achieved a fair measure of success."[75]

His wife's epitaph had been penned for him ten years before his death. The Civil War, she wrote,

> had left him with nothing but a ragged uniform, his sword, a wife, and seven children,—his health, his occupation, his place in the world, gone; his friends and comrades slain in battle; his Southern home impoverished and desolate. He had no profession, no rights as a citizen, no ability to hold office. That he conquered the fate which threatened him to destroy him,—and conquered it through the appreciation awarded him by his sometime enemies, —is a striking illustration of the possibilities afforded by our

Country; where not only can the impoverished refugees from other lands find fortune and happiness, but where her own sons, prostrate and ruined after a dreadful fratricidal strife, can bind their wounds, take up their lives again, and finally win reward for their labors.[76]

XV

An Appreciation

Roger A. Pryor led many lives: editor, diplomat, orator, congressman, general, private, lawyer, judge. His success (usually a brilliant one) in each of these roles would suggest that he was a man of many talents. Actually, such was not the case at all. He was endowed with no particular talents. But he possessed two characteristics which enabled him to succeed at whatever he chose. He could decide incisively on what should be done and he was willing to pay whatever price was necessary to implement his decision.

His successes in so many fields were not the result of brilliance, luck, or favoritism. His recipe was simple: "My only arts are, work and devotion to study."[1] When he was admitted to the New York bar, he informed his wife that "It will be study, *study, study*, ever after this!"[2] Meticulous preparation always had been his habit.

He deeply believed that there was only one way to succeed—at least for him. "I mean at least to deserve success—which is the surest way to realize it," he wrote.[3] He asked his wife: "Did you ever know any one who lived honestly, worked hard, and exerted competent talent to fail in any enterprise in life?"[4] "Study, work, unremitting study and work from early morning until late at night was his daily portion."[5]

His life seems to have been made up of a series of paradoxes. He was an instigator of war who was an apostle of peace, a notorious dueller who was a humanitarian, a hot-tempered editor who advocated peaceful reconciliation, a secessionist who ardently believed in the union, a passionate Southerner who chose his home and his friends in the North, a go-for-broke lawyer who was a judge obsessed only with justice. Actually, Pryor's career was not one of paradoxes at all. There was a central theme that ran through his life and, as the law of the Medes and the Persians, did not change. The *motif* of his existence was simple and direct: personal rights must not be violated.

This great concern for human rights characterized his entire career. The rights might be his own, as when he resigned an editorial post on the Washington *Union* when the proprietor demanded that Pryor retract an opinion. The rights might be those of a whole section of the country with its millions of people, as when he based his argument for the South's secession primarily upon deprivation of its rights. He championed the wife and child against husband (and detective); he jousted with a trust that had a monopoly *against* the people; he represented labor at a time when capital had all of the cards. Personal rights were to be safeguarded at any price. He was willing to pay the price in blood, first of all his own. Throughout his life he risked himself, whether on the duelling ground to insist upon his right to work for a political candidate, or on the battlefield to maintain for the South the right to choose its own institutions, or in the arena of his career to guarantee an anarchist freedom from illegal seizure despite the enormity of the crime alleged. He believed in the sanctity of human rights as a matter of principle, even if he was not personally involved. Thus, he led the fight in Virginia against the Know-Nothing Party with its anti-Catholic, antiforeigner program, although there were few Catholics or foreigners in Virginia at that time.

Slavery was not the main issue of the impending Civil War, declared Pryor. The fundamental principle of the Union "is subverted by a combination between a majority of the States to exclude other States from an equal participation in the common domain, and so to deny them equal advantages of expansion and development under the operation of the Federal Government." This violated "the guarantee of State sovereignty, the right reserved by each State to administer its own affairs." When a majority rides roughshod over the rights of a minority, revolution is justified. "Absolute power is the essence of tyranny, whether the power be wielded by a monarch or a multitude."[6]

"[H]e was the man who occasioned the War as much as any single man could precipitate a catastrophe that had been approaching for two decades."[7] The Civil War brought high military command to Pryor;

although he never was a rival to Lee or Jackson, he fought with distinction and was commended in the dispatches. But when he found himself in a position where he no longer was being actively used in the war effort, he threw down his commission and selected a very active regiment for his enlistment as a private. His reasoning was deceptively simple: even if the army had no need for him as a general, he would not return to civilian life, for "I had something to do with bringing on this war. I must give myself to Virginia."[8] A feeling of guilt seems to have seized him, perhaps permanently.

Little more than a month after Lee's surrender at Appomattox, Pryor conceded that the chapter on secession was closed. "We have been fairly whipped." Confederate soldiers who "do not lay down their arms and return at once to their duties as law abiding citizens should be treated as outlaws."[9] Shortly thereafter, he advised his compatriots to accept the inevitable, to grant suffrage to the Negro, to enter heartily upon the work of reconciliation and reconstruction.[10]

Was it a sense of guilt which impelled him, before other Confederate leaders, to seek to reunite the nation and to reestablish the rule of law? No other prominent Southern leader had done as much as he had to bring on the war. He explained at great length in a letter to the Richmond *Whig* in 1867 that "I have hoped in some measure, and in a quiet way, to repair the evil I contributed to bring upon the South by availing myself of every appropriate opportunity to suggest these counsels of modernization and magnanimity." His counsel to his Southern friends included "conceding to all classes the unrestricted rights guaranteed them by the laws. . . ."[11]

He was not afraid to admit a mistake or to change directions. Most of the changes in his many faceted career were externally motivated. Although at times he was a prisoner of circumstances, he never regarded this as a life sentence. When he began as a lawyer, a throat ailment ended this career before it was fairly started; but he espoused journalism with vigor. His ideas called for action, and he won election to Congress to implement his thinking. His legislative life was terminated by the war for which he was seriously responsible, and he became an army officer until (to hold his head aloft) he found it necessary to become a private. With defeat, he became just another *statloss* refugee, with no home, no friends in his new land, no vote, and no material resources; but unlike millions of other such war refugees that the world has known, he did not live out a broken life in a permanent state of shock. He acted out what he once had said about the sorely buffeted Lincoln: "I thought he never would stop getting up."[12]

He came to terms with life—and with himself. Federal generals he had opposed on the battlefield became his staunch friends after the peace. His Antietam adversary, General Hancock, subsequently was to have Pryor's support for the presidency in 1880.[13] General Butler, a Petersburg foe, became an associate in important litigation;[14] the Federal General Sickles recommended him for a New York state judgeship.[15] John D. Rockefeller, whom Pryor had attacked during a state inquiry, attended the wedding of Fanny Pryor.[16]

He threw himself wholeheartedly into whatever he did, but he still had the will and energy to be actively compassionate. His charity on the battlefield was extraordinary. After the Battle of Seven Pines, he brought whiskey and water to the enemy wounded.[17] He freed thousands of wounded and sick Northern soldiers so that they would not have to undergo the hell of prison camps.[18] He fed prisoners from his own scanty food supply.[19] He pawned his household silver to buy shoes for his captives.[20] He was marked as an overly chivalrous (that is, "soft") judge when women were before his bench.[21] He did not believe in capital punishment and, as a New York Supreme Court justice, he would not sit on a murder trial.[22]

His courage was magnificent. He fought duels on matters of principle; he was not content to be a swivel-chair general.[23] At fifty-five, he rescued a young lady from a band of ruffians;[24] at eighty-one, he attacked a youth who had provoked him physically.[25] But his moral courage was equal to his physical. He picked himself up instantly whenever he was knocked down, which was frequently. A journalist wrote about Pryor's efforts to carve out a new postbellum career in New York: "But that required courage—a higher courage than ever rebellion demanded. . . ."[26]

Pryor succeeded so magnificently in a world which dealt him numerous grievous blows because he had the courage, the will, and the strength to adapt to ever-changing circumstances.

Notes

NOTES TO CHAPTER I

1. Thomas D. Suplée, *The Life of Theodorick Bland Pryor* (San Francisco, 1879), p. 8. Unless otherwise specified, this work is the source of the genealogy in this paragraph.

2. "Virginia Council Journals," *The Virginia Magazine of History and Biography*, January, 1927, Volume XXV, p. 29. Turkey Island is a stretch of shore in the James River, close to Richmond. Paul Wilstach, *Tidewater Virginia* (Indianapolis, 1929), p. 146.

3. Cazenove Gardner Lee, Jr., *Lee Chronicle* (New York, 1957, p. 349.

4. Austin Abbott, *editor, Official Report of the Trial of Henry Ward Beecher* (New York, 1875), p. xxii.

5. Walter A. Watson, "Notes on Southside Virginia," *Bulletin of the Virginia State Library*, September, 1925, Volume XV, p. 173.

6. Sallie E. Marshall Hardy, "Some Virginia Lawyers of the Past and Present," *The Green Bag*, October 1898, Volume X, #10, p. 161.

7. Watson, "Notes on Southside Virginia," p. 174.

8. T. P. Epes, "Roger Atkinson Pryor, LL.D.," *Kaleidoscope*, 1903, Volume XI, p. 10.

9. John Herbert Claiborne, *Seventy-five Years in Old Virginia* (New York, 1904), p. 84.

10. Watson, "Notes on Southside Virginia," p. 175.

11. W. R. Turner, *Old Homes and Families in Nottoway* (Blackstone, Va., 1932), p. 24.

12. Ibid., p. 62.

13. Epes, "Roger Atkinson Pryor," p. 11.

14. Ibid., p. 10.

15. Ibid., p. 11.

16. Watson, "Notes on Southside Virginia," p. 45.

17. Suplée, *Life of Theodorick Bland Pryor,* p. 20.

18. *Who's Who in America 1910-1911* (Chicago, 1910), p. 1556.

19. Mrs. Roger A. Pryor, *My Day. Reminiscences of a Long Life* (New York, 1909), p. 9.

20. Ibid., p. 10.

21. Ibid., p. 12.

22. Ibid., p. 16.

23. Ibid., p. 65.

24. Ibid., p. 66.

25. Ibid., pp. 68 and 83.

26. *The Brown Book, 1919* (New York, 1919), p. 260.

27. Epes, "Roger Atkinson Pryor," p. 11.

28. Hardy, "Some Virginia Lawyers," p. 161.

29. Thomas J. Michie, "John Barbee Minor," *The Green Bag,* September, 1895, Volume VII, #9, p. 401.

30. Mrs. Pryor, *My Day,* p. 78.

31. Ibid., p. 68.

32. Hardy, "Some Virginia Lawyers," p. 161.

33. New York *Times,* November 6, 1898.

34. Mrs. Pryor, *My Day,* p. 169.

35. New York *Tribune,* March 15, 1919.

36. Mrs. Pryor, *My Day,* p. 84.

37. New York *Post,* March 15, 1919.

38. Claiborne, *Seventy-five Years,* p. 44.

NOTES TO CHAPTER II

1. Lester J. Cappon, *Virginia Newspapers, 1832-1935* (New York, 1936), p. 153.

2. Edward A. Wyatt IV, *Preliminary Checklist for Petersburg, 1786-1876* (Richmond, 1949), p. 253.

3. Mrs. Pryor, *My Day,* p. 84.

4. Claiborne, *Seventy-five Years,* p. 92.

5. New York *Sun,* March 15, 1919.

6. Mrs. Pryor, *My Day,* p. 85.

7. Ibid., p. 88.

8. Claiborne, *Seventy-five Years,* p. 91.

9. Wyatt, *Preliminary Checklist,* p. 259.

10. Roy Franklin Nichols, *Franklin Pierce* (Philadelphia, 1931), p. 202.

11. Ibid., p. 279.

12. Mrs. Pryor, *My Day*, p. 91.

13. Mrs. Roger A. Pryor, *Reminiscences of Peace and War* (New York, 1908), p. 4. Hereinafter this will be referred to as *Peace and War*.

14. Ibid., p. 28.

15. Ben: Perley Poore, *Perley's Reminiscences of Sixty Years in the National Metropolis* (Philadelphia, 1886), I, 429.

16. New York *Tribune*, March 23, 1902.

17. Abbott, *Trial of Henry Ward Beecher*, p. xxii.

18. Mrs. Pryor, *My Day*, p. 106.

19. Nichols, *Franklin Pierce*, p. 279.

20. Cappon, *Virginia Newspapers*, p. 171.

21. Mrs. Pryor, *Peace and War*, p. 15.

22. Clement A. Evans, *editor, Confederate Military History* (Atlanta, 1899). III, 654.

23. Henry Merritt Wriston, *Executive Agents in American Foreign Relations* (Baltimore, 1929), p. 663.

24. Mrs. Pryor, *Peace and War*, p. 26.

25. Wriston, *Executive Agents*, p. 176.

26. New York *Herald*, March 15, 1919.

27. Wriston, *Executive Agents*, p. 176.

28. Mrs. Pryor, *Peace and War*, p. 40.

29. Ibid.

30. Mrs. Pryor, *My Day*, p. 110.

31. New York *Post*, March 15, 1919.

32. New York *Herald*, March 15, 1919.

33. This description is quoted in Mrs. Pryor, *My Day*, p. 126.

34. Evans, *Confederate Military History*, III, 654.

35. Watson, "Notes on Southside Virginia," p. 176.

36. Claiborne, *Seventy-five Years*, p. 92.

37. William H. Barnwell, *The Impiety and Absurdity of Duelling* (Charleston, S.C., 1844), p. 16.

38. John Hallum, *The Diary of an Old Lawyer* (Nashville, 1895), p. 28.

39. New York *Tribune*, March 15, 1919.

40. Watson, "Notes on Southside Virginia," p. 176.

41. Harvey Wish, *George Fitzhugh, Propagandist of the Old South* (Baton Rouge, 1943), p. 145.

42. John S. Wise, "The Fire-Eaters," *Saturday Evening Post*, June 23, 1906, Volume 178, #CLXXVIII, p. 8.

43. A. W. Patterson, *The Code Duello, With Special Reference to the State of Virginia* (Richmond, 1927), p. 50.

44. New York *Sun*, March 15, 1919.

45. Douglas Southall Freeman, *Lee's Lieutenants* (New York, 1944), I, 161.

46. George Fort Milton, *The Eve of Conflict* (Boston, 1934), p. 364.

47. Frank E. Stevens, "Life of Stephen Arnold Douglas," *Journal of The Illinois State Historical Society*, Volume XVI, October 1923-January 1924, ##3-4, p. 659.

48. Henry Wilson, *History of the Rise and Fall of the Slave Power in America* (Boston, 1877), III, 177.

49. John W. Forney, *Anecdotes of Public Men* (New York 1873), p. 57.

50. For examples, see J. G. Randall, *The Civil War and Reconstruction* (Boston, 1937), p. 170; Allan Nevins, *The Emergence of Lincoln* (New York, 1950), I, 409; Burton J. Hendrick, *Lincoln's War Cabinet* (Boston, 1946), p. 24; Carl Sandburg, *Abraham Lincoln, The War Years* (New York, 1939), I, 141. Seward's speech was delivered on October 25, 1858.

51. *The Writings of Abraham Lincoln*, Arthur Brooks Lapsley, *editor* (New York, 1906), V, 95.

52. Ibid., V, 166.

53. *Congressional Globe*, December 29, 1859, p. 284.

54. *The Writings of Abraham Lincoln*, III, 1. In that day of frequent Bible quoting, all parties concerned must have known the origin of the phrase. "Every kingdom divided against itself is brought to desolation; and every city or house divided against itself shall not stand." *Matthew* 12:25.

55. Louis A. Warren, *editor, Lincoln Lore* #616, January 27, 1941, p. 1.

56. Wish, *George Fitzhugh*, p. 225.

57. Mrs. Pryor, *My Day*, p. 123.

58. Epes, "Roger Atkinson Pryor," p. 12.

59. Philip Morrison Rice, "The Know-Nothing Party in Virginia," *The Virginia Magazine of History and Biography*, January 1947, Volume 55, #1, p. 61

60. John S. Wise, *The End of an Era* (Boston, 1902), p. 53.

61. Epes, "Roger Atkinson Pryor," p. 12.

62. Randall, *Civil War and Reconstruction*, p. 79.

63. Humphrey J. Desmond, *The Know-Nothing Party* (Washington, 1904), p. 119.

64. Mrs. Pryor, *My Day*, p. 126.

65. Cappon, *Virginia Newspapers*, p. 184.

66. *Leslie's Illustrated*, April 25, 1857, p. 321.

67. Mrs. Pryor, *My Day*, p. 126.

68. In this period, many writers (particularly in the South) referred to union as the confederacy. Pryor frequently did so.

69. *Leslie's Illustrated*, April 25, 1857, p. 322.

70. See Jesse T. Carpenter, *The South as a Conscious Minority* (New York, 1930).

71. Woodrow Wilson, *Division and Reunion*, 1829-1909 (New York, 1912), p. 119.

72. See John Richard Alden, *The First South* (Baton Rouge, 1961).

73. John Withspoon du Bose, *The Life and Times of William Lowndes Yancey* (Birmingham, 1892), p. 365.

NOTES TO CHAPTER III

74. Avery O. Craven, *The Growth of Southern Nationalism, 1848-1861* (Baton Rouge, 1953), p. 281.

75. Ibid., p. 290.

76. Cappon, *Virginia Newspapers*, p. 184.

77. Lyon Gardiner Tyler, *editor, Encyclopedia of Virginia Biography* (New York, 1915), II, 125.

NOTES TO CHAPTER III

1. Claiborne, *Seventy-five Years*, p. 92.

2. William Pope Dabney, as quoted in Watson, "Notes on Southside Virginia," p. 177. John Randolph of Roanoke (1773-1833) was bitterly opposed to the Constitution of the United States when it was adopted, and Virginia sent him to Congress to see that states' rights were not violated unduly.

3. Henry T. Shanks, *The Secessionist Movement in Virginia*, 1847-1861 (Richmond, 1934), p. 128.

4. Du Bose, *Life and Times of Yancey*, p. 358.

5. Herbert Wender, *Southern Commercial Conventions* (Baltimore, 1930), p. 196.

6. Du Bose, *Life and Times of Yancey*, p. 360.

7. Alfred H. Kelly and Winfred A. Harbison, *The American Constitution* (New York, 1948), I, 263.

8. Epes, "Roger Atkinson Pryor," p. 13.

9. Wender, *Southern Commercial Conventions*, p. 214.

10. Ibid., p. 216.

11. Ibid., p. 217.

12. Ibid., p. 220.

13. John C. Calhoun of Southern Carolina championed the doctrine of nullification: any state could *nullify* a Federal statute contrary to this state's interest.

14. Henry W. Hilliard, *Politics and Pen Pictures* (New York, 1892), p. 256.

15. Hardy, "Some Virginia Lawyers," p. 161.

16. Claiborne, *Seventy-five Years*, p. 134.

17. Mrs. Pryor, *My Day*, p. 129.

18. Watson, "Notes on Southside Virginia," p. 177.

19. Wyatt, *Preliminary Checklist*, p. 259.

20. Samuel S. Cox, *Three Decades of Federal Legislation* (Providence, 1885), p. 65.

[167]

21. *Biographical Dictionary of the American Congress* (Washington, 1950), p. 264.

22. John Sherman, *Recollections of Forty Years in the House, Senate and Cabinet* (Chicago, 1895), I, 168.

23. Cox, *Three Decades of Federal Legislation*, p. 26.

24. *Congressional Globe*, December 7, 1859, p. 48.

25. Alfred R. Conkling, *The Life and Letters of Roscoe Conkling* (New York, 1889), p. 93.

26. John Sherman, *Recollections*, I, 168.

27. *Congressional Globe*, December 9, 1859, p. 49. The "act. . . . at Harper's Ferry" was John Brown's seizure of a Federal arsenal and his armed attempt to free slaves. Pryor thought that it would have been better to have kept Brown in prison rather than to have executed him. Oswald Garrison Villard, *John Brown* (Boston, 1910), p. 506.

28. *Congressional Globe*, December 29, 1859, p. 281.

29. Conkling, *Life and Letters*, p. 98.

30. John Sherman, *Recollections*, I, 177.

31. Conklin, *Life and Letters*, p. 93.

32. Cox, *Three Decades of Federal Legislation*, p. 91.

33. Mrs. Pryor, *Peace and War*, p. 42.

34. Ibid., p. 46.

35. Mrs. Pryor, *My Day*, p. 148.

36. Mrs. Pryor, *Peace and War*, p. 94.

37. Cox, *Three Decades of Federal Legislation*, p. 74.

38. David D. Porter, *Incidents and Anecdotes of the Civil War* (New York, 1885), p. 10.

39. Myrta Lockett, *Dixie after the War*, p. 109.

40. La Salle Corbell Pickett, *Across My Path* (New York, 1916), p. 141.

41. Mrs. Pryor, *Peace and War*, p. 83.

42. Claiborne, *Seventy-five Years*, p. 93.

43. Mrs. Pryor, *My Day*, p. 149.

44. *Congressional Globe*, December 7, 1859, pp. 48 and 50.

45. Ibid., December 29, 1859, p. 284.

46. Ibid., December 24, 1859, p. 246.

47. Ibid., June 6, 1860, p. 2713.

48. Ibid., February 20, 1860, p. 844.

49. Ibid., February 13, 1860, p. 749.

50. Ibid., February 14, 1860, p. 771.

51. Cox, *Three Decades of Federal Legislation*, p. 72.

52. *Congressional Globe*, December 29, 1958, p. 285.

53. Emerson David Fite, *The Presidential Campaign of 1860* (New York, 1911), p. 41.

54. *Congressional Globe*, January 28, 1861, p. 601.

55. Ibid., December 29, 1859, p. 285.

56. Ibid., December 31, 1860, p. 220.

57. Ibid., January 28, 1861, p. 603.
58. Ibid., December 29, 1859, p. 283.
59. Ibid., p. 284.
60. Ibid., June 7, 1860, p. 2641.
61. Ibid., May 31, 1860, p. 2501.
62. Ibid., December 19, 1860, p. 148.
63. Evans, *Confederate Military History*, III, 654.
64. John Sherman, *Recollections*, I, 198.
65. *Congressional Globe*, April 5, 1860, p. 203.
66. Ibid.
67. Nevins, *The Emergence of Lincoln*, II, 124.
68. *Congressional Globe*, April 11, 1860, p. 1668.
69. *Appleton's Cyclopedia of American Biography* (New York, 1900), V, 90.
70. Wise, "The Fire-Eaters," p. 8.
71. New York *Times*, May 15, 1919.
72. Carl Schurz, *The Reminiscences of* (New York, 1907), II, 166.
73. *Appleton's Cyclopedia*, V, 90.
74. Avery O. Craven, *The Coming of the Civil War* (New York, 1950), p. 421.
75. New York *Times*, May 15, 1919.
76. Alphonse B. Miller, *Thaddeus Stevens* (New York, 1939), p. 21.

NOTES TO CHAPTER IV

1. *Congressional Globe*, June 6, 1860, p. 2709.
2. M. Halstead, *Caucuses of 1860* (Columbus, 1860), p. 121.
3. New York *Times*, May 15, 1919.
4. Margaret Kean Monteiro, "The Presidential Election of 1860 in Virginia," *Richmond College Historical Papers*, June 1916, Volume I, #2, p. 248.
5. Ibid., p. 251.
6. Epes, "Roger Atkinson Pryor," p. 13.
7. W. R. Turner, *Old Homes and Families in Nottoway* (Blackstone, Va., 1932), p. 267.
8. Monteiro, "The Presidential Election," p. 256.
9. Abbott, *Trial of Henry Ward Beecher*, p. xxiii.
10. Mary Boykin Chesnut, *A Diary from Dixie* (Boston, 1949), p. 1.
11. Ibid., p. 2.

12. Randall, *Civil War and Reconstruction*, p. 183.

13. Ibid., p. 184.

14. Mrs. Pryor, *My Day*, p. 153.

15. Porter, *Incidents and Anecdotes*, p. 8.

16. Mrs. Pryor, *My Day*, p. 154.

17. J. G. de Roulhac Hamilton, "Lincoln's Election An Immediate Menace to Slavery in the States?", *American Historical Review*. July 1932, Volume XXXVII, #4, p. 700.

18. Arthur C. Cole, "Lincoln's Election An Immediate Menace to Slavery in the States?", *American Historical Review*. July 1931, Volume XXXVI, #7, p. 767.

19. Woodrow Wilson, *Division and Reunion*, p. 208.

20. Edward A. Pollard, *The Lost Cause* (New York, 1867), p. 47.

21. Randall, *Civil War and Reconstruction*, p. 189.

22. Roger A. Pryor, *Essays and Addresses* (New York, 1912), p. 26.

23. Ollinger Crenshaw, *The Slave States in the Presidential Election of 1860* (Baltimore, 1945), p. 79.

24. January 19, 1860.

25. *Congressional Globe*, January 20, 1860, p. 540.

26. Alexander Harris, *A Review of the Political Conflict in America* (New York, 1876), p. 200.

27. Randall, *Civil War and Reconstruction*, p. 202.

28. *Official Records of the War of the Rebellion* (Washington, 1880-1901), I Series, Volume LI, Part 2, p. 3. Hereinafter cited as *Official Records*.

29. Ibid., I, LI, 2, p. 4.

30. A. B. Miller, *Thaddeus Stevens*, p. 128.

31. *Congressional Globe*, January 12, 1861, p. 346.

32. Ibid., February 26, 1861, p. 1227.

33. Ibid., February 25, 1861, p. 1190.

34. Ibid.

35. *Congressional Globe*, February 21, 1861, p. 1107. General Winfield Scott was a Southerner who stayed with the Union, as did David Glasgow Farragut, George Thomas, Robert Anderson, and certain others.

36. Suplée, *Life of Theodorick Bland Pryor*, p. 25.

37. *Congressional Globe*, February 26, 1861, p. 1227.

38. Pryor, *Essays*, p. 11.

39. *Congressional Globe*, January 28, 1861, p. 602.

40. Harris, *Review of Political Conflict*, p. 197.

41. Clement Eaton, "Henry A. Wise and the Virginia Fire Eaters of 1856," *Mississippi Valley Historical Review*, March 1935, Volume XXI, #4, p. 505n.

42. Turner, *Old Homes*, p. 267.

43. New York *Times*, July 17, 1908.

44. Albert Bigelow Paine, *Th. Nast, His Period and His Pictures* (New York, 1904), p. 73.

45. Cox, *Three Decades of Federal Legislation*, p. 117.

46. Randall, *Civil War and Reconstruction*, p. 247.

47. Burton J. Hendrick, *The Lees of Virginia* (Boston, 1935), p. 425.

48. La Salle Pickett, *editor, The Heart of a Soldier* (New York, 1913), p. 35.

49. Clyde C. Webster, "John Minor Botts, Anti-Secessionist," *Richmond College Historical Papers*, June 1915, Volume I, #1, p. 9.

50. W. Wilson, *Division and Reunion*, p. 215.

51. J. E. Cairnes, *The Slave Power: Its Character, Career and Probable Designs* (London, 1863), p. 24.

52. *The Writings of Abraham Lincoln*, V. 266.

53. Cox, *Three Decades of Federal Legislation*, p. 100.

NOTES TO CHAPTER V

1. *Official Records*, I, LI, 2, p. 263.

2. Cox, *Three Decades of Federal Legislation*, p. 64.

3. James G. Blaine, *Thirty Years of Congress* (Norwich, Conn., 1884), I, p. 243.

4. Mrs. Pryor, *My Day*, p. 155.

5. *Official Records*, IV, III, p. 1187n.

6. Watson, "Notes on Southside Virginia," p. 177.

7. Esther 5:13.

8. *The Writings of Abraham Lincoln*, V, p. 253.

9. Ralph Haswell Lutz, "Rudolf Schleiden and the Visit to Richmond, April 25, 1861," *Annual Report of the American Historical Association for the Year 1915* (Washington, 1917), p. 211.

10. Edward A. Pollard, *The First Year of the War* (New York, 1864), p. 51.

11. James Chester, "Inside Sumter in '61," *Battles and Leaders of the Civil War* (New York, 1887), I, p. 52.

12. Pollard, *The First Year of the War*, p. 53.

13. D. E. Huger Smith, *A Charlestonian's Recollections, 1846-1913*, (Charleston, S.C., 1950), p. 70.

14. Ashley Halsey, Jr., "Who Fired The First Shot?", *The Saturday Evening Post*, December 17, 1960, Volume 233, #25, p. 83.

15. Chesnut, *A Diary from Dixie*, p. 31.

16. Wise, *The End of an Era*, p. 330.

17. Randall, *Civil War and Reconstruction*, p. 239.

18. Robert W. Winston, *High Stakes and Hair Trigger. The Life of Jefferson Davis* (New York, 1930), p. 185.

19. The Vice-President of the United States.

20. New York *Tribune*, April 17, 1861.

21. Cox, *Three Decades of Federal Legislation*, p. 149.

22. H. Wilson, *Rise and Fall of Slave Power*, III, p. 208.

23. Chesnut, *A Diary from Dixie*, p. 37.

24. Manly Wade Wellman, *They Took Their Stand. The Founders of the Confederacy* (New York, 1959), p. 81.

25. New York *Tribune*, March 15, 1919.

26. New York *Times*, March 15, 1919.

27. New York *Herald*, March 16, 1919.

28. Brooklyn *Daily Eagle*, March 15, 1919.

29. Mrs. Pryor, *My Day*, p. 161.

30. Alfred Roman, *The Military Operations of General Beauregard* (New York, 1884), I, p. 42.

31. *Official Records*, I, LIII, p. 142.

32. Evans, *Confederate Military History*, III, p. 654.

33. A. R. Chisholm, "Notes on the Surrender of Fort Sumter," *Battles and Leaders of the Civil War* (New York, 1887), I, p. 82.

34. New York *Tribune*, April 19, 1861.

35. Alexander H. Stephens, *A Constitutional View of the Late War Between The States; Its Causes, Character, Conduct and Results* (Philadelphia, 1870), II, 38.

36. Horace Greeley, *The American Conflict* (Hartford, Conn., 1864), I, 442.

37. Nathaniel W. Stephenson, *The Day of the Confederacy* (New Haven, 1920), p. 16.

38. John Minor Botts, *The Great Rebellion: Its Secret History, Rise, Progress, and Disastrous Failure* (New York, 1866), p. 203.

39. The Union Secretary of State.

40. William E. Dodd, *Statesmen of the Old South* (New York, 1911), p. 221.

41. Greeley, *The American Conflict*, I, p. 443.

42. Ashley Halsey, Jr., "South Carolina Began Preparing for War in 1851," *Civil War Times Illustrated*, April 1962, Volume I, #1, p. 8.

43. Stephen D. Lee, "The First Step in the War," *Battles and Leaders of the Civil War* (New York, 1887), I, p. 76.

44. Mrs. Pryor, *Peace and War, supra*, p. 121.

45. Avery Craven, *Edmund Ruffin, Southerner* (New York, 1932), p. 90.

46. Wyatt, *Preliminary Checklist*, p. 257.

47. Wellman, *They Took Their Stand*, p. 87. Who actually *did* fire this historic shot is still the subject of some controversy. See Halsey, "Who Fired The First Shot?", p. 22.

49. Greeley, *The American Conflict*, I, p. 443.

50. S. D. Lee, "The First Step in the War," I, p. 76.

51. Chesnut, *A Diary from Dixie*, p. 36.

52. Evans, *Confederate Military History*, III, p. 654.

53. Chester, "Inside Sumter in '61,", I, p. 71.
54. *Official Records*, I, I, p. 15.
55. New York *Tribune*, April 19, 1861.
56. Samuel Wylie Crawford, *The Genesis of the Civil War* (New York, 1887), p. 442.
57. Abner Doubleday, *Reminiscences of Forts Sumter and Moultrie in 1860-'61* (New York, 1876), p. 169.
58. *Official Records*, I, I, p. 28.
59. Ibid., I, I, p. 35.
60. *The Writings of Abraham Lincoln*, V, p. 285.
61. Wise, *The End of An Era*, p. 159.
62. Randall, *Civil War and Reconstruction*, p. 248.
63. Blaine, *Thirty Years of Congress*, I, p. 301.

NOTES TO CHAPTER VI

1. *Official Records*, IV, I, p. 630.
2. Mrs. Pryor, *Peace and War*, p. 132.
3. G. Moxley Sorrel, *Recollections of a Confederate Staff Officer* (Jackson, Tenn., 1958), p. 44.
4. Pickett, *Heart of a Soldier*, p. 38.
5. Mrs. Pryor, *My Day*, p. 165.
6. Ibid., p. 182.
7. Sorrel, *Recollections of a Confederate Staff Officer*, p. 23.
8. Arthur Fremantle, *Three Months in the Southern States* (New York, 1864), p. 293.
9. William T. Sherman, *Memoirs* (New York, 1889), II, p. 383.
10. Ashley Halsey, Jr., "South Carolina Began Preparing for War in 1851," p. 9.
11. J. B. Jones, *A Rebel War Clerk's Diary* (Philadelphia, 1866), I, p. 46.
12. John Bach McMaster, *A History of the United States During Lincoln's Administration* (New York, 1927), p. 190.
13. W. H. Morgan, *Reminiscences of the War of 1861-5* (Lynchburg, Va., 1911), p. 33.
14. W. Sherman, II, p. 381.
15. *The Writings of Abraham Lincoln*, VI, p. 314.
16. New York *Tribune*, April 17, 1861. One irresistibly is reminded of William S. Gilbert's very model of a modern major-general (British), who

vouchsafed that he knew "more of tactics than a novice in a nunnery." *The Pirates of Penzance*, Act I.

17. *Official Records*, I, II, p. 797. The capital had not yet been shifted from Montgomery.

18. *Official Records*, I, XVIII, p. 790.

19. Ibid., I, XVIII, p. 888.

20. Mrs. Pryor, *Peace and War*, p. 213.

21. Mrs. Pryor, *My Day*, p. 163.

22. *Confederate Veteran*, March 1908, Volume XVI, #3, p. 127.

23. Suplée, *The Life of Theodorick Bland Pryor*, p. 49.

24. Mrs. Pryor, *My Day*, p. 166.

25. James D. McCabe, Jr., *The Grayjackets: And How They Lived, Fought and Died for Dixie* (Richmond, 1876), p. 192.

26. *Official Records*, IV, III, p. 1189.

27. Alfred Hoyt Bill, *The Beleaguered City* (New York, 1946), p. 170.

28. Jones, *A Rebel War Clerk's Diary*, II, p. 347.

29. E. Merton Coulter, *The Confederate States of America, 1861-1865* (Baton Rouge, 1950), pp. 141, 143.

30. Evans, *Confederate Military History*, III, p. 655.

31. "Proceedings of First Confederate Congress—First Session," *Southern Historical Society Papers*, June 1923, New Series, No. VI, Whole Number XLIV, p. 46.

32. *Official Records*, IV, II, pp. 446-448.

33. "Proceedings of First Confederate Congress," p. 152.

34. Ibid.

35. G. T. Beauregard, "The Campaign of Shiloh," *Battles and Leaders of the Civil War* (New York, 1887), I, p. 568.

36. *Official Records*, I, V, p. 1048.

37. Ibid., I, VII, p. 880.

38. A distinguished Brooklyn clergyman and journalist. See Chapter IX.

39. Joseph S. Auerbach, *The Bar of Other Days* (New York, 1940), p. 199.

40. J. F. C. Fuller, *Decisive Battles of the U.S.A.* (New York, 1953), p. 186.

41. Sorrel, *Recollections of a Confederate Staff Officer*, pp. 56-58.

42. *Official Records*, I, LI, 1, p. 91.

43. Ibid., I, XL, 1, p. 567.

44. Ibid., I, XI, 1, p. 569.

45. Mrs. Pryor, *Peace and War*, p. 166.

46. Sorrel, *Recollections of a Confederate Staff Officer*, p. 26.

47. Fuller, *Decisive Battles of the U.S.A.*, pp. 187-188.

48. Sorrel, *Recollections of a Confederate Staff Officer*, p. 54.

49. Randall, *Civil War and Reconstruction*, p. 295.

50. *Official Records*, I, XL, 1, p. 945.

51. Frank Moore, editor, *The Rebellion Record* (Washington, 1862-1871), V, p. 97.

52. *Official Records*, I, XL, 1, p. 941.

53. Sorrel, *Recollections of a Confederate Staff Officer*, p. 67.

54. George B. McClellan, *McClellan's Own Story* (New York, 1887), p. 338.

55. Fuller, *Decisive Battles of the U.S.A.*, p. 195.

56. *Confederate Veteran*, 1899, Volume VII, #2, p. 56.

57. Fuller, *Decisive Battles of the U.S.A.*, p. 205.

58. *Official Records*, I, XI, 2, p. 781.

59. Ibid., I, XI, II, p. 759.

60. Mrs. Pryor, *Peace and War*, p. 182.

61. Mrs. Pryor, *My Day*, p. 168.

62. Joseph B. Mitchell, *Decisive Battles of the Civil War* (New York, 1955), p. 86.

63. William Allan, *The Army of Northern Virginia in 1862* (Boston, 1892), p. 296.

64. *Official Records*, I, XII, 2, pp. 601-602.

65. McCabe, *The Grayjackets*, pp. 192-193.

66. New York *Times*, March 15, 1919.

67. Mrs. Pryor, *My Day*, p. 175.

68. Ibid.

69. Sorrel, *Recollections of a Confederate Staff Officer*, p. 104.

70. Ibid., p. 108.

71. *Official Records*, I, XXX, 2, p. 861.

72. Sorrel, *Recollections of a Confederate Staff Officer*, p. 48.

73. Walter H. Hebert, *Fighting Joe Hooker* (Indianapolis, 1944), pp. 155-159.

74. *Official Records*, I, XXL, p. 1032.

75. Ibid., I, XIX, 1, p. 712.

76. Ibid., I, XXI, p. 1017.

77. Ibid., I, XXI, p. 1036.

78. Ibid., I, XVIII, p. 145.

79. Ibid., I, LI, 2, p. 667.

80. Ibid., I, XVIII, p. 845.

81. Ibid., I, XXVII, 3, p. 874.

82. This was a word Lee used very infrequently. Generally he used such an expression as "those people."

83. *Official Records*, I, XXV, 2, p. 624.

84. Ibid., I, IX, p. 468.

85. Mrs. Pryor, *My Day*, p. 190.

86. Dunbar Rowland, editor, *Jefferson Davis, Constitutionalist, His Letters, Papers and Speeches* (Jackson, Miss., 1923), V, p. 449.

87. Richmond *Times-Dispatch*, March 15, 1919.

88. Cox, *Three Decades of Federal Legislation*, p. 92.

89. Evans, *Confederate Military*, III, p. 655.

90. Hudson Strode, *Jefferson Davis, Confederate President* (New York, 1959), p. 440.

91. Sorrel, *Recollections of a Confederate Staff Officer*, p. 63.

92. Evans, *Confederate Military History*, III, p. 655.

93. Mrs. Pryor, *My Day*, p. 191.

94. Richmond *Times-Dispatch*, March 15, 1919.

95. Mrs. Pryor, *Peace and War*, p. 241.

96. Ibid., p. 242.

97. Wise, *The End of An Era*, pp. 335, 336.

98. Mrs. Pryor, *My Day*, p. 198. Jubal Early was a Confederate general, "of a snarling, rasping disposition . . ." Sorrel, *Recollections of a Confederate Staff Officer*, p. 43.

99. Mrs. Pryor, *My Day*, p. 193.

100. John C. Stiles, "Some Confederate Officers," *Confederate Veteran*, August, 1924, Volume XXXII, #8, p. 316.

101. Walter Goerlitz, *History of the German General Staff* (New York, 1953), p. 358.

102. Edward Younger, editor, *Inside the Confederate Government. The Diary of Robert Garlick Hill Kean* (New York, 1957), p. 96.

103. Jones, *A Rebel War Clerk's Diary*, II, p. 20.

NOTES TO CHAPTER VII

1. Epes, "Roger Atkinson Pryor," p. 14.

2. Mrs. Pryor, *Peace and War*, p. 288.

3. Mrs. Pryor, *My Day*, p. 193.

4. Ibid., p. 198.

5. Watson, "Notes on Southside Virginia," p. 175.

6. Supplée, *The Life of Theodorick Bland Pryor*, p. 55.

7. *Official Records*, XXXVI, 2, p. 239.

8. Jones, *A Rebel War Clerk's Diary*, II, p. 196.

9. Ibid., II, p. 197.

10. Douglas Southall Freeman, *R.E. Lee* (New York, 1936), III, p. 275.

11. Walter Harrison, *Pickett's Men* (New York, 1870), p. 124.

12. G. T. Beauregard, "The Defence of Drewry's Bluff," *Battles and Leaders of the Civil War* (New York 1884-7), IV, p. 196.

13. Johnson Hagood, *Memoirs of the War of Secession* (Columbia, S.C., 1910), p. 221.

14. *Official Records*, I, LI, 2, p. 242.

15. Mrs. Pryor, *My Day*, p. 202.

16. Ibid., p. 237.

17. Supplée, *The Life of Theodorick Bland Pryor*, p. 59.

18. Mrs. Pryor, *My Day*, p. 210.

19. Ibid., p. 206.

20. C. Wesley Howard, *Sketch of Cobb Legion Cavalry* (n.p., n.d. [Atlanta, 1901 (?)]), p. 12.

21. Richmond *Express*, November 30, 1864, as quoted in Jones, *op. cit.*, II, p. 342. Actually, the Union Secretary of War, Stanton, was said by friends to have disapproved of the ruse by which the capture had been effected. Daniel B. Lucas, *Memoir of John Yates Beall* (Montreal, 1865), p. 56.

22. New York *Post*, November 30, 1864.

23. Mrs. Pryor, *Peace and War*, p. 307.

24. *Official Records*, I, XLII, 3, p. 721.

25. Ibid., I, XLII, 3, p. 734.

26. Ibid., I, XLII, 3, p. 739.

27. Ibid., I, XLII, 3, p. 750.

28. Ibid., I, XLII, 3, p. 753.

29. Brooklyn *Eagle*, November 29, 1864. Captain H. O. Dudly of Company C, Eleventh New Hampshire Volunteers, had ordered Pryor's capture in the belief that he was an *officer* who could have been exchanged for Captain Burrage. *Official Records*, I, XLII, 3, p. 722.

30. Mrs. Pryor, *My Day*, p. 219.

31. New York *Post*, November 30, 1864.

32. Ibid.

33. *Harper's Weekly*, September 17, 1861, p. 571.

34. Mrs. Pryor, *My Day*, p. 222.

35. Ibid., p. 223.

36. Mrs. Pryor, *Peace and War*, p. 309.

37. Roy P. Basler and others, editors, *The Collected Works of Abraham Lincoln* (New Brunswick, N.J., 1953), VIII, p. 314n.

38. *Official Records*, II, VIII, p. 191.

39. James H. McNeilly, "John Yates Beall," *Confederate Veteran*, Volume VII, #2, 1899, p. 68.

40. Allan Nevins, editor, *The Diary of George Templeton Strong* (New York, 1952), III, p. 521.

41. *Official Records*, II, VIII, p. 83.

42. McNeilly, "John Yates Beall," p. 68. "A warm friendship sprang up between Beall and Pryor, and among his dying requests he desired a memento to be presented to Gen. Pryor." Lucas, *Memory of Beall*, p. 56.

43. Mrs. Pryor, *Peace and War*, p. 312.

44. Blair Niles, *The James* (New York, 1939), p. 259.

45. Mrs. Pryor, *My Day*, p. 229.

46. Mrs. Pryor, *Peace and War*, pp. 327 and 340.

47. *The Collected Works of Abraham Lincoln*, VIII, p. 314n.

48. Ibid., p. 314.

49. Ward Hill Lamon, *Recollections of Abraham Lincoln, 1847-1865* (Washington, 1911), p. 224.

50. Ibid., p. 225.

51. *The Collected Works of Abraham Lincoln*, VIII, p. 314.

52. New York *Times*, July 20, 1915.

53. McClellan, *McClellan's Own Story*, p. 338.

54. *The Writings of Abraham Lincoln*, III, p. 1; V, p. 95.

55. New York *Times*, March 5, 1865.

56. Margaret Leech, *Reveille in Washington, 1860-1865* (New York, 1941), p. 357.

57. Forney, *Anecdotes of Public Men*, p. 38.

58. New York *Times*, March 5, 1865.

59. *Official Records*, II, VIII, p. 191.

60. Ibid., I, XLVI, 2, p. 668. At City Point also was situated the family home of the Epes family, Pryor's maternal ancestors. Mrs. Pryor, *Peace and War*, p. 136.

61. *The Collected Works of Abraham Lincoln, supra*, VIII, p. 317.

62. *Official Records*, II, VIII, p. 313. Robert Ould was the Confederate Agent of Exchange.

63. Ibid., II, VIII, p. 317.

64. Jones, *A Rebel War Clerk's Diary*, II, p. 438.

65. Mrs. Pryor, *My Day*, p. 252.

66. Wise, *End of An Era*, p. 342.

67. Mrs. Pryor, *Peace and War*, p. 350.

68. Ibid., p. 352.

69. *Official Records*, I, XLVI, 3, p. 521.

70. Mrs. Pryor, *My Day*, p. 257.

71. Ibid., p. 259.

72. Suplée, *The Life of Theodorick Bland Pryor*, p. 67.

NOTES TO CHAPTER VIII

1. Mary Tucker Magill, *Women, or, Chronicles Of The Late War* (Baltimore, 1871), p. 379.

2. Mrs. Pryor, *My Day*, p. 263.

3. Ibid., p. 265.

4. Ibid., p. 258.

5. Carl Sandburg, *Abraham Lincoln, The War Years* (New York, 1936), IV, p. 344.

6. New York *Tribune*, March 15, 1919.

7. Mrs. Pryor, *Peace and War*, p. 390.

8. Richmond *Times-Dispatch*, March 15, 1919.

9. Mrs. Pryor, *My Day*, p. 274.

10. Ibid., p. 278.

11. Ibid., p. 272.

12. *Congressional Globe*, January 28, 1861, p. 602.

13. J. T. Trowbridge, *The South: A Tour of Its Battle-Fields And Ruined Cities* (Hartford, 1866), p. 585.

14. Pollard, *The Lost Cause*, p. 743.

15. E. Merton Coulter, *The South during Reconstruction* (Baton Rouge, 1947), p. 16.

16. Paul H. Buck, *The Road to Reunion, 1865-1900* (Boston, 1937), p. 34.

17. H. J. Eckinrode and Byron Conrad, *James Longstreet. Lee's War Horse* (Chapel Hill, N.C., 1936), p. 359.

18. West Virginia.

19. Wise, *The End of an Era*, p. 462.

20. Chesnut, *A Diary from Dixie*, p. 538.

21. Myrta Lockett Avary, *Dixie after the War* (New York, 1906), p. 157.

22. Mrs. Pryor, *Peace and War*, p. 372.

23. Mrs. Pryor, *My Day*, p. 278.

24. Mrs. Pryor, *Peace and War*, p. 398.

25. New York *Times*, May 21, 1865.

26. Abbott, *Trial of Henry Ward Beecher*, p. xxiii.

27. New York *Times*, February 16, 1912.

28. New York *Tribune*, March 15, 1919.

29. Claiborne, *Seventy-five Years*, p. 93.

30. Coulter, *The South during Reconstruction, supra*, p. 187.

31. Mrs. Pryor, *My Day*, p. 280.

32. *Biographical Dictionary of the American Congress*, p. 2038.

33. Doubleday, *Reminiscences of Forts Sumter and Moultrie*, p. 98.

34. Samuel Augustus Pleasants, *Fernando Wood of New York* (New York, 1948), p. 119.

35. Ibid., p. 124.

36. *Biographical Dictionary of the American Congress*, p. 2038.

37. Denis Tilden Lynch, *"Boss" Tweed* (New York, 1927), p. 222.

38. Richmond *Times-Dispatch*, March 15, 1919.

39. Mrs. Pryor, *My Day*, p. 281.

40. Mrs. Pryor, *Peace and War*, p. 399.

41. December 12, 1865.

42. Mrs. Pryor, *My Day*, p. 282.

43. Ibid., p. 284.

44. New York *Times*, March 15, 1919.

45. Mrs. Pryor, *My Day*, p. 294.

46. Ibid., p. 284.

47. *Trow's New York City Directory 1867* (New York, 1866), p. 819.

48. *Catalogue of the Books in the Library of New York Law Institute* (New York, 1874), p. xi.

49. Mrs. Pryor, *My Day*, p. 285.
50. Ibid., p. 286.
51. Ibid., p. 294.
52. Ibid., p. 295.
53. Ibid., p. 351.
54. Mrs. Pryor, *Peace and War*, p. 403.
55. Mrs. Pryor, *My Day*, p. 291.
56. Ibid., p. 302.
57. Tyler, *Encyclopedia of Virginia Biography*, IV, p. 5.
58. New York *Times*, November 6, 1898.
59. This was part of the silver service Pryor had received in 1856 from the Democratic Party in Virginia for his work in the Know-Nothing campaign. Epes, "Roger Atkinson Pryor," p. 12.
60. Mrs. Pryor, *My Day*, p. 298.
61. Ibid., p. 300.
62. Suplée, *The Life of Theodorick Bland Pryor*, pp. 67, 69, 72.
63. Ibid., p. 78.
64. Ibid., p. 79.
65. *Trow's New York City Directory 1868* (New York, 1867), p. 835.
66. Mrs. Pryor, *My Day*, pp. 303 and 305.
67. Ibid., p. 306.
68. Ibid., p. 330.
69. G. M. Hopkins, *Atlas of The City of Brooklyn, 1880* (Philadelphia, 1880), V, Plate C.
70. Mrs. Pryor, *My Day*, p. 332.
71. Ibid., p. 343.
72. Ibid., p. 316.
73. Ibid., p. 331.
74. Claiborne, *Seventy-five Years*, p. 93.
75. Gideon Welles, *Diary* (Boston, 1911), III, pp. 172, 174
76. Mrs. Pryor, *My Day*, p. 319.
77. Ibid., p. 339.
78. Ibid., p. 399.
79. Ibid., p. 451.
80. Ibid., p. 326.
81. Suplée, *The Life of Theodorick Blend Pryor*, p. 85.
82. Mrs. Pryor, *My Day*, p. 343.
83. Suplée, *The Life of Theodorick Bland Pryor*, p. 141.
84. *United States Census 1870*, 1st Ward, Brooklyn, p. 101, Schedule 1.
85. Suplée, *The Life of Theodorick Bland Pryor*, p. 146.
86. Ibid., pp. 152 and 156.
87. Ibid., pp. 173, 175, and 177.
88. Ibid., pp. 178 and 183.
89. Ibid., pp. 184-186 and 189.

NOTES TO CHAPTER IX

1. Roger A. Pryor, *The Religious and the Secular Culture* (New York, 1873), p. 25.

2. Ibid., p. 23.

3. Ibid., p. 8.

4. *Trow's New York City Directory 1874* (New York, 1873), p. 1055.

5. See Robert S. Holzman, *Stormy Ben Butler* (New York, 1954).

6. Edward Field, editor, *State of Rhode Island and Providence Plantations at the End of the Century: A History* (Boston, 1902), III, p. 316.

7. *National Cyclopedia of American Biography* (New York, 1898), IX, p. 147.

8. David McAdam *et al.*, editors, *History of the Bench and Bar of New York* (New York, 1897), II, p. 309.

9. Edward Winslow Martin, *Behind the Scenes in Washington* (Washington, 1873), p. 206.

10. James Wilford Garner, *Reconstruction in Mississippi* (New York, 1901), p. 298.

11. Benjamin F. Butler Manuscript Collection in the Library of Congress, April 3, 1876.

12. Ibid., April 2, 1876.

13. Garner, *Reconstruction in Mississippi*, p. 405.

14. Claude Bowers, *The Tragic Era* (Boston, 1929), p. 457.

15. Abbott, *Trial of Henry Ward Beecher*, p. xxiv.

16. Ibid., p. 115.

17. Ibid., pp. 79, 85, and 86.

18. Chester L. Barrows, *William M. Evarts* (Chapel Hill, N.C., 1941), p. 287.

19. *Tilton v. Beecher*, 59 N.Y. 176 (Ct. App., 1874)

20. J. W. Donovan, *Modern Jury Trials and Advocates* (New York, 1881), p. 413.

21. Joseph S. Auerbach, *The Bar of Other Days* (New York, 1940), p. 193.

22. On July 2, after 52 ballots, the jury was discharged.

23. Donovan, *Modern Jury Trials*, p. 412.

24. Abbott, *Trial of Henry Ward Beecher*, p. xxiii. Sketches of the attorney by E. W.

25. *1875 Census, 2d Election District, First Ward*, p. 16.

26. Suplée, *The Life of Theodorick Bland Pryor*, p. 170.

27. *Patten v. The New York Elevated Railroad Company*, 3 Abbott (New Cases) 306 (Cm. Pl., 1877).

28. *Story v. The New York Elevated Railroad Company*, 90 N.Y. 122 (Ct. App., 1882).

29. *Lahr v. The Metropolitan Elevated Railway Co.*, 104 N.Y. 268 (Ct. App., 1887).

30. *New York Elevated Railroad Company v. Fifth National Bank*, 135 U.S. 432 (1890).

31. *Kennedy v. Kennedy*, 73 N.Y. 369 (Ct. App., 1878).

32. *The People ex rel. Thomas Kelly v. The Common Council of the City of Brooklyn*, 77 N.Y. 503 (Ct. App., 1879).

33. *Trow's New York City Directory 1879* (New York, 1878), p. 1179.

34. C. Vann Woodward, *Reunion and Reaction. The Compromise of 1877 and the End of Reconstruction* (Boston, 1951), p. 211.

35. Coulter, *The South during Reconstruction*, p. 376.

36. Wade Hampton of South Carolina and Governor Francis T. Nicholls of Louisiana were "Redeemers" who gave their solemn pledges in the Compromise of 1877 to protect the Negroes' rights. C. Vann Woodward, *Origins of the New South* (Baton Rouge, 1951), p. 209.

37. New York *Tribune*, April 26, 1877.

38. Mrs. Pryor, *My Day*, p. 367.

39. Brooklyn *Eagle*, May 31, 1877.

40. New York *Times*, May 31, 1877.

41. New York *Tribune*, May 31, 1877.

42. Henry R. Stiles, editor, *The Civil, Political, Professional and Ecclesiastical History and Commercial and Industrial Record of the County of Kings and the City of Brooklyn, N.Y.* (Brooklyn, 1884), II, p. 1247.

43. Brooklyn *Eagle*, May 31, 1877.

44. Quoted in New York *Times*, June 7, 1877.

45. Mrs. Pryor, *My Day*, p. 368.

46. Quoted in Mrs. Pryor, *My Day, supra*, p. 375.

47. Coulter, *The South during Reconstruction*, p. 386.

48. New York *Times*, July 19, 1908.

49. Mrs. Pryor, *My Day*, p. 351.

50. *Biographical Dictionary of the American Congress*, p. 1707.

51. Bowers, *The Tragic Era*, p. 484.

52. Freeman, *R. E. Lee*, IV, p. 202n.

53. Ibid., IV, p. 200.

54. Coulter, *The South during Reconstruction*, p. 386.

55. Freeman, *R. E. Lee*, IV, p. 381.

56. Coulter, *The South during Reconstruction*, p. 386.

57. *Congressional Record*, April 16, 1880, p. 2479.

58. Ibid., March 11, 1880, p. 1493.

59. Ibid., March 27, 1880, p. 1906.

60. New York *Times*, April 17, 1880.

61. *Congressional Record*, March 11, 1880, p. 1493.

62. Mrs. Pryor, *My Day*, p. 376.

63. *1880 Census, 2nd Enumeration District, 1st Election District of 1st Ward*, p. 64.

64. Mrs. Pryor, *My Day*, p. 371.

65. June 30, 1880.

66. New York *Tribune*, November 9, 1880.

67. Mrs. Pryor, *My Day*, p. 372.

NOTES TO CHAPTER X

1. Theodore Clarke Smith, *The Life and Letters of James Garfield* (New Haven, 1925), II, p. 1039.

2. John I. Davenport, *History of the Forged "Morey Letter"* (New York, 1884), p. 8.

3. Ibid., pp. 11 and 13.

4. Ibid., pp. 19 and 24.

5. *People v. Philp et al.*, Court of Oyer and Terminer.

6. Allan Nevins, *Grover Cleveland* (New York, 1932), p. 101.

7. New York *Tribune*, May 14, 1883.

8. *Hoyt v. Hoyt et al.*, 45 Hun 590 (S.C., 1887).

9. 112 N.Y. 493 (Ct. App., 1889).

10. *Hoyt v. Jackson*, 3 Demarest 388 (N.Y. County Surrogate's Court, 1885).

11. Butler Manuscript, December 27, 1881.

12. James Wilton Brooks, *History of the Court of Common Pleas* (New York, 1896), p. 128.

13. Butler Manuscript, January 31, 1884.

14. P. J. P. Tynan, *The Irish National Invincibles* (New York, 1894), p. 402.

15. John Adye Curran, *Reminiscences* (New York, 1915), p. 193.

16. Justin McCarthy, *Ireland Since The Union* (London, 1887), p. 323.

17. Ibid., p. 274.

18. Mrs. Pryor, *My Day*, p. 387.

19. New York *Times*, November 8, 1883.

20. Mrs. Pryor, *My Day*, p. 384.

21. Ibid., p. 385.

22. Ibid., p. 387.

23. Ibid., p. 388.

24. McCarthy, *Ireland*, p. 274.

25. Mrs. Pryor, *My Day*, p. 388.

26. Mrs. Pryor, *Peace and War*, p. 340.

27. Cox, *Three Decades of Federal Legislation*, p. 92.

28. Stiles, *The Civil, Political, Professional and Ecclesiastical History*, II, p. 1247.

29. August 9, 1884.

30. *Harper's Weekly*, July 5, 1884, p. 443. Actually, Boss Kelly preferred Benjamin F. Butler, the Anti-Monopoly candidate. DeAlva Stanwood Alexander, *Four Famous New Yorkers* (New York, 1923), p. 42.

31. *Trow's New York City Directory 1886* (New York, 1885), p. 1554.

32. Mrs. Pryor, *My Day*, p. 394.

33. New York *Times*, February 26, 1886.

34. Henry Collins Brown, editor, *Valentine's Manual of Old New York. 1927* (New York, 1926), p. 90.

35. McAdam, *History of the Bench and Bar*, I, p. 324.

36. New York *Herald*, March 2, 1886.

37. Ibid., March 6, 1886.

38. Ibid., February 26, 1886.

39. Ibid., March 2, 1886.

40. Ibid.

41. New York *Herald*, March 4, 1886.

42. Brown, *Valentine's Manual*, p. 90.

43. New York *Herald*, March 6, 1886.

44. Ibid.

45. Brown, *Valentine's Manual*, p. 92.

46. New York *Tribune*, May 14, 1893.

47. Ibid., May 4, 1886.

48. *Spies et al. v. People*, 12 Northeastern Reports. 865 (Ill. S.C., 1887).

49. Michael J. Schaack, *Anarchy and Anarchists* (Chicago, 1889), p. 620.

50. Geo. N. McLean, *The Rise and Fall of Anarchy in America* (Chicago, 1883), p. 200.

51. *Commonwealth*, October 15, 1887, Volume 3, #92, p. 331.

52. Alan Calmer, *Labor Agitator. The Story of Albert R. Parsons* (New York, 1937), p. 115.

53. Henry David, *The History Of The Haymarket Affair* (New York, 1936), p. 380.

54. Ibid., p. 382.

55. He was referring to his military occupation of New Orleans in 1862. See Holzman, *Stormy Ben Butler, supra.*

56. McLean, *Rise and Fall of Anarchy*, p. 205.

57. *Spies v. Illinois*, 123 U.S. 131 (1887).

58. Calmar, *Labor Agitator*, p. 114.

NOTES TO CHAPTER XI

1. Brooks, *History of the Court of Common Pleas*, p. 129.
2. Mrs. Pryor, *My Day*, p. 447.
3. Ibid., p. 407.
4. Epes, "Roger Atkinson Pryor", p. 15.
5. Mrs. Pryor, *My Day*, p. 447.
6. Pryor, *Essays and Addresses*, p. 51.
7. Justin McCarthy, Rossiter Johnson, and Albert Ellery Bergh, editors, *Modern Eloquence* (Philadelphia, 1900), III, p. 959.
8. Ibid., III, p. 962.
9. New York *Tribune*, February 20, 1889.
10. *Who's Who in New York 1918* (New York, 1918), p. 876.
11. Notable Virginia Bar Addresses (Charlottesville, Va., 1938), p. 266.
12. Mrs. Pryor, *My Day*, p. 450.
13. Pryor, *Essays and Addresses*, p. 85.
14. New York *Herald*, March 17, 1889.
15. March 18, 1889.
16. Mrs. Pryor, *My Day*, p. 392.
17. *Official Records*, II, VIII, p. 191.
18. Mrs. Pryor, *My Day*, p. 380.
19. Ibid., p. 377.
20. Ibid., p. 401.
21. New York *Times*, May 31, 1877.
22. *Who's Who in America 1903-1905* (Chicago, 1903), p. 1201.
23. Turner, *Old Homes and Families in Nottoway, supra*, p. 58.
24. Allan Nevins, *John D. Rockefeller* (New York, 1941), II, p. 118.
25. New York *Herald*, February 28, 1888.
26. Ibid.
27. New York *Herald*, March 1, 1888.
28. New York *Times*, March 15, 1919.
29. Pryor, *Essays and Addresses, supra*, p. 151.
30. 54 Hun 354 (S.C., 1889).
31. Pryor, *Essays and Addresses*, p. 156.
32. Ibid., p. 160.
33. Ibid., 194.
34. Ibid., p. 244.
35. 121 N.Y. 582 (Ct. App., 1890).
36. New York *Times*, September 21, 1890.
37. Roger A. Pryor, *The Foundations of Professional Success* (Chicago, 1911), p. 4.
38. Alfred Henry Lewis, *Richard Croker* (New York, 1901), p. 292.
39. New York *Sun*, March 15, 1919.
40. New York *Times*, September 21, 1890.
41. September 21, 1890.

42. New York *Times*, October 2, 1890.
43. John Russell Young, *Men and Memories* (New York, 1901), p. 326.
44. Brooks, *History of the Court of Common Pleas*, p. 128.
45. Mrs. Pryor, *My Day*, p. 450.
46. Epes, "Roger Atkinson Pryor," p. 17.

NOTES TO CHAPTER XII

1. *In re Blakeslee*, 11 N.Y.S. 950 (Cm. Pl., 1890).
2. *Brush et al. v. Manhattan Railway Company and The Metropolitan Elevated Railway Company*, 13 N.Y.S. 908 (Cm. Pl., 1890).
3. *Bernheimer et al. v. Manhattan Railway Company*, 13 N.Y.S. 913 (Cm. Pl., 1890).
4. Epes, "Roger Atkinson Pryor," p. 15.
5. Mrs. Pryor, *My Day*, p. 450.
6. New York *Sun*, March 15, 1919.
7. Epes, "Roger Atkinson Pryor," p. 10.
8. New York *Tribune*, October 13, 1891.
9. Epes, "Roger Atkinson Pryor," p. 16.
10. New York *Tribune*, May 14, 1893.
11. Constitution of 1895, Article 6, Section 5.
12. New York *Tribune*, February 10, 1896.
13. *Hurwitz v. Hurwitz et al.*, 31 N.Y.S. 25 (Cm. Pl., 1894). One is reminded of a song by a lawyer-librettist of that period:

> "In the reign of James the Second,
> It was generally reckoned
> As a very serious crime . . ."
> William S. Gilbert, *Trial by Jury*

14. *Watson v. Russell*, 28 N.Y.S. 26 (Cm. Pl., 1894).
15. *Tallman v. Earle*, 13 N.Y.S. 805 (Cm. Pl., 1891).
16. *Fromme et al. v. Gray*, 36 N.Y.S. 1107 (Cm Pl., 1895).
17. *Brown v. Baldwin & Gleason Company, Limited*, 13 N.Y.S. 893 (Cm. Pl., 1891).
18. *Hoey v. Gilroy*, 14 N.Y.S. 159 (Cm. Pl., 1891).
19. *Hasbrouck v. Stokes et al.*, 13 N.Y.S. 333 (Cm. Pl., 1891).
20. *Powell v. Flechter*, 18 N.Y.S. 451 (Cm. Pl., 1892).
21. *Fahr v. Manhattan Railway Company*, 29 N.Y.S. 1 (Cm. Pl., 1894).

22. *Hawes v. Gas Consumers' Benefit Company*, 12 N.Y.S. 924 (Cm. Pl., 1891).

23. *Walter et al. v. Rafel et al.*, 28 N.Y.S. 10 (Cm. Pl., 1894).

24. *Vanderpool v. Gorman*, 22 N.Y.S. 541 (Cm. Pl., 1893).

25. *Kruse v. Seeger & Guernsey Company*, 16 N.Y.S. 529 (Cm. Pl., 1891).

26. *Millie v. Manhattan Railway Company*, 25 N.Y.S. 753 (Cm. Pl., 1893).

27. New York *Tribune*, May 14, 1893.

28. *Hardegg v. Willards*, 33 N.Y.S. 25 (Cm. Pl., 1895).

29. *Clark v. Andrews et al.*, 19 N.Y.S. 211 (Cm. Pl., 1892).

30. *Di Messiah v. Gern*, 30 N.Y.S. 824 (Cm. Pl., 1894).

31. *Hoey v. Gilroy*, 14 N.Y.S. 159 (Cm. Pl., 1891).

32. *Kirk et al. v. McCusker*, 22 N.Y.S. 780 (Cm. Pl., 1893).

33. *Davis v. Davis*, 22 N.Y.S. 191 (Cm. Pl., 1893).

34. *Bernard v. United Life Insurance Association*, 33 N.Y.S. 22 (Cm. Pl., 1895).

35. *Levy v. Schreyer*, 43 N.Y.S. 199 (S.C., 1897).

36. *Morris v. Barrisford*, 29 N.Y.S. 17 (Cm. Pl., 1894).

37. *Knarr v. Bates et al.*, 35 N.Y.S. 1060 (Cm. Pl., 1895).

38. *Lechowitzer v. Hamburg-American Packet Co.*, 28 N.Y.S. 577 (Cm. Pl., 1894).

39. *Mayor, etc., of the City of New York v. Bigelow*, 34 N.Y.S. 92 (Cm. Pl., 1895).

40. *Kiernan v. Metropolitan Life Insurance Co.*, 34 N.Y.S. 95 (Cm. Pl., 1895).

41. *Frankfort v. Manhattan Railway Company*, 33 N.Y.S. 36 (Cm. Pl., 1895).

42. *Bernheimer et al. v. Manhattan Railway Company*, 13 N.Y.S. 913 (Cm. Pl., 1890).

43. *Mead et al. v. Hartwell et al.*, 31 N.Y.S. 674 (Cm. Pl., 1895).

44. *Yale et al. v. Dart et al.*, 13 N.Y.S. 277 (Cm. Pl., 1891).

45. *People ex rel. Claussen v. Murray et al.*, 38 N.Y.S. 609 (S.C., 1896). Judge Pryor had handed down a similar decision in *People ex rel. Gentilesco v. Board of Excise Commissioners*, 27 N.Y.S. 983 (Cm. Pl., 1894).

46. *Cantor v. Tattersall's of New York, Limited*, 34 N.Y.S. 96 (Cm. Pl., 1895).

47. *Jung v. Keuffel et al.*, 32 N.Y.S. 1136 (Cm. Pl., 1895).

48. *Garvey v. United States Horse & Cattle Show Society*, 38 N.Y.S. 171 (Cm. Pl., 1895).

49. *Wallach v. Manhattan Railroad Company et al.*, 28 N.Y.S. 483 (Cm. Pl., 1894).

NOTES TO CHAPTER XIII

1. *Bondy et al. v. Collier*, 33 N.Y.S. 996 (Cm. Pl., 1895).
2. *In re The Agudath Hakehiloth of New York*, 42 N.Y.S. 985 (S.C., 1896).
3. New York *Times*, December 29, 1896.
4. December 28, 1896.
5. *Fromme et al. v. Gray*, 36 N.Y.S. 1107 (Cm. Pl., 1895).
6. *Nevada National Bank et al. v. Cregan et al.*, 40 N.Y.S. 1065 (S.C., 1896).
7. *People ex rel. Devery v. Martin et al.*, 33 N.Y.S. 1000 (Cm. Pl., 1895).
8. *People ex rel. Glennon v. Martin et al.*, 33 N.Y.S. 1007 (Cm. Pl., 1895).
9. *Gidion v. Dwyer*, 40 N.Y.S. 1053 (S.C., 1896).
10. *Helwig v. Second Avenue Railroad Company*, 29 N.Y.S. 9 (Cm. Pl., 1894).
11. *Ames et al. v. McNally*, 26 N.Y.S. 7 (Cm. Pl., 1893).
12. *Myers v. Dean*, 31 N.Y.S. 119 (Cm. Pl., 1894).
13. *Bidwell et al. v. Overton*, 13 N.Y.S. 274 (Cm. Pl., 1891).
14. *In re Elias et al.*, 40 N.Y.S. 910 (S.C., 1896).
15. *Sternback v. Friedman et al.*, 50 N.Y.S. 1025 (S.C., 1898).
16. *Anderson v. Manhattan Railway Company*, 21 N.Y.S. 1 (Cm. Pl., 1892).
17. *Helwig v. Second Avenue Railroad Company*, 29 N.Y.S. 9 (Cm. Pl., 1894).
18. *Karger v. Karger*, 44 N.Y.S. 220 (S.C., 1897).
19. *Perry v. Perry*, 39 N.Y.S. 863 (S.C., 1896).
20. *Fanning v. Fanning*, 20 N.Y.S. 849 (Cm. Pl., 1892).
21. *Shrady v. Logan*, 40 N.Y.S. 1010 (S.C., 1896).
22. *Vincent v. Vincent*, 17 N.Y.S. 497 (Cm. Pl., 1891).
23. *Di Messiah v. Gern*, 30 N.Y.S. 824 (Cm. Pl., 1894).
24. New York *World*, December 24, 1898.
25. New York *Sun*, March 15, 1919.
26. New York *World*, December 24, 1898.
27. *Dignan v. Dignan*, 40 N.Y.S. 320 (S.C., 1896).
28. *Keegan v. Sage*, 25 N.Y.S. 78 (Cm. Pl., 1893).
29. *Irving v. Britton*, 28 N.Y.S. 529 (Cm. Pl., 1894).
30. *Health Department of the City of New York v. Rector, Church-Wardens, and Vestrymen of Trinity Church*, 17 N.Y.S. 510 (Cm. Pl., 1892).
31. New York *World*, December 24, 1898.
32. Mrs. Pryor, *My Day*, p. 453.
33. New York *Sun*, March 15, 1919.
34. *Dumois et al. v. Hill et al.*, 37 N.Y.S. 1093 (S.C., App. Div., 1896).
35. New York *Law Journal*, March 18, 1919.
36. Pryor, *Essays and Addresses*, p. 92.

37. Ibid., p. 117.
38. New York *Tribune*, December 11, 1898.
39. Ibid., December 24, 1898.
40. New York *World*, December 24, 1898.
41. New York *Post*, March 15, 1919.
42. New York *World*, December 24, 1898.

NOTES TO CHAPTER XIV

1. Tyler, *Encyclopedia of Virginia Biography*, IV, p. 5.
2. *National Cyclopedia of American Biography*, XXXVIII, p. 202.
3. *Catalogue of the Sale of Paintings and Drawings Owned By William de Leftwich Dodge, February 23, 1897* (New York, 1897).
4. New York *Times*, April 1, 1897.
5. New York *Tribune*, April 1, 1897.
6. New York *Times*, April 1, 1897.
7. This letter is now owned by Mrs. Hunter Kimbrough, the daughter of Fanny Pryor Dodge, who graciously permitted its use here.
8. New York *Tribune*, November 9, 1898.
9. Epes, "Roger Atkinson Pryor," p. 12.
10. New York *Tribune*, December 25, 1898.
11. Grace Mayer, *Story Of A City* (New York, 1958), p. 354.
12. *Who's Who in America 1910-1911* (Chicago, 1910), p. 1556.
13. *Who's Who in New York 1909* (New York, 1908), p. 1068.
14. Mrs. Pryor, *My Day*, p. 421.
15. *Confederate Veteran*, November, 1920, Volume XXVIII, #11, p. 421.
16. July 1905, Volume X, #4, p. 925.
17. Mrs. Pickett, *Across My Path*, p. 142.
18. Mrs. Roger A. Pryor, *The Mother of Washington and Her Times* (New York, 1903).
19. Roger A. Pryor, *Essays and Addresses*.
20. Mrs. Roger A. Pryor, *The Birth Of The Nation. Jamestown, 1607* (New York, 1907).
21. New York *Times*, June 27, 1902.
22. Ibid., June 28, 1902.
23. New York *Tribune*, April 15, 1899.
24. Matthew P. Breen, *Thirty Years of New York Politics* (New York, 1899), p. 814.
25. New York *Tribune*, April 15, 1899.

26. *Who's Who in America 1903-1905* (Chicago, 1903), p. 1201.

27. Mrs. Pryor, *Peace and War.*

28. Mrs. Pryor, *My Day.*

29.New York *Tribune*, March 23, 1902.

30. *Confederate Veteran*, August, 1906, #18, p. 322.

31. D. C. Kelley, "Gen. Robert Hatton," *Confederate Veteran*, 1899, Volume VII, No. 12, p. 554.

32. New York *Times*, July 19, 1908.

33. *Loc. cit.*

34. New York *Sun*, March 15, 1919.

35. Unpaged pamphlet, *To General and Mrs. Roger A. Pryor.*

36. At the Democratic National Convention in Charleston, South Carolina, in June, 1860, Massachusetts Delegate Benjamin F. Butler had voted forty-three times for Jefferson Davis of Mississippi for the presidential nominee. Holzman, *Stormy Ben Butler*, p. 24.

37. New York *Times*, July 19, 1908.

38. New York *Herald*, March 15, 1919.

39. New York *Times*, July 19, 1908.

40. Hardy, "Some Virginia Lawyers," p. 161.

41. Minutes of the Board of Directors, December 7, 1909.

42. This letter was supplied to the author by Mrs. Hunter Kimbrough, Pryor's granddaughter.

43. *Who's Who in New York 1918* (New York, 1918), p. 876.

44. This certificate was furnished to the author by Mrs. Hunter Kimbrough.

45. Brooks, *History of the Court of Common Pleas*, p. 129.

46. New York *Sun*, March 31, 1919.

47. Roger A. Pryor, *Essays and Addresses*, unnumbered page (actual p. 5).

48. New York *Times*, February 16, 1912.

49. New York *Law Journal*, March 18, 1919.

50. New York *Times*, March 15, 1919.

51. Mrs. Pryor, *My Day*, p. 399.

52. New York *Times*, February 16, 1912.

53. September 10, 1912. The letter was supplied to the author by the addressee, now Mrs. Hunter Kimbrough.

54. Letter supplied by Sara Dodge Kimbrough.

55. Ibid.

56. *Who's Who in New York 1918* (New York, 1918), p. 876.

57. New York *Times*, July 20, 1915.

58. New York *Times*, April 19, 1914.

59. New York *Times*, July 20, 1915.

60. A separate treaty of peace was signed at Brest-Litovsk on March 3, 1918.

61. New York *Times*, July 20, 1915.

62. New York *Times*, July 25, 1915.
63. Holograph letter dated October 9, 1914, now owned by the author.
64. *The Writings of Abraham Lincoln*, VII, p. 331.
65. New York *Times*, July 20, 1915.
66. New York *Sun*, March 15, 1919.
67. Richmond *Times-Dispatch*, March 15, 1919.
68. New York *Herald*, March 15, 1919.
69. New York *Times*, April 2, 1919.
70. New York *Law Journal*, March 18, 1919.
71. Ibid.
72. Ibid.
73. New York *Sun*, March 15, 1919.
74. Brooklyn *Eagle*, March 15, 1919.
75. Epes, "Roger Atkinson Pryor," p. 17.
76. Mrs. Pryor, *My Day*, p. 453.

NOTES TO CHAPTER XV

1. Mrs. Pryor, *My Day*, p. 299.
2. Ibid., p. 284.
3. Ibid., p. 285.
4. Ibid., p. 294.
5. Ibid., p. 334.
6. *Congressional Globe*, January 28, 1861, p. 602.
7. New York *Times*, July 19, 1908.
8. Mrs. Pryor, *Peace and War*, page 242.
9. New York *Times*, May 21, 1865.
10. Abbott, *Trial of Henry Ward Beecher*, p. xxiii.
11. Mrs. Pryor, *My Day*, p. 326.
12. New York *Tribune*, March 15, 1919.
13. Ibid., June 30, 1880.
14. Benjamin F. Butler Manuscript, April 3, 1876.
15. New York *Herald*, February 28, 1888.
16. New York *Times*, April 1, 1897.
17. McClellan, *McClellan's Own Story*, p. 338.
18. New York *Times*, March 15, 1919.
19. Lamon, *Recollections of Abraham Lincoln*, p. 225.
20. Mrs. Pryor, *My Day*, p. 298.
21. New York *World*, December 24, 1898.

22. New York *Times*, July 20, 1915.
23. McCabe, *The Grayjackets*, p. 193.
24. Mrs. Pryor, *My Day*, p. 389.
25. New York *Sun*, March 15, 1919.
26. Mrs. Pryor, *My Day*, p. 352.

Bibliography

MANUSCRIPT SOURCES

The Library of Congress in Washington possesses the Benjamin F. Butler Manuscript, consisting of letters and other material, arranged chronologically in manuscript boxes. Included are letters from Pryor to Butler.

The original United States Census Reports for Brooklyn in 1870, 1875, and 1880 were examined in the Kings County Court House.

OFFICIAL PUBLICATIONS

The *Official Records of the War of the Rebellion* was published by the Government Printing Office in Washington between 1880 and 1901. This work consists of 128 volumes. It is comprised primarily of dispatches and orders of the commanders and other officers in the field.

Substantial reference has been made to the published reports of New York cases in which Pryor participated as attorney or judge. Reference also has been made to the United States and Illinois reports of the courts.

Considerable material on the verbatim transcripts of debates in the House of Representatives was obtained from the *Congressional Globe* for the Thirty-sixth Congress. The *Congressional Record* was used for certain later periods.

[193]

NEWSPAPERS

Frequent reference was made to contemporary newspapers, as mentioned in footnotes in the text. Contemporary national weeklies were utilized, as indicated in the footnotes.

BOOKS AND ARTICLES

Abbott, Austin, editor, *Official Report of the Trial of Henry Ward Beecher*. New York, 1875.

Alden, John Richard, *The First South*. Baton Rouge, La., 1961.

Allan, William, *The Army of Northern Virginia in 1862*. Boston, 1892.

Ambler, Charles Henry, *Sectionalism in Virginia From 1776 to 1861*. Chicago, 1910.

Appleton's Cyclopedia of American Biography. New York, 1900.

Auerbach, Joseph S., *The Bar of Other Days*. New York, 1940.

Avary, Myrta Lockett, *Dixie after the War*. New York, 1906.

Barnwell, William H., *The Impiety and Absurdity of Duelling*. Charleston, 1844.

Barrows, Chester L., *William M. Evarts*. Chapel Hill, N.C., 1941.

Beauregard, G. T., "The Campaign of Shiloh." Clarence C. Buel and Robert Underwood Johnson, editors, *Battles and Leaders of the Civil War*. New York, 1887.

————, "The Defence of Drewry's Bluff." Same source as the preceding item.

Bill, Alfred Hoyt, *The Beleaguered City*. New York, 1946.

Biographical Dictionary of the American Congress. Washington, 1950.

Blaine, James G., *Twenty Years of Congress*. Norwich, Conn., 1884.

Botts, John Minor, *The Great Rebellion: Its Secret History, Rise, Progress, and Disastrous Failure*. New York, 1866.

Bowers, Claude, *The Tragic Era*. Boston, 1929.

Breen, Matthew P., *Thirty Years of New York Politics*. New York, 1899.

Brooks, James Wilton, *History of the Court of Common Pleas*. New York, 1896.

Brown, Henry Collins, editor, *Valentine's Manual of Old New York*. *1927*. New York, 1926.

The Brown Book, 1919. New York, 1919.

Buck, Paul H., *The Road to Reunion, 1865-1900.* Boston, 1937.

Cairnes, J. E., *The Slave Power: Its Character, Career and Probable Designs.* London, 1863.

Calmer, Alan, *Labor Agitator. The Story of Albert L. Parsons.* New York, 1937.

Campbell, Mrs. A. A., in *Confederate Veteran,* November 1920, XXVIII, 421.

Cappon, Lester J., *Virginia Newspapers, 1821-1935.* New York, 1936.

Carpenter, Jesse T., *The South as a Conscious Minority, 1789-1861.* New York, 1930.

Chesnut, Mary Boykin, *A Diary from Dixie.* Boston, 1949.

Chester, James, "Inside Sumter in '61." Clarence C. Buel and Robert Underwood Johnson, editors, *Battles and Leaders of the Civil War.* New York, 1887.

Chisholm, A. R., "Notes on the Surrender of Fort Sumter." Same source as the preceding item.

Claiborne, John Herbert, *Seventy-five Years in Old Virginia.* New York, 1904.

Cole, Arthur C., "Lincoln's Election an Immediate Menace to Slavery in the States?" *American Historical Review,* July 1931, XXXVI, 740.

Commonwealth, October 15, 1887, III, 331.

Conkling, Alfred R., *The Life and Letters of Roscoe Conkling.* New York, 1889.

Coulter, E. Merton, *The Confederate States of America, 1861-1865.* Baton Rouge, 1950.

———, *The South during Reconstruction.* Baton Rouge, 1947.

Cox, Samuel S., *Three Decades of Federal Legislation.* Providence, 1885.

Craven, Avery, *The Coming of the Civil War.* New York, 1950.

———, *The Growth of Southern Nationalism, 1848-1861.* Baton Rouge, 1953.

———, *Edmund Ruffin, Southerner.* New York, 1932.

Crawford, Samuel Wylie, *The Genesis of the Civil War.* New York, 1887.

Crenshaw, Ollinger, *The Slave States in the Presidential Election of 1860.* Baltimore, 1945.

[195]

Curran, John Adye, *Reminiscences*. New York, 1915.

David, Henry, *The History of the Haymarket Affair*. New York, 1936.

Desmond, Humphrey J., *The Know-Nothing Party*. Washington, 1904.

Dictionary of American Biography. New York, 1928.

Dodd, William E., *Statesmen of the Old South*. New York, 1911.

Dodge, William de Leftwich, *Catalogue of Sale of Art*. New York, 1897.

Donovan, J. W., *Modern Jury Trials and Advocates*. New York, 1881.

Doubleday, Abner, *Reminiscences of Forts Sumter and Moultrie in 1860-'61*. New York, 1876.

Du Bose, John Witherspoon, *The Life and Times of William Lowndes Yancey*. Birmingham, Ala., 1892.

Eaton, Clement, "Henry A. Wise and the Virginia Fire Eaters of 1856." *Mississippi Valley Historical Review*, March 1935, XXI, 495.

Eckinrode, H. J. and Conrad, Byron, *James Longstreet. Lee's War Horse*. Chapel Hill, N.C., 1936.

Epes, T. P., "Roger Atkinson Pryor, LL.D." *Kaleidoscope*. 1903, XI, 9.

Evans, Clement, editor, *Confederate Military History*. Atlanta, 1899.

Field, Edward, editor, *State of Rhode Island and Providence Plantations at the End of the Century: A History*. Boston, 1902.

Fite, Emerson David, *The Presidential Campaign of 1860*. New York, 1911.

Forney, John W., *Anecdotes of Public Men*. New York, 1873.

Freeman, Douglas Southall, *R. E. Lee*. New York, 1936.

———, *Lee's Lieutenants*. New York, 1944.

Fremantle, Arthur, *Three Months in the Southern States*. New York, 1864.

Fuller, J. F. C., *Decisive Battles of the U. S. A.* New York, 1953.

Garner, James Wilford, *Reconstruction in Mississippi*. New York, 1901.

Goerlitz, Walter, *History of the German General Staff*. New York, 1953.

Greeley, Horace, *The American Conflict*. Hartford, Conn., 1864.

Hagood, Johnson, *Memoirs of the War of Secession*. Columbia, S.C., 1910.

Hallum, John, *The Diary of an Old Lawyer*. Nashville, 1895.

Halsey, Ashley, Jr., "South Carolina Began Preparing for War in 1851." *Civil War Times Illustrated*, April 1962, I, 8.

———, "Who Fired the First Shot?" *The Saturday Evening Post*, December 17, 1960, CCXXXIII, 22.

Halstead, M., *Caucuses of 1860.* Columbus, 1860.

Hamilton, J. G. de Roulhac, "Lincoln's Election an Immediate Menace to Slavery in the States?" *American Historical Review*, July 1932, XXXVII, 700.

Hardy, Sallie E. Marshall, "Some Virginia Lawyers of the Past and Present." *The Green Bag*, 1898, X, 149.

Harris, Alexander, *A Review of the Political Conflict in America.* New York, 1876.

Harrison, Walter, *Pickett's Men.* New York, 1870.

Hebert, Walter H., *Fighting Joe Hooker.* Indianapolis, 1944.

Hendrick, Burton J., *The Lees of Virginia.* Boston, 1935.

———, *Lincoln's War Cabinet.* Boston, 1946.

Hill, Frederick Trevor, *Decisive Battles of the Law.* New York, 1907.

Hilliard, Henry W., *Politics and Pen Pictures.* New York, 1892.

Holt, Henry, *Garrulities of an Octogenerian Editor*, Boston, 1923.

Holzman, Robert S., *Stormy Ben Butler.* New York, 1954.

Howard, C. Wesley, *Sketch of Cobb Legion Cavalry* (n.p., n.d. [Atlanta 1901 (?)]).

Hopkins, G. M. *Atlas of the City of Brooklyn, 1880.* Philadelphia, 1880.

Jones, J. B., *A Rebel War Clerk's Diary.* Philadelphia, 1866.

Kelley, D. C., "Gen. Robert Hatton." *Confederate Veteran*, 1899, VII, 554.

Kelly, Alfred H. and Harbison, Winfred A., *The American Constitution.* New York, 1948.

Lamon, Ward Hill, *Recollections of Abraham Lincoln, 1847-1865.* Chicago, 1895.

Lee, Cazenove Gardner, Jr., *Lee Chronicle.* New York, 1957.

Lee, Stephen D., "The First Step in the War." Clarence C. Buel and Robert Underwood Johnson, editors, *Battles and Leaders of the Civil War.* New York, 1887.

Leech, Margaret, *Reveille in Washington. 1860-1885.* New York, 1941.

Lewis, Alfred Henry, *Richard Croker.* New York, 1901.

Lincoln, Abraham, *The Collected Works of Abraham Lincoln*. Roy P. Basler and others, editors, New Brunswick, N.J., 1953.

Lincoln, Abraham, *The Writings of Abraham Lincoln*. Arthur Brooks Lapsley, editor. New York, 1906.

Lucas, Daniel B., *Memoir of John Yates Beall*. Montreal, 1865.

Lutz, Ralph Haswell, "Rudolf Schleiden and The Visit to Richmond, April 25, 1861." *Annual Report of the American Historical Association for the Year 1915.* Washington, 1917.

Lynch, Denis Tilden, *"Boss" Tweed.* New York, 1927.

Magill, Mary Tucker, *Women, or, Chronicles of the Late War.* Baltimore, 1871.

Martin, Edward Winslow, *Behind the Scenes in Washington.* Washington, 1873.

McAdam, Davis and others, editors, *History of the Bench and Bar of New York.* New York, 1897.

[McCabe, James D., Jr.], *The Grayjackets: And How They Lived, Fought and Died for Dixie.* Richmond, 1867.

McCarthy, Justin, *Ireland since the Union.* London, 1887.

McCarthy, Justin; Johnson, Rossiter; and Bergh, Albert Ellery, associate editors, *Modern Eloquence.* Philadelphia, 1900.

McClellan, George B., *McClellan's Own Story.* New York, 1887.

McLean, Geo. N., *The Rise and Fall of Anarchy in America*, Chicago, 1883.

McMaster, John Bach, *A History of the United States during Lincoln's Administration.* New York, 1927.

McNeilly, James H., "John Yates Beall." *Confederate Veteran*, 1899, VII, 66.

Michie, Thomas J., "John Barbee Minor." *The Green Bag*, 1895, VII, 401.

Miller, Alphone B., *Thaddeus Stevens.* New York, 1939.

Milton, George Fort, *The Eve of Conflict.* Boston, 1934.

Mitchell, Joseph B., *Decisive Battles of the Civil War.* New York, 1955.

Monteiro, Margaret Kean, "The Presidential Election of 1860 in Virginia." *Richmond College Historical Papers*, June 1916, I, 222.

Moore, Frank, editor, *The Rebellion Record.* Washington, 1862-71.

Morgan, C. H., *Reminiscences of the War of 1861-5.* Lynchburg, Va., 1911.

National Cyclopedia of American Biography. New York, 1898.

Nevins, Allan, *The Emergence of Lincoln.* New York, 1950.

———, *Grover Cleveland; A Study in Courage.* New York, 1932.

———, *John D. Rockefeller.* New York, 1941.

New York Law Institute, *Catalogue of the Books in the Library of,* New York, 1874.

Nichols, Roy Franklin, *Franklin Pierce.* Philadelphia, 1931.

Niles, Blair, *The James.* New York, 1939.

Notable Virginia Bar Addresses. Charlottesville, Va., 1938.

Paine, Albert Bigelow, *Th. Nast, His Period and His Pictures.* New York, 1904.

Patterson, A. W., *The Code Duello, with special Reference to the State of Virginia.* Richmond, 1927.

Pickett, La Salle Corbell, *Across My Path.* New York, 1916.

———, *The Heart of a Soldier.* New York, 1913.

Pleasants, Samuel Augustus, *Fernando Wood of New York.* New York, 1948.

Pollard, Edward A., *The First Year of the War.* New York, 1864.

———, *The Lost Cause.* New York, 1867.

Poore, Ben: Perley, *Perley's Reminscences of Sixty Years in the National Metropolis.* Philadelphia, 1886.

Porter, David D., *Incidents and Anecdotes of the Civil War.* New York, 1885.

"Proceedings of First Confederate Congress—First Session." *Southern Historical Society Papers,* June 1923, New Series, VI, 46.

Pryor, Roger A., *Essays and Addresses.* New York, 1912.

———, *The Foundations of Professional Success.* Chicago, 1911.

———, *The Religious and The Secular Culture.* New York, 1873.

Pryor, Mrs. Roger, *The Birth of the Nation. Jamestown, 1607.* New York, 1907.

———, *The Mother of Washington and Her Times.* New York, 1903.

———, *My Day. Reminiscences of a Long Life.* New York, 1909.

———, *Reminiscences of Peace and War.* New York, 1908.

Randall, J. G., *The Civil War and Reconstruction.* Boston, 1937.

Rice, Philip Morrison, "The Know-Nothing Party in Virginia." *The Virginia Magazine of History and Biography,* January 1947, LV, 61.

Roman, Alfred, *The Military Operations of General Beauregard*. New York, 1884.

Rowland, Dunbar, editor, *Jefferson Davis, Constitutionalist, His Letters, Papers and Speeches*. Jackson, Miss., 1923.

Sandburg, Carl, *Abraham Lincoln, the War Years*. New York, 1936.

Schaack, Michael J., *Anarchy and Anarchists*. Chicago, 1889.

Schurz, Carl, *The Reminiscences of Carl Schurz*. New York, 1907.

Shanks, Henry T., *The Secession Movement in Virginia, 1847-1861*. Richmond, 1934.

Sherman, John, *Recollections of Forty Years in The House, Senate and Cabinet*. Chicago, 1895.

Sherman, William T., *Memoirs*. New York, 1889.

Smith, D. E. Huger, *A Charlestonian's Recollections, 1846-1913*. Charleston, 1950.

Sorrel, G. Moxley, *Recollections of a Confederate Staff Officer*. Jackson, Tenn., 1958.

Stephens, Alexander H., *A Constitutional View of the Late War Between The States; Its Causes, Character, Conduct and Results*. Philadelphia, 1870.

Stephenson, Nathaniel W., *The Day of the Confederacy*. New Haven, 1920.

Stevens, Frank E., "Life of Stephen Arnold Douglas." *Journal of the Illinois State Historical Society*, October 1923-January 1924, XVI, 247.

Stiles, Henry R., editor, *The Civil, Political, Professional and Ecclesiastical History and Commercial and Industrial Records of the County of Kings and the City of Brooklyn, N.Y.* Brooklyn, 1884.

Strode, Hudson, *Jefferson Davis, Confederate President*. New York, 1959.

Strong, George Templeton, *The Diary of George Templeton Strong*. New York, 1952.

Suplée, Thomas D., *The Life of Theodorick Bland Pryor*. San Francisco, 1879.

Trow's New York City Directory . . . New York, 1867-1898.

Trowbridge, J. T., *The South: A Tour of Its Battle-Fields and Ruined Cities*. Hartford, 1866.

Turner, W. R., *Old Homes and Families in Nottoway*. Blackstone, Va., 1932.

———, "Some Early Nottoway County History." *The Virginia Magazine of History And Biography*, July 1937, XLV, 260.

Tyler, Lyon Gardiner, editor, *Encyclopedia of Virginia Biography*. New York, 1915.

Tynan, P. J. P., *The Irish Invincibles*. New York, 1894.

Villard, Oswald Garrison, *John Brown*. Boston, 1910.

Warren, Louis A., editor, *Lincoln Lore* No. 616, January 27, 1941, p. 1.

Watson, Walter A., "Notes on Southside Virginia." *Bulletin of the Virginia State Library*, September 1925, XV, 173.

Webster, Clyde C., "John Minor Botts, Anti-Secessionist." *Richmond College Historical Papers*, June 1915, I, 9.

Welles, Gideon, *Diary*. Boston, 1911.

Wellman, Many Wade, *They Took Their Stand. The Founders of the Confederacy*. New York, 1959.

Wender, Herbert, *Southern Commercial Conventions*. Baltimore, 1930.

Who's Who In America . . . Chicago, 1903; 1910.

Who's Who In New York . . . New York, 1908; 1918.

Wilson, Henry, *History of the Rise and Fall of the Slave Power in America*. Boston, 1877.

Wilson, Woodrow, *Division and Reunion, 1829-1909*. New York, 1912.

Wilstach, Paul, *Tidewater Virginia*. Indianapolis, 1929.

Winston, Robert W., *High Stakes and Hair Trigger. The Life of Jefferson Davis*. New York, 1930.

Wise, John S., *The End of an Era*. Boston, 1902.

———, "The Fire-Eaters." *The Saturday Evening Post*, June 23, 1906, CLXXVIII, 8.

Wish, Harvey, *George Fitzhugh, Propagandist of the Old South*. Baton Rouge, 1943.

Woodward, C. Vann, *Origins of the New South*. Baton Rouge, 1951.

———, *Reunion and Reaction. The Compromise of 1877 and the End of Reconstruction*. Boston, 1951.

Wriston, Henry Merritt, *Executive Agents in American Foreign Relations*. Baltimore, 1929.

Wyatt, Edward A., IV, *Preliminary Checklist for Petersburg, 1786-1876*. Richmond, 1949.

Young, John Russell, *Men and Memoirs*. New York, 1901.

Younger, Edward, editor, *Inside the Confederate Government. The Diary of Robert Garlick Hill Kean*. New York, 1957.

Index

Welles, Gideon, secretary of the navy, 95
Wessels, H.W., general, 77
Whitney, Henry C., attorney, 21
Wilcox, C.M., C.S.A. general, 77
Williams, John S., general, 77
Williamsburg, Battle of, 66
Wilson, Woodrow, U.S. president, 150, 155
Wise, Henry A., governor-attorney, 22, 130

Wood, Benjamin, publisher, 89-91, 95
Wood, Fernando, mayor, 89-90
Wright, Alex S., general, 84
Wright, H.G., general, 84

Yancey, William Lowndes, congressman, 26-27
Young, John Russell, journalist, 108, 130